B. P. Pratten

The Psalter

A revised edition of the Scottish metrical version of the Psalms, with additional

Psalm-versions

B. P. Pratten

The Psalter

A revised edition of the Scottish metrical version of the Psalms, with additional Psalm-versions

ISBN/EAN: 9783337241315

Printed in Europe, USA, Canada, Australia, Japan

Cover: Foto ©Lupo / pixelio.de

More available books at **www.hansebooks.com**

THE PSALTER:

A REVISED EDITION

OF THE

SCOTTISH METRICAL VERSION OF THE PSALMS,

WITH

ADDITIONAL PSALM-VERSIONS.

PREPARED AND PUBLISHED BY

AUTHORITY OF THE

GENERAL ASSEMBLY OF THE PRESBYTERIAN CHURCH

IN IRELAND.

BLACKIE & SON
89 TALBOT STREET, DUBLIN, AND
97 DONEGAL STREET, BELFAST.
1880.

PREFACE.

In this Psalter the Scottish Metrical Version of the Psalms has been revised.

The time, it was believed, had come for attempting to remove the blemishes which mar to some extent that admirable version. As it is now more than two hundred years old, several of its words and phrases, and not a few of its grammatical forms, have become antiquated; while, through the progress of Hebrew scholarship and the labours of critical expositors, some of its renderings have been shown to be inaccurate.

In the present work an attempt has been made to remove these blemishes by emendations of those portions where there are erroneous renderings, errors of syntax, faulty rhymes, obsolete words, or want of correspondence between the rhythm of sense and the rhythm of sound. And while the Old Version, out of regard for the place which it has in the memory and affections of the people, has been very tenderly dealt with, it is hoped that most of its graver blemishes have been removed, and that something has been done to make it a more faithful conveyance of the original and a more suitable vehicle of the Church's praise. The additional Psalm-Versions give a little more variety of metre than is to be found in the Scottish Version.

THE PSALMS.

PSALM I. Dunfermline, 15.

1 THAT man hath perfect blessedness
    Who walketh not astray
In counsel of ungodly men,
    Nor stands in sinners' way,
Nor sitteth in the scorner's chair:
2   But placeth his delight
Upon God's law, and meditates
    On his law day and night.

3 He shall be like a tree that hath
    Been planted by a river,
Which in its season yields its fruit,
    And its leaf fadeth never:
And all he doth shall prosper well.
4   The wicked are not so;
But like they are unto the chaff,
    Which wind drives to and fro.

5 In judgment therefore shall not stand
    Such as ungodly are;
Nor in the assembly of the just
    Shall wicked men appear.
6 Because the way of godly men
    Unto the Lord is known;
Whereas the way of wicked men
    Shall quite be overthrown.

PSALM II. New London, 3 s.

1 WHY rage the heathen? and vain things
    Why do the people mind?
2 Kings of the earth do set themselves,
    And princes are combined,
To plot against the Lord, and his
    Anointed, saying thus,
3 Let us asunder break their bands,
    And cast their cords from us.

4 He that in heaven sits shall laugh;
    The Lord shall scorn them all.
5 Then shall he speak to them in wrath,
    In rage he vex them shall.
6 Yet I my King appointed have
    Upon my holy hill;
On Zion mount his throne is set,
    Established by my will.

7 The sure decree I will declare:
    The Lord hath said to me,
Thou art mine only Son; this day
    I have begotten thee.
8 Ask of me, and for heritage
    The heathen I'll make thine;
And for possession I to thee
    Will give earth's utmost line.

9 Thou with a rod of iron shalt
    Beat down and break them all;
Them, as a potter's vessel, thou
    Shalt dash in pieces small.
10 Now therefore, kings, be wise; be taught,
    Ye judges of the earth:

11 Serve ye the Lord in holy fear;
   Join trembling with your mirth.

12 Kiss ye the Son, lest in his ire
   Ye perish from the way;
   For suddenly his wrath may burn:
   Blest all that on him stay.

PSALM III. Eden, 17.

1 O LORD, how are my foes increased!
   Against me many rise.
2 Many say of my soul, For him
   In God no succour lies.
3 Yet thou my shield and glory art,
   The uplifter of mine head.
4 I cried, and from his holy hill
   The Lord me answer made.

5 I laid me down and slept, I waked;
   For God sustained me.
6 I will not fear though thousands ten
   Set round against me be.
7 Arise, O Lord; save me, my God;
   For thou hast struck my foes
   Upon the cheek; the wicked's teeth
   Hast broken by thy blows.

8 Salvation surely doth belong
   Unto the Lord alone;
   Thy blessing, Lord, for evermore
   Thy people is upon.

PSALM IV. Abbey, 8.

1 GIVE ear unto me when I call,
   God of my righteousness;

    Have mercy, hear my prayer; thou hast
       Enlarged me in distress.
2 O ye the sons of men! how long
     Will ye love vanities?
   How long my glory turn to shame,
     And will ye follow lies?

3 But know, that for himself the Lord
     The godly man doth choose:
   The Lord, when I on him do call,
     To hear will not refuse.
4 Fear, and sin not; talk with your heart
     On bed, and silent be.
5 Offerings present of righteousness,
     And in the Lord trust ye.

6 O who will show us any good?
     Is that which many say:
   But of thy countenance the light,
     Lord, lift on us alway.
7 Upon my heart bestowed by thee,
     More gladness I have found
   Than they, even then, when corn and wine
     Did most with them abound.

8 I will both lay me down in peace,
     And quiet sleep will take;
   Because thou only me to dwell
     In safety, Lord, dost make.

PSALM V.   *Kilmarnock, 28.*

1 GIVE ear unto my words, O Lord,
     My meditation weigh.
2 Hear my loud cry, my King, my God;
     For I to thee will pray.

3 Lord, thou shalt early hear my voice:
    I early will direct
  My prayer to thee; and, looking up,
    An answer will expect.

4 For thou art not a God that doth
    In wickedness delight;
  Neither shall evil dwell with thee,
5   Nor fools stand in thy sight.
  All evil-doers thou dost hate,
6   Cutt'st off that liars be:
  The bloody and deceitful man
    Abhorred is by thee.

7 But I into thy house will come
    In thine abundant grace;
  And I will worship in thy fear
    Toward thy holy place.
8 Lord, lead me in thy righteousness,
    For foes do lie in wait:
  Thy way, wherein I am to walk,
    Before my face make straight.

9 For in their mouth there is no truth,
    Their inward part is vile;
  Their throat's an open sepulchre,
    Their tongue is full of guile.
10 O God, condemn them; let them be
    By their own counsel quelled:
  Them for their many sins cast out,
    For they 'gainst thee rebelled.

11 But let all joy that trust in thee,
    For aye lift up their voice,
  For them thou sav'st: in thee let all
    That love thy name rejoice.

12 For, Lord, unto the righteous man
    Thou wilt thy blessing yield:
With favour thou wilt compass him
    About, as with a shield.

PSALM VI.—1st Version. <small>Soldau, 66.</small>

1 LORD, in thy wrath rebuke me not;
    Nor in thy hot rage chasten me.
2 Lord, pity me, for I am weak:
    Heal me, for my bones vexed be.
3 My soul is also vexed sore;
    But, Lord, how long stay wilt thou make?
4 Return, O Lord, my soul set free;
    O save me for thy mercies' sake.

5 Because those that deceased are
    Of thee shall no remembrance have;
    And who is he that will to thee
    Give praises lying in the grave?
6 I with my groaning weary am,
    And all the night till morn appears,
    Through grief I make my bed to swim,
    And water all my couch with tears.

7 Mine eye, consumed with grief, grows old,
    Because of all mine enemies.
8 Hence from me, evil-doers all;
    For God hath heard my weeping cries.
9 God hath my supplication heard;
    By him my prayer received shall be.
10 Shamed and sore vexed be all my foes,
    Turned back and shamed suddenly.

PSALM VI.—2nd Version. Bangor, 9.

1 IN thy great indignation, Lord,
    Do thou rebuke me not;
Nor on me lay thy chastening hand
    In thy displeasure hot.
2 Lord, pity me, for I am weak;
    Have mercy upon me:
And heal thou me, O Lord, because
    My bones much vexed be.

3 My soul is vexed sore: but, Lord,
    How long stay wilt thou make?
4 Return, O Lord, my soul set free,
    Save for thy mercy's sake.
5 Because of thee in death there shall
    No more remembrance be:
Of those that in the grave do lie,
    Who shall give thanks to thee?

6 I with my groaning weary am;
    All night till morn appears,
Through grief I make my bed to swim,
    My couch to flow with tears.
7 By reason of my vexing grief
    Mine eye consumed is;
It waxeth old, because of all
    That are mine enemies.

8 But now, depart from me all ye
    That work iniquity:
Because the Lord hath heard my voice
    When I did mourn and cry.
9 Unto my supplication's voice
    The Lord hath lent his ear;

When to the Lord my prayer I make,
  He graciously will hear.

10 Let all be troubled and asham'd
  That enemies are to me;
Let them turn back, and suddenly
  Ashamed let them be.

PSALM VII. Esslingen, 19.

1 O LORD my God, in thee do I
  My confidence repose;
Save and deliver me from all
  My persecuting foes;
2 Lest that the enemy my soul
  Should, like a lion, tear,
In pieces rending it, while there
  Is no deliverer.

3 O Lord my God, if it be so
  That I committed this;
If it be so that in my hands
  Iniquity there is;
4 If I rewarded ill to him
  That was at peace with me;
(Yea, even the man that without cause
  My foe was I did free;)

5 Then let the foe pursue and take
  My soul, and my life thrust
Down to the earth, and let him lay
  Mine honour in the dust.
6 Rise in thy wrath, Lord, raise thyself,
  For my foes raging be;
And, to the judgment which thou hast
  Commanded, wake for me.

7 Of nations the assembled host
    Around thee shall draw nigh;
  And over them do thou return
    Unto thy place on high.
8 Jehovah shall the people judge;
    My judge, Jehovah, be,
  After my righteousness and mine
    Integrity in me.

9 O let the wicked's mischief end;
    The righteous fortify;
  Because the righteous God art thou
    Who heart and reins dost try.
10 In God, who saves the upright in heart,
    Is my defence and stay.
11 God is a righteous Judge, and God
    Is angry every day.

12 If he do not repent and turn,
    Then he his sword will whet;
  His bow he hath already bent,
    And hath it ready set:
13 He also hath for him prepared
    The instruments of death;
  Against the persecutors he
    His shafts ordained hath.

14 Behold, he with iniquity
    Doth travail as in birth;
  A mischief he conceived hath,
    And falsehood shall bring forth.
15 He made a pit, and digged it deep,
    Another there to take;
  But he is fallen into the ditch
    Which he himself did make.

16 On his own head shall be returned
    The mischief he hath wrought;
  The violence that he hath done,
    Shall on himself be brought.
17 According to his righteousness
    The Lord I'll magnify;
  And praise will sing unto his name,
    Who is the Lord most high.

PSALM VIII.—1st Version. St. Peter, 49.

1 HOW excellent in all the earth,
    Lord, our Lord, is thy name!
  Who hast thy glory far advanced
    Above the starry frame.
2 From infants' and from sucklings' mouth
    Thou power didst ordain,
  Because of foes, that so thou mightst
    The vengeful foe restrain.

3 When I look up unto thy heavens,
    Which thine own fingers framed,
  Unto the moon and to the stars,
    Which were by thee ordained;
4 Then say I, What is man, that he
    Remembered is by thee?
  Or what the son of man, that thou
    So kind to him shouldst be?

5 For thou a little lower hast
    Him than the angels made;
  With glory and with dignity
    Thou crowned hast his head.
6 Of thy hands' works thou madest him lord;
    All 'neath his feet didst lay,

7 All sheep and oxen, yea, and beasts
    That in the field do stray;

8 Fowl of the air, fish of the sea,
    All that pass through the same.
9 How excellent in all the earth,
    Lord, our Lord, is thy name!

PSALM VIII.—2nd Version. <small>Goss, 7s.</small>

1 O LORD, our Lord, how excellent
    In all the earth thy name!
  Who hast thy glory set above
    The starry frame.
2 From infants' and from sucklings' mouths
    Is strength by thee ordained,
  That so the avenger may be quelled,
    The foe restrained.

3 When I behold thy spacious heavens,
    The work of thine own hand,
  The moon and stars in order set
    By thy command;
4 O, what is man, that thou shouldst him
    In kind remembrance bear?
  Or what the son of man, that thou
    For him shouldst care?

5 For thou a little lower hast
    Him than the angels made;
  With honour and with glory thou
    Hast crowned his head.
6 Lord of thy works thou hast him made;
    All unto him must yield,
  All sheep and oxen, yea, and beasts
    Which roam the field.

7 Fowl of the air, fish of the sea,
  All that pass through the same;
    O Lord, our Lord, in all the earth
    How great thy name!

PSALM IX. Kaltenthal, 27.

1 LORD, thee I'll praise with all my heart,
    Thy wonders all proclaim.
2 In thee, most High, I'll greatly joy,
    And sing unto thy name.
3 When back my foes were turned, they fell,
    And perished at thy sight:
4 For thou maintainst my right and cause;
    Enthroned sittst judging right.

5 The heathen thou rebuked hast,
    The wicked overthrown;
  Thou hast put out their names, that they
    May never more be known.
6 The desolations are complete
    That fell the foe upon;
  Their cities thou hast razed quite,
    Their memory is gone.

7 The Lord for ever doth endure;
    For judgment sets his throne;
8 In righteousness to judge the world,
    Justice to give each one.
9 So shall the Lord a refuge be
    For those that are oppressed;
  A refuge will he be for them,
    What time they are distressed.

10 And they that know thy name in thee
    Their confidence will place:

  For thou hast not forsaken them
   That truly seek thy face.
11 O sing ye praises to the Lord
   That dwells in Zion hill;
  Among the people everywhere
   His deeds declare ye still.

12 When he enquireth after blood,
   He doth remember them:
  The afflicted he doth not forget
   That call upon his name.
13 Lord, pity me; behold the grief
   Which I from foes sustain;
  Even thou, who from the gates of death
   Dost raise me up again:

14 That I in Zion's daughter's gates
   May all thy praise relate;
  And that I may exult with joy
   In thy salvation great.
15 Sunk are the heathen in the pit
   Which they themselves prepared;
  And in the net which they have hid
   Their own feet fast are snared.

16 The Lord is by the judgment known
   Which he himself hath wrought:
  The sinners' hands do make the snares
   Wherewith themselves are caught.
17 The wicked shall be turned back
   Into death's dark abode;
  And all the nations that forget
   The great and mighty God.

18 For they that needy are shall not
   Forgotten be alway;

The expectation of the poor
　　　　Shall not be lost for aye.
19 Arise, Lord, let not man prevail;
　　　Judge heathen in thy sight;
20 That they may know themselves but men,
　　　The nations, Lord, affright.

PSALM X. Dundee, 14.

1 WHEREFORE is it that thou, O Lord,
　　　　Dost stand from us afar?
　　And wherefore hidest thou thyself
　　　　When times so troublous are?
2 The wicked in his loftiness
　　　Doth persecute the poor:
　　In the devices they have framed
　　　Let them be taken sure.

3 The wicked of his heart's desire
　　　Doth talk with boastful word;
　　The covetous renounceth, yea,
　　　He doth despise the Lord.
4 The wicked in his haughtiness
　　　Upon God doth not call;
　　And in the counsels of his heart
　　　There is no God at all.

5 His ways at all times grievous are;
　　　Thy judgments from his sight
　　Removed are: at all his foes
　　　He puffeth with despite.
6 Within his heart he thus hath said,
　　　I shall not moved be;
　　And no adversity at all
　　　Shall ever come to me.

7 His mouth with cursing, fraud, and wrong
    Is filled abundantly;
  And underneath his tongue there is
    Mischief and vanity.
8 He closely sits in villages;
    He slays the innocent:
  Against the poor that pass him by
    His cruel eyes are bent.

9 He lion-like lurks in his den;
    He waits the poor to take,
  And when he draws him in his net,
    His prey he doth him make.
10 Himself he humbleth very low,
    He croucheth down withal,
  That so a multitude of poor
    May by his strong ones fall.

11 He thus hath said within his heart,
    God hath it quite forgot;
  He hides his countenance, and he
    For ever sees it not.
12 O Lord, do thou arise; O God,
    Lift up thine hand on high:
  Put not the meek afflicted ones
    Out of thy memory.

13 Why is it that the wicked man
    Doth God thus still despise?
  Because that God will it require
    He in his heart denies.
14 Thou hast it seen; for wrong and wrath
    Thou seest to repay:
  The poor commits himself to thee;
    Thou art the orphan's stay.

15 The arm break of the wicked man,
    And of the evil one;
  Do thou seek out his wickedness,
    Until thou findest none.
16 The Lord is king through ages all,
    Even to eternity;
  The heathen people from his land
    Are perished utterly.

17 O Lord, of those that humble are
    Thou the desire didst hear;
  Thou wilt prepare their heart, and thou
    To hear wilt bend thine ear;
18 To judge the fatherless and those
    That are oppressed sore;
  That man, who is but of the earth,
    May them oppress no more.

PSALM XI. York, S4.

1 I IN the Lord do put my trust;
    How is it then that ye
  Say to my soul, Even as a bird
    Unto your mountain flee?
2 For, lo, the wicked bend their bow,
    Their shafts on string they fit,
  That those who upright are in heart
    They privily may hit.

3 If the foundations be destroyed,
    What hath the righteous done?
4 God in his holy temple is,
    In heaven is his throne.
5 His eyes behold, his eyelids try
    Men's sons. The just he proves:

    But his soul hates the wicked man,
      And him that violence loves.

6 Snares, fire and brimstone, furious storms,
    On sinners he shall rain:
  This, as the portion of their cup,
    Doth unto them pertain.
7 Because the Lord most righteous doth
    In righteousness delight;
  They shall his countenance behold
  Who are in heart upright.

PSALM XII. Elgin, 18.

1 HELP, Lord, because the godly man
    Doth daily fade away;
  And from among the sons of men
    The faithful do decay.
2 Unto his neighbour every one
    Doth utter vanity:
  They with a double heart do speak,
    And lips of flattery.

3 God shall cut off all flattering lips,
    Tongues that speak proudly thus,
4 Our tongues prevail; our lips are ours:
    Who is lord over us?
5 For the oppression of the poor,
    For him in need that sighs,
  To save him from his scornful foes,
    God saith, I will arise.

6 Jehovah's words are words most pure;
    They are like silver tried
  In earthen furnace, seven times
    That hath been purified.

7 Lord, thou shalt them preserve and keep
   For ever from this race.
8 On all sides walk the wicked, when
   Vile men are high in place.

PSALM XIII.—1st Version. Martyrdom, 3).

1 HOW long wilt thou forget me, Lord?
     Shall it forever be?
  O how long shall it be that thou
     Wilt hide thy face from me?
2 How long take counsel in my soul,
     Still sad in heart, shall I?
  How long exalted over me
     Shall be mine enemy?

3 O Lord my God, consider well,
     And answer to me make:
  Mine eyes enlighten, lest the sleep
     Of death me overtake.
4 Lest that mine enemy should say,
     Against him I prevail;
  And those that trouble me rejoice,
     When I am moved and fail.

5 But I have all my confidence
     Upon thy mercy set;
  My heart within me shall rejoice
     In thy salvation great.
6 Unto Jehovah then will I
     Sing praises cheerfully,
  Because he hath his bounty shown
     To me abundantly.

PSALM XIII.—2nd Version.   Aurelia, 76.

1 HOW long wilt thou forget me?
    O Lord, for evermore?
For ever wilt thou let me
    Thine absent face deplore?
How long in fruitless wailing
    Shall I consume the day?
And thus how long prevailing
    My vaunting foe bear sway?

2 O, do not thou forsake me!
    Enlighten thou my gloom;
Lest fatal sleep o'ertake me,
    The death-sleep of the tomb:
Lest then my foe insulting
    Should boast of his success,
And impious men exulting
    Triumph in my distress.

3 Lord, in my tribulation
    I trust thy mercy still,
And surely thy salvation
    My heart with joy shall fill.
Thine aid thou didst afford me,
    Thy praises I will sing;
And for his mercies toward me
    Will bless my God and king.

PSALM XIV.   Moravia, 32.

1 THAT there is not a God, the fool
    Doth in his heart conclude:
They are corrupt, their works are vile,
    Not one of them doth good.

2 The Lord upon the sons of men
   From heaven did look abroad,
To see if any understood,
   And did seek after God.

3 Corrupt they altogether are,
   They all aside are gone;
And there is none that doeth good,
   Yea, sure there is not one.
4 These workers of iniquity
   Do they not know at all,
That they my people eat as bread,
   Nor on Jehovah call?

5 There feared they much; for God is with
   The whole race of the just.
6 You shame the counsel of the poor,
   Because the Lord's his trust.
7 Let Israel's help from Zion come:
   When back the Lord shall bring
His captives, Jacob shall rejoice,
   And Israel shall sing.

PSALM XV. Tallis, 53.

1 WITHIN thy tabernacle, Lord,
   Who shall abide with thee?
And in thy high and holy hill
   Who shall a dweller be?
2 The man that walketh uprightly,
   And worketh righteousness,
And as he thinketh in his heart,
   So doth he truth express.

3 Who doth not slander with his tongue,
   Nor to his friend doth hurt;

>   Nor yet against his neighbour doth
>   Take up an ill report.
> 4 In whose eyes vile men are despised;
>   But those the Lord that fear
>   He honoureth; and changeth not,
>   Though to his hurt he swear.
>
> 5 His coin puts not to usury,
>   Nor take reward will he
>   Against the guiltless. Who doth thus
>   Shall never moved be.

PSALM XVI. St. Paul, 4S.

> 1 LORD, keep me, for I trust in thee;
>   To God this was my cry,
> 2 Thou art my Lord, and above thee
>   Not any good have I.
> 3 To saints on earth, The excellent,
>   There my delight's all placed;
> 4 Their sorrows shall be multiplied
>   To other gods that haste:
>
>   Of their drink-offerings of blood
>   No offering will I make;
>   Their very names into my lips
>   I will not even take.
> 5 Of mine inheritance and cup
>   The Lord's the portion sure;
>   The lot that fallen is to me
>   Thou dost maintain secure.
>
> 6 Unto me happily the lines
>   In pleasant places fell;
>   Yea, the inheritance I have
>   In beauty doth excel.

7 I bless the Lord, because he doth
   By counsel me conduct;
 And in the seasons of the night
   My reins do me instruct.

8 Before me still the Lord I set:
   Since it is so that he
 Doth ever stand at my right hand,
   I shall not moved be.
9 Because of this my heart is glad,
   And joy shall be expressed
 Even by my glory; and my flesh
   In confidence shall rest.

10 Because my soul unto the grave
    Shall not be left by thee;
  And thou wilt not thine Holy One
    Corruption give to see.
11 Thou wilt me show the path of life:
    Of joy there is full store
  Before thy face; in thy right hand
    Are pleasures evermore.

PSALM XVII. Gräfenberg, 25.

1 LORD, hear the right, regard my cry,
   Unto my prayer give heed,
 That doth not in hypocrisy
   From feigned lips proceed.
2 And from before thy presence let
   My judgment come to me;
 Turn thou thine eyes to upright things,
   Look thou on equity.

3 My heart thou provest, and by night
   Dost visit and me try,

But findest nought; for my intent
  My mouth doth not belie.
4 As for men's works, I, by the word
  That from thy lips doth flow,
Have kept myself out of the paths
  Wherein destroyers go.

5 Hold up my goings, Lord, me guide
  In those thy paths divine,
So that my footsteps may not slide
  Out of those ways of thine.
6 I called have on thee, O God,
  Because thou wilt me hear:
That thou may'st hearken to my speech,
  To me incline thine ear.

7 Thy wondrous loving-kindness show,
  Thou that, by thy right hand,
Sav'st them that trust in thee from those
  That up against them stand.
8 As the apple of the eye me keep;
  In thy wings' shade me hide
9 From wasting deadly foes, who me
  Beset on every side.

10 In their own fat they are inclosed;
   Their mouth speaks loftily.
11 Our steps they compass, and to earth
   Down bowing set their eye.
12 He like unto a lion is
   That's greedy of his prey,
Or lion young, which lurking doth
   In secret places stay.

13 Arise, and disappoint my foe,
   And cast him down, O Lord:

  And from the wicked man my soul
   Deliver by thy sword.
14 From worldly men, Lord, by thy hand
   Let me delivered be,
  Who only in this present life
   Their part and portion see;

  Whom with thy treasure thou dost fill:
   They many sons receive;
  And of their great abundance they
   Unto their children leave.
15 But as for me, I thine own face
   In righteousness will see;
  And with thy likeness, when I wake,
   I satisfied shall be.

PSALM XVIII.   *Bedford, 10.*

1 THEE will I love, O Lord, my strength.
2 My fortress is the Lord,
  My rock, and he that doth to me
   Deliverance afford:
  My God, my strength, whom I will trust,
   A buckler unto me,
  The horn of my salvation sure,
   And my high tower, is he.

3 Unto the Lord, who worthy is
   Of praises, will I cry;
  And then shall I preserved be
   Safe from mine enemy.
4 The cords of death encompassed me,
   Sin's floods made me afraid;
5 Bands of the grave were round me drawn,
   Death's snares were on me laid.

6 I in distress called on the Lord,
    Cry to my God did I;
  He from his temple heard my voice,
    To his ears came my cry.
7 Earth as affrighted then did shake,
    Trembling upon it seized:
  The hills' foundations moved were,
    Because he was displeased.

8 Up from his nostrils came a smoke,
    And from his mouth there came
  Devouring fire, and coals by it
    Were turned into flame.
9 He also bowed down the heavens,
    And thence he did descend;
  And thickest clouds of darkness did
    Under his feet attend.

10 And he upon a cherub rode,
    And thereon he did fly;
  Yea, on the swift wings of the wind
    His flight was from on high.
11 He darkness made his secret place:
    About him, for his tent,
  Dark waters were, and thickest clouds
    Of the airy firmament.

12 And at the brightness of that light,
    Which was before his eye,
  His thick clouds passed away, hailstones
    And coals of fire did fly.
13 Jehovah also in the heavens
    Did thunder in his ire;
  And there the Highest gave his voice,
    Hailstones and coals of fire.

14 Yea, he his arrows sent abroad,
    And them he scattered;
His lightnings also he shot out,
    And them discomfited.
15 The waters' channels then were seen,
    The world's foundations vast
At thy rebuke discovered were,
    And at thy nostrils' blast.

16 And from above the Lord sent down,
    And took me from below;
From many waters he me drew,
    Which would me overflow.
17 He rescued me from my strong foes,
    And such as did me hate;
Because he saw that they for me
    Too strong were and too great.

18 They came upon me in the day
    Of my calamity;
But even then the Lord himself
    A stay was unto me.
19 Unto a place of liberty
    And room he hath me brought;
Because he took delight in me,
    He my deliverance wrought.

20 According to my righteousness
    He did me recompense;
He me repaid according to
    My hands' pure innocence.
21 For I the Lord's ways kept, nor from
    My God turned wickedly.
22 His judgments were before me, I
    His laws put not from me.

23 Sincere before him was my heart,
   Upright with him was I;
 And watchfully I kept myself
   From mine iniquity.
24 According to my righteousness
   The Lord did me requite;
 After the cleanness of my hands
   Appearing in his sight.

25 Thou to the gracious showest grace,
   To just men just thou art;
26 Pure to the pure, but froward still
   To men of froward heart.
27 For thou wilt the afflicted save
   In grief that low do lie;
 But wilt bring down the countenance
   Of those whose looks are high.

28 For thou thyself wilt light my lamp,
   That it shall shine full bright:
 The Lord my God will also make
   My darkness to be light.
29 By thee through troops of men I break,
   And them discomfit all;
 And, by my God assisting me,
   I overleap a wall.

30 As for God, perfect is his way;
   Jehovah's word is tried;
 He is a buckler to all those
   Who do in him confide.
31 Who but the Lord is God? but he
   Who is a rock and stay?
32 'Tis God that girdeth me with strength,
   And perfect makes my way.

33 He made my feet swift as the hinds',
     On my heights made me stand;
34 My hands he taught to war, my arms
     A bow of brass did bend.
35 The shield of thy salvation thou
     Upon me didst bestow:
   Thy right hand held me up, and great
     Thy kindness made me grow.

36 And in my way my steps thou hast
     Enlarged under me,
   That I go safely, and my feet
     Are kept from sliding free.
37 Mine enemies I did pursue,
     And them did overtake;
   Nor did I turn again till I
     An end of them did make.

38 I wounded them, they could not rise;
     They 'neath my feet did fall.
39 Thou girdedst me with strength for war;
     My foes thou broughtst down all:
40 And thou hast given me the necks
     Of all mine enemies,
   That I might utterly destroy
     Those who against me rise.

41 They in their trouble cried for help,
     But there was none to save;
   Yea, they did cry unto the Lord,
     But he no answer gave.
42 Then did I beat them small as dust
     Before the wind that flies;
   And I did cast them out like dirt
     Upon the street that lies.

43 Thou madest me free from people's strife,
  The heathen's head to be:
 A people whom I have not known
  Shall service do to me.
44 At hearing they shall me obey,
  To me they shall submit.
45 Strangers for fear shall fade away
  Who in their strongholds sit.

46 Jehovah lives, blessed be my Rock;
  God, who me saves, praised be.
47 God doth avenge me, and subdue
  The people under me.
48 He saves me from mine enemies;
  Yea, thou hast lifted me
 Above my foes, and from the man
  Of violence set me free.

49 Therefore to thee will I give thanks
  The heathen folk among;
 And to thy name, O Lord, I will
  Give praises in a song.
50 He great deliverance gives his king:
  He mercy doth extend
 To David, his anointed one,
  And his seed without end.

PSALM XIX.—1st Version. St Anne, 43.

1 THE heavens God's glory do declare,
  The skies his hand-works preach:
2 Day utters speech to day, and night
  To night doth knowledge teach.
3 There is no speech nor tongue to which
  Their voice doth not extend:

4 Their line is gone through all the earth,
   Their words to the world's end.
5 There he a tabernacle hath
   Erected for the sun;
 Who comes like bridegroom from his tent,
   Like strong man joys to run.
6 From heaven's end he goeth forth,
   Circling to the end again;
 And there is nothing from his heat
   That hidden doth remain.
7 God's law is perfect, and converts
   The soul in sin that lies:
 God's testimony is most sure,
   And makes the simple wise.
8 The statutes of the Lord are right,
   And do rejoice the heart:
 The Lord's command is pure, and doth
   Light to the eyes impart.
9 Unspotted is the fear of God,
   And doth endure for ever:
 The judgments of the Lord are true
   And righteous altogether.
10 They more than gold, yea, much fine gold,
    To be desired are:
 Than honey, honey from the comb
    That droppeth, sweeter far.
11 Moreover, they thy servant warn
    How he his life should frame:
 A great reward provided is
    For them that keep the same.
12 Who can his errors understand?
    From secret faults me cleanse:

13 Thy servant keep thou also back
    From all presumptuous sins;

    And do not suffer them to have
    Dominion over me:
I shall be righteous then, and clear
    From great transgression be.

14 The words which from my mouth proceed,
    The thoughts sent from my heart,
Accept, O Lord, for thou my strength
    And my Redeemer art.

PSALM XIX.—2nd Version.   Bevan, 71

1   THE lofty heavens proclaim
        The majesty of God;
    The firmament displays
    His handiwork abroad:
Day unto day doth utter speech,
And night to night doth knowledge teach.

2   Aloud they do not speak,
    They utter forth no word,
    Nor into language break;
    Yet is their witness heard:
Their line through all the earth extends,
Their words to earth's remotest ends.

3   In them he hath prepared
    A dwelling for the sun;
    Which, as a mighty man,
    Exults his race to run;
And, bridegroom-like in his array,
Comes from his chamber, bringing day.

4   His daily going forth
    Is from the end of heaven;

          The firmament to him
          Is for his circuit given.
        He to its end returns again;
        Hid from his heat can nought remain.

5   The Lord's law is complete;
          It makes the soul arise:
          The Lord's decree is sure;
          It makes the simple wise:
        The statutes of the Lord are right,
        Imparting to the heart delight.

6   The Lord's command is pure;
          Light on the eyes it pours:
          The Lord's fear is unstained;
          For ever it endures:
        The judgments of the Lord are true,
        And altogether righteous, too.

7   More to be prized than gold,
          Yea, much fine gold, they are;
          Than honey from the comb
          That droppeth, sweeter far.
        They also warn thy servant, Lord;
        In keeping them is great reward.

8   Who can his errors know?
          From secret faults me cleanse:
          Keep thou thy servant back
          From all presumptuous sins:
        Let them not triumph over me;
        Then shall I pure and upright be.

9   Yea, then I shall be free
          From much and heinous sin.

O let the words I speak,
   And all my thoughts within,
Be acceptable, Lord, to thee,
   Who strength and Saviour art to me.

PSALM XX. Corona, 13.

1 JEHOVAH hear thee in the day
   When trouble he doth send;
And let the name of Jacob's God
   Thee from all ill defend.
2 O let him help send from above,
   Out of his sanctuary;
From Zion, his own holy hill,
   Let him give strength to thee.

3 Let him remember all thy gifts,
   Accept thy sacrifice:
4 Grant thee thine heart's wish, and fulfil
   Thy thoughts and counsel wise.
5 In thy salvation we will joy;
   In our God's name we will
Display our banners: and the Lord
   Thy prayers all fulfil.

6 Now know I God his king doth save:
   He from his holy heaven
Will hear him, with the saving strength
   By his own right hand given.
7 In chariots some put confidence,
   On horses some rely;
But we the Lord's name mention will,
   Who is our God most high.

8 We rise and upright stand, when they
   Are bowed down and fall.

9 Deliver, Lord; O let the King
   Us hear, when we do call.

PSALM XXI.
St. James, 43.

1 JEHOVAH, in thy strength the king
      Shall very joyful be:
   And in thy saving help rejoice
      How fervently shall he!
2 Thou hast bestowed upon him
      All that his heart would have;
   And thou from him didst not withhold
      Whate'er his lips did crave.

3 For thou with blessings dost him meet
      Of goodness manifold;
   And thou hast set upon his head
      A crown of purest gold.
4 When he desired life of thee,
      Thou life to him didst give;
   Even such a length of days, that he
      For evermore should live.

5 In that salvation wrought by thee
      His glory is made great;
   Honour and comely majesty
      Thou hast upon him set.
6 Because that thou for evermore
      Most blessed hast him made;
   And thou hast with thy countenance
      Made him exceeding glad.

7 Because the king upon the Lord
      His confidence doth lay;
   And through the grace of the Most High
      Shall not be moved away.

8 Thine hand shall all those men find out
 That enemies are to thee;
 Even thy right hand shall find out those
 Of thee that haters be.

9 Like fiery oven thou shalt them make,
 When kindled is thine ire;
 The Lord in wrath shall swallow them,
 Devour them shall the fire.

10 Their fruit from earth thou shalt destroy,
 Their seed men from among:
11 For they beyond their might 'gainst thee
 Did mischief plot and wrong.

12 Thou therefore shalt make them turn back,
 When thou thy shafts shalt place
 Upon thy strings, made ready all
 To fly against their face.
13 In thy almighty strength, O Lord,
 Do thou exalted be:
 So shall we sing with joyful hearts,
 Thy power praise shall we.

PSALM XXII. *Dundee, 14.*

1 MY God, my God, wherefore is it
 Thou hast forsaken me?
 Why from my help so far, and from
 My cry of agony?
2 All day, my God, to thee I cry,
 Yet am not heard by thee;
 And in the season of the night
 I cannot silent be.

3 But thou art holy, thou that dost
 Inhabit Israel's praise.

4 Our fathers hoped in thee, they hoped,
   And thou didst them release.
5 When unto thee they sent their cry,
   To them deliverance came:
Because they put their trust in thee,
   They were not put to shame.

6 But as for me, a worm I am,
   And as no man am prized;
Reproach of men I am, and by
   The people am despised.
7 All that me see laugh me to scorn;
   Shoot out the lip do they;
They nod and shake their heads at me,
   And, mocking, thus do say,

8 He trusted in the Lord, that he
   Would free him by his might;
Let him deliver him, since he
   Had in him such delight.
9 But thou art he out of the womb
   That didst me safely take;
When I was on my mother's breasts,
   Thou me to trust didst make.

10 And I was cast upon thy care,
   Even from my birth till now;
And from my mother's womb my God
   And my support art thou.
11 Be not far off, for trouble's near,
   And none to help is found.
12 Bulls many compass me, strong bulls
   Of Bashan me surround.

13 Their mouths they opened wide on me,
   Upon me gape did they,

  Like to a lion ravening
   And roaring for his prey.
14 Like water I'm poured out, my bones
   All out of joint do part:
  Amidst my bowels, as the wax,
   So melted is my heart.

15 My strength is like a potsherd dried;
   My tongue it cleaveth fast
  Unto my jaws; and to the dust
   Of death thou brought me hast.
16 For dogs have compassed me about:
   The wicked, that did meet
  In their assembly, me enclosed:
   They pierced my hands and feet.

17 I all my bones may tell; they do
   Upon me look and stare.
18 Upon my vesture lots they cast,
   My clothes among them share.
19 But be not far, O Lord, my strength;
   Haste to give help to me.
20 From sword my soul, from power of dogs
   My darling, set thou free.

21 From the devouring lion's mouth,
   My life do thou defend;
  To save from horns of unicorns
   Thou dost me answer send.
        Jackson, 26.
22 Among those that my brethren are
   I will declare thy name;
  Amidst the congregation I
   Thy praises will proclaim.

23 Praise ye the Lord who do him fear;
    Him glorify all ye
The seed of Jacob; fear him all
    That Israel's children be.
24 For he despised not nor abhorred
    The afflicted's misery;
Nor from him hid his face, but heard,
    When he to him did cry.

25 Within the congregation great
    My praise shall be of thee;
My vows before them that him fear
    Shall be performed by me.
26 The meek shall eat, and shall be filled;
    They also praise shall give
Unto the Lord that do him seek:
    Your heart shall ever live.

27 All ends of the earth remember shall,
    And turn unto the Lord;
The kindreds of the nations all
    Thee homage shall accord.
28 Because the kingdom to the Lord
    Doth appertain as his;
Likewise among the nations all,
    The Governor he is.

29 Earth's fat ones eat, and worship shall:
    All who to dust descend
Shall bow to him; none of them can
    His soul from death defend.
30 A seed shall service do to him;
    Unto the Lord it shall
A generation reckoned be,
    Even to ages all.

31 They shall come forth, and shall declare
    His truth and righteousness
Unto a people yet unborn,
    And that he hath done this.

PSALM XXIII. St. Peter, 49.

1 THE Lord's my shepherd, I'll not want.
2   He makes me down to lie
In pastures green: he leadeth me
    The quiet waters by.
3 My soul he doth restore again;
    And me to walk doth make
Within the paths of righteousness,
    Even for his own name's sake.

4 Yea, though I walk in death's dark vale,
    Yet will I fear none ill:
For thou art with me; and thy rod
    And staff me comfort still.
5 My table thou hast furnished
    In presence of my foes;
My head thou dost with oil anoint,
    And my cup overflows.

6 Goodness and mercy all my life
    Shall surely follow me:
And in God's house for evermore
    My dwelling-place shall be.

PSALM XXIV. Newlands, 35.

1 THE earth belongs unto the Lord,
    And all that it contains;
The world that is inhabited,
    And all that there remains.

2 For the foundations of the same
    He on the seas did lay,
And he hath it established
    Upon the floods to stay.

3 Who is the man that shall ascend
    Into the hill of God?
Or who within his holy place
    Shall have a firm abode?

4 Whose hands are clean, whose heart is pure,
    And unto vanity
Who hath not lifted up his soul,
    Nor sworn deceitfully.

5 This is the man who shall receive
    The blessing from the Lord;
The God of his salvation shall
    Him righteousness accord.

6 This is the generation who
    Do after him inquire;
They Jacob are, who seek thy face
    With their whole hearts' desire.

7 Ye gates, lift up your heads on high;
    Ye doors that last for aye,
Be lifted up, that so the King
    Of glory enter may.

8 But who of glory is the King?
    The mighty Lord is this;
Even that same Lord that great in might
    And strong in battle is.

9 Ye gates, lift up your heads; ye doors,
    Doors that do last for aye,
Be lifted up, that so the King
    Of glory enter may.

10 But who is he that is the King
      Of glory? who is this?
    The Lord of hosts, and none but he,
      The King of glory is.

PSALM XXV.—1st Version. St. Bride, 3.

1 TO thee I lift my soul;
2   O Lord, I trust in thee:
    My God, let me not be ashamed,
      Nor foes exult o'er me.
3 Let none that wait on thee
      Be put to shame at all;
    But those that without cause transgress,
      Let shame upon them fall.

4 Show me thy ways, O Lord;
      Thy paths O teach thou me:
5 And do thou lead me in thy truth,
      Therein my teacher be:
    For thou art God that dost
      To me salvation send,
    And I upon thee all the day
      Expecting do attend.

6 Thy tender mercies, Lord,
      To mind do thou recall,
    And loving-kindnesses, for they
      Have been through ages all.
7 My sins and faults of youth
      Do thou, O Lord, forget:
    After thy mercy think on me,
      And for thy goodness great.

8 God good and upright is;
      The way he'll sinners show.

9 The meek in judgment he will guide,
    And make his path to know.
10 The whole paths of the Lord
    Are truth and mercy sure,
  To those that do his covenant keep,
    And testimonies pure.

11 Now, for thine own name's sake,
    O Lord, I thee entreat
  To pardon mine iniquity;
    For it is very great.

St. Michael, 4.

12 What man is he that fears
    The Lord, and doth him serve?
  Him shall he teach the way that he
    Shall choose, and still observe.

13 His soul shall dwell at ease;
    And his posterity
  Shall flourish still, and of the earth
    Inheritors shall be.
14 With those that fear him is
    The secret of the Lord;
  The knowledge of his covenant
    He will to them afford.

15 Mine eyes upon the Lord
    Continually are set;
  For he it is that shall bring forth
    My feet out of the net.
16 Turn unto me thy face,
    And to me mercy show;
  Because that I am desolate,
    And am brought very low.

17 My heart's griefs are increased:
    Me from distress relieve.
18 See mine affliction and my pain,
    And all my sins forgive.
19 Consider thou my foes,
    Because they many be;
  And it a cruel hatred is
    Which they do bear to me.

20 O do thou keep my soul,
    Do thou deliver me;
  And let me never be ashamed,
    Because I trust in thee.
21 Let truth and right me keep,
    For I on thee attend.
22 Redemption, Lord, to Israel
    From all his troubles send.

PSALM XXV.—2nd Version. St. Paul, 48.

1 TO thee I lift my soul, O Lord;
2   My God, I trust in thee:
  Let me not be ashamed; let not
    My foes exult o'er me.
3 Yea, let thou none ashamed be
    That do on thee attend:
  Ashamed let them be, O Lord,
    Who without cause offend.

4 Thy ways, Lord, show; teach me thy paths;
5   Lead me in truth, teach me:
  For of my safety thou art God;
    All day I wait on thee.
6 Thy mercies that most tender are
    To mind, O Lord, recall,

And loving-kindnesses; for they
  Have been through ages all.
7 Let not the errors of my youth,
  Nor sins, remembered be:
In mercy, for thy goodness' sake,
  O Lord, remember me.
8 Since good and upright is the Lord,
  The way he'll sinners show;
9 The meek in judgment he will guide,
  And make his path to know.

10 The whole paths of the Lord our God
  Are truth and mercy sure,
To such as keep his covenant,
  And testimonies pure.
11 Now, for thine own name's sake, O Lord,
  I humbly thee entreat
To pardon mine iniquity;
  For it is very great.

12 Who fears the Lord? him shall he teach
  The way that he shall choose.
13 His soul shall dwell at ease; his seed
  The earth, as heirs, shall use.
14 The secret of the Lord is with
  Such as do fear his name;
And he his holy covenant
  Will manifest to them.

15 Towards the Lord my waiting eyes
  Continually are set;
For he it is that shall bring forth
  My feet out of the net.
16 O turn thee unto me, my God,
  And mercy to me show;

For I am lone and desolate,
And am brought very low.

17 Enlarged the griefs are of mine heart;
Me from distress relieve.
18 See mine affliction and my pain,
And all my sins forgive.
19 Consider thou mine enemies,
Because they many be;
And it a cruel hatred is
Which they do bear to me.

20 O do thou keep my soul; O God,
Do thou deliver me:
Let me not be ashamed; for I
Do put my trust in thee.
21 Let truth and uprightness me keep,
For I on thee attend.
22 Redemption, Lord, to Israel
From all his troubles send.

PSALM XXVI. Abbey, S.

1 JUDGE me, O Lord, for I have walked
In mine integrity:
I trusted also in the Lord;
Slide therefore shall not I.
2 Examine me, and do me prove;
Try heart and reins, O God:
3 For thy love is before mine eyes,
Thy truth's paths I have trod.

4 With persons vain I have not sat,
Nor with dissemblers gone:
5 The assembly of ill men I hate;
To sit with such I shun.

6 Mine hands in innocence, O Lord,
   I'll wash and purify;
So to thine holy altar go
   And compass it will I:

7 That I with voice of thanksgiving
   May publish and declare,
And tell of all thy mighty works,
   That great and wondrous are.

8 The habitation of thy house,
   Lord, I have loved well;
Yea, in that place I do delight
   Where doth thine honour dwell.

9 With sinners gather not my soul,
   And such as blood would spill:
10 Whose hands devices mischievous,
   Whose right hand bribes do fill.
11 But as for me, I will walk on
   In mine integrity:
Do thou redeem me, and, O Lord,
   Be merciful to me.

12 My foot upon an even place
   Doth stand with steadfastness:
Within the congregations I
   Jehovah's name will bless.

PSALM XXVII.—1st Version. St. Bartholomew, 44.

1 THE Lord's my light and saving health;
      Who shall make me dismayed?
My life's strength is the Lord; of whom
      Then shall I be afraid?
2 What time mine enemies and foes,
      Most wicked persons all,

To eat my flesh against me rose,
   They stumbled and did fall.
3 Against me though an host encamp,
   My heart yet fearless is:
Though war against me rise, I will
   Be confident in this.
4 One thing I of the Lord desired,
   And will seek to obtain,
That all days of my life I may
   Within God's house remain;

That I the beauty of the Lord
   Behold may and admire,
And that I in his holy place
   May reverently inquire.
5 For he in his pavilion shall
   Me hide in evil days;
In secret of his tent me hide,
   And on a rock me raise.

6 And now even at this present time
   Mine head shall lifted be
Above all those that are my foes,
   And round encompass me:
Then offerings of joyfulness
   Into his house I'll bring;
And I will sing unto the Lord,
   Yea, I will praises sing.

7 O Lord, give ear unto my voice,
   When I do cry to thee;
Upon me also mercy have,
   And do thou answer me.
8 When thou didst say, Seek ye my face,
   Then unto thee reply

>   Thus did my heart, Above all things
>   Thy face, Lord, seek will I.

9 Far from me hide not thou thy face;
    Put not away from thee
  Thy servant in thy wrath: thou hast
    An helper been to me.
  O God, who my salvation art,
    Leave me not, nor forsake;
10 Though father, mother, both me leave,
    The Lord me up will take.

11 O Lord, instruct me in thy way,
    To me a leader be
  In a plain path, because of those
    That hatred bear to me.
12 Give me not to mine enemies' will;
    For witnesses that lie
  Against me risen are, and such
    As breathe out cruelty.

13 I fainted had, unless that I
    Believed had to see
  The Lord's own goodness in the land
    Of them that living be.
14 Wait on the Lord, and be thou strong,
    And he shall strength afford
  Unto thine heart; yea, do thou wait,
    I say, upon the Lord.

PSALM XXVII.—2nd Version. St. John, 73.

1 JEHOVAH is my light,
    And my salvation he;
  Who then shall me affright?
    The Lord is unto me

My life's sure stronghold, ever near;
Of whom then shall I stand in fear?

2 When wicked men, my foes
  And adversaries all,
  To eat my flesh arose,
  They stumbled and did fall.
Though hosts surround, I will not quail;
In this I trust, though war assail.

3 For one thing did I pray,
  This I'll seek to obtain,
  That all my life I may
  In the Lord's house remain;
Jehovah's beauty to admire,
And in his temple to inquire.

4 Within his tent he will
  Me hide in evil days,
  Me in his tent conceal,
  And on a rock me raise.
And now my head shall lifted be
Above my foes that compass me.

5 Into his courts with joy
  I'll sacrifices bring;
  Songs shall my lips employ,
  Praise to the Lord I'll sing.
Lord, hear me when I cry to thee;
On me have mercy; answer me.

6 Thou saidst, Seek ye my face;
  Then did my heart reply,
  In thine abundant grace,
  Thy face, Lord, seek will I.

  In wrath hide not thy face from me,
  Nor put thy servant far from thee.

7 My help of old art thou,
   To thee I me betake;
   O God, my Saviour, now
   Leave me not, nor forsake.
  When father, mother, both me leave,
  The Lord himself will me receive.

8 Teach me, O Lord, thy way;
   Me in a plain path guide,
   For foes my steps survey:
   Me give not to their pride:
  For false accusers 'gainst me rise,
  And such as breathe out cruelties.

9 I fainted had unless
   I had believed to see
   The Lord's own graciousness
   'Mong them that living be.
  Wait on the Lord; be strong of heart;
  Yea, wait, and he shall strength impart.

PSALM XXVIII.—1st Version. Gloucester, C4.

1 TO thee I'll cry, O Lord, my rock;
  Hold not thy peace to me;
 Lest like those who to death go down
  I by thy silence be.

2 The voice hear of my humble prayers,
  When unto thee I cry;
 When to thy holy oracle
  I lift my hands on high.

3 With ill men draw me not away
  That work iniquity;

That speak peace to their friends, while in
    Their hearts doth mischief lie.
4 Give them according to their deeds,
    And evil of their way;
After the work of their own hands
    Do thou to them repay.

5 God shall not build, but them destroy,
    Who would not understand
The Lord's own works, nor did regard
    The doing of his hand.
6 For ever blessed be the Lord,
    For graciously he heard
The voice of my petitions, and
    My prayers did regard.

7 The Lord's my strength and shield; my heart
    Upon him did rely;
And I am helped: hence my heart
    Doth joy exceedingly;
And with my song I will him praise.
8   Their strength is God alone:
He also is the saving strength
    Of his anointed one.

9 O thine own people do thou save.
    Bless thine inheritance;
Them also do thou feed, and them
    For evermore advance.

PSALM XXVIII.—2nd Version. <small>Eisenach, 60.</small>

1 TO thee, Jehovah, will I cry,
    My rock; O, be not silent now!
Lest, if thou hold thy peace, I be
    Like those who in the pit lie low.

2 O, hear my supplication's voice,
    When unto thee for help I cry,
When to thy holy oracle
    I lift my pleading hands on high.

3 O, with the wicked draw me not
    Away, nor with the men of sin;
Who to their neighbours speak of peace,
    But evil is their heart within.

4 Give them according to their deed,
    Their evil doings all reward;
Give them according to their works,
    Return them their desert, O Lord.

5 Since they Jehovah's mighty acts,
    And doings of his hands disdain,
He will destroy them in his wrath,
    And never build them up again.

6 Blest be Jehovah! He hath heard
    My supplication's voice in heaven;
Jehovah is my strength and shield;
    I trusted him, he help hath given.

7 And therefore shall my heart exult,
    My song shall of his praises be.
He is their strength; the saving strength
    Of his anointed one is he.

8 O, save the nation of thy love,
    O, bless thy chosen heritage;
Feed them and lead them as a flock,
    Lift thou them up from age to age.

PSALM XXIX.—1st Version. Zwingle, 55.

1 GIVE ye unto the Lord, ye sons
    That of the mighty be,

All strength and glory to the Lord
  With cheerfulness give ye.
2 O give ye glory to the Lord,
  And his great name adore;
And in the beauty of holiness
  Bow down the Lord before.

3 The Lord's voice on the waters is;
  The God of majesty
Doth thunder, and on multitudes
  Of waters sitteth he.
4 A mighty voice it is that comes
  Out from the Lord most high;
The voice of the great Lord is full
  Of glorious majesty.

5 The voice of the Eternal doth
  Asunder cedars tear;
Jehovah doth the cedars break
  That Lebanon doth bear.
6 He makes them like a calf to skip,
  Even that great Lebanon,
And, like to a young unicorn,
  The mountain Sirion.

7 The Lord's voice cleaves the flames of fire;
8   The desert it doth shake:
The Lord doth make the wilderness
  Of Kadesh all to quake.
9 The Lord's voice makes the hinds to calve,
  It makes the forest bare:
And in his temple every one
  His glory doth declare.

10 The Lord sat on the flood; the Lord
  Sits King, and ever shall.

11 The Lord will give his people strength,
    And with peace bless them all.

PSALM XXIX.—2nd Version. Roxburgh, 88.

1 GIVE ye to Jehovah, O sons of the mighty,
    Give ye to Jehovah the glory and power;
  Give ye to Jehovah the honour and glory;
    In beauty of holiness kneel and adore.
2 The voice of Jehovah comes down on the waters;   [nigh:
    In thunder the God of the glory draws
  Lo, over the waves of the wide flowing waters
    Jehovah as King is enthronéd on high!

3 The voice of Jehovah is mighty, is mighty;
    The voice of Jehovah in majesty speaks:
  The voice of Jehovah the cedars is breaking;
    Jehovah the cedars of Lebanon breaks.
4 Like young heifers sporting, they skip when he speaketh;
    Lo, Lebanon leaps at the sound of his name!
  Like son of the unicorn Sirion is skipping;
    The voice of Jehovah divideth the flame.

5 The voice of Jehovah—it shaketh the desert;
    The desert of Kadesh it shaketh with fear:
  The hind of the field into travail-pangs casteth:
    The voice of Jehovah the forest strips bare.
6 Each one, in his temple, his glory proclaimeth.
    He sat on the flood; he is King on his throne.
  Jehovah all strength to his people imparteth;
    Jehovah with peace ever blesseth his own.

PSALM XXX.—1st Version. Gauntlett, 23.

1 LORD, I will thee extol, for thou
    Hast lifted me on high,
And over me thou to rejoice
    Madest not mine enemy.
2 O thou who art the Lord my God,
    I in distress to thee
With loud cries lifted up my voice,
    And thou hast healed me.

3 O Lord, my soul thou hast brought up
    And rescued from the grave;
That I to death should not go down,
    Alive thou didst me save.
4 O ye that are his holy ones,
    Sing praise unto the Lord;
And unto him give thanks, when ye
    His holiness record.

5 For but a moment lasts his wrath;
    Life in his favour lies:
Weeping may for a night endure,
    At morn doth joy arise.
6 In my prosperity I said
    That nothing shall me move:
7 O Lord, thou hast my mountain made
    To stand strong by thy love.

Thou didst thy face hide; then was I
    Sore troubled and dismayed:
8 I cried to thee, O Lord, to thee
    I supplication made:
9 What profit is there in my blood,
    When I to death go down?

> Shall dust give praises unto thee?
> Shall it thy truth make known?

10 Hear, Lord, have mercy; help me, Lord;
11   Thou didst from sackcloth free;
> My grief to dancing thou hast turned,
> With gladness girded me;

12 That sing thy praise my glory may,
> And never silent be.
> O Lord my God, for evermore
> I will give thanks to thee.

PSALM XXX.—2nd Version. Dykes, 72.

1   LORD, I will thee extol;
> For thou hast set me free,
> And over me to rule
> Made not mine enemy.
> To thee, O Lord my God, I cried;
> And thou hast health and strength supplied.

2   Thou hast my soul restored,
> When I was near the grave;
> And from the pit, O Lord,
> Alive thou didst me save.
> O ye his saints, sing to the Lord;
> With thanks his holiness record.

3   Soon is his anger past;
> Life in his favour lies:
> Tears for a night may last,
> At morn shall joy arise.
> I said in my prosperity,
> I surely never moved shall be.

4   My mountain, by thy grace,
> Thou madest to stand in power;

   Thou didst withdraw thy face,
   And I was troubled sore.
 To thee, O Lord, with cries I prayed;
 I to the Lord petition made.

5   What shall my blood avail,
   When I to grave go down?
   Shall dust thy praises tell;
   Shall it thy truth make known?
 Hear me, O Lord, and mercy send;
 Thy help to me, O Lord, extend.

6   My mourning thou at last
   Hast into dancing turned:
   And thou for sackcloth hast
   With gladness me adorned;
 That sing to thee my glory may.
 Lord, thee my God I'll praise for aye.

PSALM XXXI.   Kilmarnock, 2s.

1 IN thee, O Lord, I put my trust;
  Shamed let me never be:
 According to thy righteousness
  Do thou deliver me.
2 Bow down thine ear to me, with speed
  Send me deliverance:
 To save me, my strong rock be thou,
  And my house of defence.
3 Because thou art my rock, and thee
  I for my fortress take;
 Do thou me therefore lead and guide,
  Even for thine own name's sake.
4 And, since thou art my strength, do thou
  Pull me out of the net,

Which they in subtlety for me
  So privily have set.
5 Into thy hand I do commit
  My spirit; thou art he,
  O thou, Jehovah, God of truth,
  Who hast redeemed me.
6 Those that do lying vanities
  Regard I have abhorred:
  But as for me, my confidence
  Is fixed upon the Lord.
7 I'll in thy mercy greatly joy:
  For thou my miseries
  Considered hast; thou hast my soul
  Known in adversities;
8 And thou hast not inclosed me
  Within the enemy's hand;
  And by thee have my feet been made
  In a large place to stand.

9 O Lord, upon me mercy have,
  For trouble is on me:
  Mine eye, my belly, and my soul,
  With grief consumed be.
10 Because my life with grief is spent,
  My years with sighs and groans:
  My strength doth fail; and for my sin
  Consumed are my bones.
11 I through my foes all was a scorn,
  And to my neighbours near
  A great reproach have I become,
  And to my friends a fear:
12 And when they saw me walk abroad,
  They from my presence fled;

    I like a broken vessel am,
      Forgotten as one dead.
13 For slanders I of many heard;
      Fear compassed me, while they
    Against me did consult, and plot
      To take my life away.
14 But as for me, O Lord, my trust
      Upon thee I have laid;
    And I to thee, Thou art my God,
      Have confidently said.
15 My times are wholly in thy hand:
      Do thou deliver me
    From their hands that mine enemies
      And persecutors be.
16 Thy countenance to shine do thou
      Upon thy servant make;
    And unto me salvation give,
      For thy great mercies' sake.
17 Let me not be ashamed, O Lord,
      For on thee called I have:
    Let wicked men be shamed, let them
      Be silent in the grave.
18 To silence put the lying lips,
      That grievous things do say,
    And hard reports, in pride and scorn,
      On righteous men do lay.
19 How great's thy goodness thou for them
      That fear thee keep'st in store,
    And wrought'st for them that trust in thee
      The sons of men before!
20 In secret of thy presence thou
      Shalt hide them from man's pride:

From strife of tongues thou closely shalt,
　　As in a tent, them hide.
21 All praise and thanks be to the Lord:
　　For he hath magnified
　His wondrous love to me within
　　A city fortified.
22 For, From thine eyes cut off I am,
　　I in my haste had said;
　My voice yet heard'st thou, when to thee
　　With cries my moan I made.

23 O love the Lord, all ye his saints;
　　Because the Lord doth guard
　The faithful, and he plenteously
　　Proud doers doth reward.
24 Be of good courage, and he strength
　　Unto your heart shall send,
　All ye whose hope and confidence
　　Upon the Lord depend.

PSALM XXXII. Newington, 34.

1 O BLESSED is the man to whom
　　Is freely pardoned
　All the transgression he hath done,
　　Whose sin is covered.
2 Blest is the man to whom the Lord
　　Imputeth not his sin,
　And in whose spirit is no guile,
　　Nor fraud is found therein.

3 When I from speaking did refrain,
　　And silent was my tongue,
　My bones then waxed old, because
　　I cried out all day long.

4 Because on me both day and night
    Thine hand did heavy lie,
So that my moisture turned is
    To summer's drought thereby.

5 I thereupon have unto thee
    My sin acknowledged,
And likewise mine iniquity.
    I have not covered:
I will confess unto the Lord
    My trespasses, said I;
And of my sin thou freely didst
    Forgive the iniquity.

6 For this shall every godly one
    His prayer make to thee;
In such a time he shall thee seek,
    As found thou mayest be.
Surely, when floods of waters great
    Do swell up to the brim,
They shall not overwhelm his soul,
    Nor once come near to him.

7 Thou art my hiding-place, thou shalt
    From trouble keep me free:
Thou with songs of deliverance
    About shalt compass me.

8 I will instruct thee, and thee teach
    The way that thou shalt go;
And, with mine eye upon thee set,
    I will direction show.

9 Then be not like the horse or mule,
    Which do not understand;
Whose mouth, that they may come to thee,
    A bridle must command.

10 Unto the man that wicked is
　　His sorrows shall abound;
　But him that trusteth in the Lord
　　Mercy shall compass round.

11 Ye righteous, in the Lord be glad,
　　In him do ye rejoice:
　All ye that upright are in heart,
　　For joy lift up your voice.

PSALM XXXIII. St. David, 45.

1 YE righteous, in the Lord rejoice;
　　It comely is and right,
　That upright men with thankful voice
　　Should praise the Lord of might.
2 Jehovah praise with harp, to him
　　Sing with the psaltery;
　Upon a ten-stringed instrument
　　Make ye sweet melody.

3 A new song to him sing, and play
　　With loud noise skilfully;
4 For right's the Lord's word, all his work
　　Is done in verity.
5 To judgment and to righteousness
　　A love he beareth still;
　The loving-kindness of the Lord
　　The earth throughout doth fill.

6 The heavens by Jehovah's word
　　Did their beginning take;
　And by the breathing of his mouth
　　He all their hosts did make.
7 The waters of the seas he brings
　　Together as an heap;

And in storehouses, as it were,
   He layeth up the deep.
8 Let earth, and all that live therein,
   With reverence fear the Lord;
  Let all the world's inhabitants
   Dread him with one accord.
9 For he did speak the word, and done
   It was without delay;
  Established it firmly stood,
   Whatever he did say.
10 The Lord the counsel brings to nought
   Which heathen folk do take;
  And what the people do devise
   Of none effect doth make.
11 O but the counsel of the Lord
   Doth stand for ever sure;
  And of his heart the purposes
   From age to age endure.
12 That nation blessed is, whose God
   Jehovah is, and those
  A blessed people are, whom for
   His heritage he chose.
13 The Lord from heaven looks; he sees
   All sons of men full well:
14 He views all from his dwelling-place
   That in the earth do dwell.
15 He forms their hearts alike, and all
   Their doings he observes.
16 Great hosts save not a king, much strength
   No mighty man preserves.
17 An horse for safety and defence
   Is a deceitful thing;

    And by the greatness of his strength
      Can no deliverance bring.
18 Behold, on those that do him fear
      The Lord doth set his eye;
    Even those who on his mercy do
      With confidence rely;
19 From death to free their soul, in dearth
      Life unto them to yield.
20 Our soul doth wait upon the Lord;
      He is our help and shield.

21 Since in his holy name we trust,
      Our heart shall joyful be.
22 Lord, let thy mercy be on us,
      As we do hope in thee.

PSALM XXXIV. St. Bartholomew, 44.

1 GOD will I bless all times; his praise
      My mouth shall still express.
2 My soul shall boast in God: the meek
      Shall hear with joyfulness.
3 Extol the Lord with me, let us
      His name together praise;
4 I sought the Lord, he heard, and did
      Above all fears me raise.

5 They looked to him and lightened were:
      Their faces were not shamed;
6 This poor man cried, God heard, and him
      From all distress redeemed.
7 The angel of the Lord encamps,
      And round encompasseth
    All those about that do him fear,
      And them delivereth.

8 O taste and see that God is good:
   Who trusts in him is blessed.
 9 Fear God his saints: none that him **fear**
   Shall be with want oppressed.
10 The lions young may hungry be,
     And they may lack their food:
   But they that truly seek the Lord
     Shall not lack any good.

11 O children, hither do ye come,
     And unto me give ear;
   I shall you teach to understand
     How ye the Lord should fear.
12 What man is he that life desires,
     To see good would live long?
13 Thy lips refrain from speaking guile,
     And from ill words thy tongue.

14 Depart from ill, do good, seek peace,
     Pursue it earnestly.
15 God's eyes are on the just; his ears
     Are open to their cry.
16 The face of God is set against
     Those that do wickedly,
   That he may quite out from the earth
     Cut off their memory.

17 The righteous cry unto the Lord,
     He unto them gives ear;
   And they out of their troubles all
     By him delivered are.
18 The Lord is ever nigh to them
     In heart that broken be;
   Those who in spirit contrite are
     He saveth graciously.

19 The troubles that afflict the just
    In number many be;
  But yet at length out of them all
    The Lord doth set him free.
20 He carefully his bones doth keep,
    Whatever may befall;
  That not so much as one of them
    Can broken be at all.

21 Ill shall the wicked slay; condemned
    Shall be who hate the just.
22 The Lord redeems his servants' souls;
    None perish that him trust.

PSALM XXXV.   Esslingen, 19.

1 PLEAD, Lord, with those that plead;
    and fight
  With those that fight with me.
2 Of shield and buckler take thou hold,
    Stand up mine help to be.
3 Draw also out the spear, and stop
    My persecutors' way;
  And in thy mercy, to my soul,
    I'm thy salvation, say.

4 Let them confounded be and shamed
    That for my soul have sought:
  Who plot my hurt turned back be they,
    And to confusion brought.
5 Let them be like unto the chaff
    That flies before the wind;
  And let the angel of the Lord
    Pursue them hard behind.

6 With darkness cover thou their way,
    And let it slippery prove;
    And let the angel of the Lord
    Pursue them from above.
7 For without cause have they for me
    In secret hid their snare;
    And they a pit without a cause
    Did for my soul prepare.

8 Let ruin seize him unawares;
    His net he hid withal
    Himself let catch; and in the same
    Destruction let him fall.
9 My soul in God shall joy, and glad
    In his salvation be:
10 And all my bones shall say, O Lord,
    Who is like unto thee,

    Who dost the poor set free from him
        That is for him too strong;
    The poor and needy from the man
        That spoils and does him wrong?
11 False witnesses arose; 'gainst me
    Things that I knew not laid:
12 They to the spoiling of my soul
    Me ill for good repaid.

13 But as for me, when they were sick,
    In sackcloth sad I mourned;
    My humbled soul did fast, my prayer
    Into my bosom turned.
14 I bore myself as for a friend,
    Or brother dear to me;
    As one who for a mother mourns,
    I bowed down heavily.

15 But in my trouble they rejoiced,
   And they together met;
  The abjects vile together did
   Themselves against me set.
  I knew it not; they did me tear,
   And quiet would not be.
16 With mocking hypocrites at feasts
   They gnashed their teeth at me.

17 How long, Lord, look'st thou on? from
   Destructions they intend   [those
  Rescue my soul, from lions young
   My darling do defend.
18 I will give thanks to thee, O Lord,
   Within the assembly great;
  And where much people gathered are
   Thy praises forth will set.

19 Let not my wrongful enemies
   Proudly rejoice o'er me;
  Nor let them wink with scornful eye,
   Who hate me causelessly.
20 For peace they do not speak at all:
   But crafty plots prepare
  Against all those within the land
   That meek and quiet are.

21 Their mouths they open wide at me,
   They say, Ha, ha! we see:
22 Lord, thou hast seen, hold not thy peace;
   Lord, be not far from me.
23 Stir up thyself; wake, that thou may'st
   Judgment to me afford,
  Even to my cause, O thou that art
   My only God and Lord.

24 O Lord my God, do thou me judge
 After thy righteousness;
And let them not their joy o'er me
 Triumphantly express:
25 Nor let them say within their hearts,
 Ah, we would have it thus;
Nor suffer them to say, Lo, he
 Is swallowed up by us.

26 Shamed and confounded be they all
 That at my hurt are glad;
Let those against me that do boast
 With shame and scorn be clad.
27 Let them who love my righteous cause
 With gladness shout, nor cease
To say, The Lord be magnified,
 Who loves his servant's peace.

28 Thy righteousness shall also be
 Declared by my tongue;
The praises that belong to thee
 Speak shall it all day long.

PSALM XXXVI. French, &c.

1 THE wicked man's transgression speaks
 Within my heart and says,
Undoubtedly the fear of God
 Is not before his eyes.
2 Because himself he flattereth
 In his own blinded eyes
The hatefulness shall not be found
 Of his iniquities.

3 Words from his mouth proceeding are,
 Fraud and iniquity:

He to be wise, and to do good,
　　Hath left off utterly.
4 He mischief, lying on his bed,
　　Most cunningly doth plot:
　He sets himself in ways not good,
　　Ill he abhorreth not.

5 Thy mercy, Lord, is in the heavens;
　　Thy truth doth reach the clouds;
6 Thy justice is like mountains great;
　　Thy judgments deep as floods:
　Lord, thou preservest man and beast.
7 　How precious is thy grace!
　Therefore in shadow of thy wings
　　Men's sons their trust shall place.

8 They with the fatness of thy house
　　Shall be well satisfied;
　From rivers of thy pleasures thou
　　Wilt drink to them provide.
9 Because of life the fountain pure
　　Remains alone with thee;
　And in that purest light of thine
　　We clearly light shall see.

10 Thy loving-kindness unto them
　　Continue that thee know;
　And still on men upright in heart
　　Thy righteousness bestow.
11 And suffer not the foot of pride
　　To trample upon me;
　And by the hand of wicked men
　　Thrust forth let me not be.

12 There fallen to the earth are they
　　That work iniquities:

Cast down they are, and never shall
    Be able to arise.

PSALM XXXVII Leicester, 29.

1 FOR evil-doers fret thou not
    Thyself unquietly;
Nor do thou envy bear to those
    That work iniquity.
2 For, even like unto the grass,
    Soon be cut down shall they;
And, like the green and tender herb,
    They wither shall away.

3 Set thou thy trust upon the Lord,
    And be thou doing good;
And so thou in the land shalt dwell,
    And verily have food.
4 Delight thyself in God; he'll give
    Thine heart's desire to thee.
5 Thy way to God commit, him trust,
    It bring to pass shall he.

6 And, like unto the light, he shall
    Thy righteousness display;
And he thy judgment shall bring forth,
    Like noon-tide of the day.
7 Rest in the Lord, and patiently
    Wait for him: do not fret
For him who, prospering in his way,
    Success in sin doth get.

8 Let anger cease within thy heart,
    And wrath forsake thou too:
Fret not thyself in any wise,
    That evil thou shouldst do.

9 For those that evil-doers are
    Shall be cut off and fall:
  But those that wait upon the Lord
    The earth inherit shall.

10 For yet a little while, and then
    The wicked shall not be;
  His place thou shalt consider well,
    But it thou shalt not see.
11 But by inheritance the earth
    The meek ones shall possess:
  They also shall delight themselves
    In an abundant peace.

12 The wicked gnashes with his teeth,
    And plots the just to slay;
13 The Lord shall laugh at him, because
    At hand he sees his day.
14 The wicked have drawn out the sword,
    And bent their bow, to slay
  The poor and needy, and to kill
    Men of an upright way.

15 But their own sword, which they have
    Shall enter their own heart;   [drawn,
  Their bows which they have bent shall
    And into pieces part.   [break,
16 A little that a just man hath
    Is more and better far
  Than is the wealth of many such
    As vile and wicked are.

17 For sinners' arms shall broken be;
    The Lord the just sustains.
18 The Lord doth know the just man's ways;
    Their heritage remains.

19 They shall not be ashamed when they
     The evil time do see;
   And when the days of famine are
     They satisfied shall be.
20 But wicked men, Jehovah's foes,
     As fat of lambs, decay;
   They shall consume, yea, into smoke
     They shall consume away.
21 The wicked borrows, but the same
     Again he doth not pay:
   Whereas the righteous mercy shows,
     And gives his own away.
22 For such as blessed be of him
     The earth inherit shall;
   And they that cursed are of him
     Shall be destroyed all.
23 A good man's footsteps by the Lord
     Are ordered aright;
   And in the way wherein he walks
     He greatly doth delight.
24 Although he fall, yet shall he not
     Be cast down utterly;
   Because the Lord with his own hand
     Upholds him mightily.
25 I have been young, and now am old,
     Yet have I never seen
   The just man left, nor that his seed
     For bread have beggars been.
26 He's ever merciful, and lends:
     His seed is blest therefore.
27 Depart from evil, and do good,
     And dwell for evermore.

28 For God loves judgment, and his saints
    Leaves not in any case;
  They are kept ever: but cut off
    Shall be the sinner's race.

29 The just inherit shall the land,
    And ever in it dwell;
30 The just man's mouth doth wisdom speak;
    His tongue doth judgment tell.
31 His God's law is within his heart;
    His steps slide not away.
32 The wicked man doth watch the just,
    And seeketh him to slay.

33 Yet him the Lord will not forsake,
    Nor leave him in his hands:
  The righteous will he not condemn,
    When he in judgment stands.
34 Wait on the Lord, and keep his way,
    And thee exalt shall he
  Earth to inherit; when cut off
    The wicked thou shalt see.

35 I saw the wicked great in power
    Spread like a green bay-tree:
36 He passed, yea, was not: him I sought,
    But found he could not be.
37 Mark thou the perfect, and behold
    The man of uprightness;
  Because that surely of this man
    The latter end is peace.

38 But those men that transgressors are
    Shall be destroyed together;
  The latter end of wicked men
    Shall be cut off for ever.

39 But the salvation of the just
    Is from the Lord above;
  He in the time of their distress
    Their stay and strength doth prove.

40 The Lord shall help and rescue them;
    He shall them free and save
  From wicked men; because in him
    Their confidence they have.

PSALM XXXVIII.   *Bangor, 9.*

1 IN thy great indignation, Lord,
    Do thou rebuke me not;
  Nor on me lay thy chastening hand,
    In thy displeasure hot.
2 For in me fast thine arrows stick,
    Thine hand doth press me sore:
3 And in my flesh there is no health,
    Nor soundness any more.

  This grief I have, because thy wrath
    Is forth against me gone;
  And in my bones there is no rest,
    For sin that I have done.
4 Because gone o'er mine head my sins
    And my transgressions be;
  And, as a weighty burden, they
    Too heavy are for me.

5 My wounds corrupt and noisome are;
    My folly makes it so.
6 I troubled am, and much bowed down;
    All day I mourning go.
7 For a disease that loathsome is
    So fills my loins with pain,

That in my weak and weary flesh
   No soundness doth remain.
8 So very feeble and infirm,
   And sorely crushed am I,
That, through disquiet of my heart,
   I make loud moan and cry.
9 O Lord, before thine eyes is all
   That is desired by me:
And of my heart the secret groans
   Not hidden are from thee.
10 My heart doth pant incessantly,
   My strength doth quite decay;
As for mine eyes, their wonted light
   Is from me gone away.
11 My lovers and my friends do stand
   Far distant from my sore;
And those do stand aloof that were
   Kinsmen and kind before.

12 Yea, they that seek my life lay snares;
   Who seek to do me wrong
Speak mischief, and deceitful things
   Imagine all day long.
13 But, as one deaf that heareth not,
   I suffered all to pass;
I as a dumb man did become,
   Whose mouth not opened was:
14 As one that hears not, in whose mouth
   Are no reproofs at all.
15 For, Lord, I hope in thee; my God,
   Thou'lt hear me when I call.
16 For I said, Hear me, lest they should
   Rejoice o'er me with pride;

And o'er me magnify themselves,
   What time my foot doth slide.

17 Because I ready am to halt,
   My grief I ever see:
18 For I'll declare my sin, and grieve
   For mine iniquity.
19 But yet my foes are full of life,
   And strong are they beside;
   And they that hate me wrongfully
   Are greatly multiplied.

20 And they for good that render ill
   As enemies me withstood;
   Yea, even for this, because that I
   Do follow what is good.
21 Forsake me not, O Lord; my God,
   Far from me never be.
22 O Lord, thou my salvation art,
   Haste to give help to me.

PSALM XXXIX.—1st Version. St. Mary, 47.

1 I SAID, I will look to my ways,
     Lest with my tongue I sin:
   In sight of wicked men my mouth
     With bridle I'll keep in.
2 With silence I as dumb became,
     I did myself restrain
   Even from good; but then the more
     Increased was my pain.

3 My heart within me waxed hot,
     And while I mused long,
   A fire within me kindled was;
     Then spake I with my tongue.

4 Mine end and measure of my days,
    O Lord, unto me show
What is the same; that I thereby
    How frail I am may know.

5 Lo, thou my days an handbreadth mad'st;
    Mine age is nought with thee:
Sure each man in his best estate
    Is wholly vanity.

6 Sure each man walks in a vain show;
    They vex themselves in vain:
He heaps up wealth, and doth not know
    To whom it shall pertain.

7 And now, O Lord, what wait I for?
    My hope is fixed on thee.
8 Free me from all my trespasses,
    The fool's scorn make not me.
9 Dumb am I, opening not my mouth,
    Because this work is thine.
10 O, take thy stroke away from me;
    By thy hand's blow I pine.

11 When with rebukes thou dost correct
    Man for iniquity,
Like moth thou dost his beauty waste:
    Each man is vanity.
12 Regard my cry, Lord, at my tears
    And prayers not silent be:
I sojourn as my fathers all,
    And stranger am with thee.

13 O spare thou me, that I my strength
    Recover may again,
Before that hence I do depart,
    And here no more remain.

PSALM XXXIX.—2nd Version. <small>Mentz, 80.</small>

1 I WILL of my ways be heedful,
    That I sin not with my tongue;
For my mouth a curb is needful,
    While the wicked round me throng.
2 Thus I said, and dumb remainéd;
    From my lips no sound was heard;
From good words I even refrainéd,
    But my inmost soul was stirred.

3 Long my heart was in me burning,
    Ere the smothered flame out-brake,
And, the enkindled words returning,
    Thus impatiently I spake:
4 Teach me, Lord, the number meting
    Of my days, how brief it is;
Make me see and know how fleeting,
    Vain and sad a life is this.

5 Life a span is at the longest;
    Mine is nothing, Lord, to thee;
In his best estate and strongest
    Man is only vanity.
6 Yea, he fleeting past us goeth
    In a shadow brief and vain,
Heaping riches; but none knoweth
    Who shall gather them again.

7 And where, Lord, is my reliance?
    All my hope is fixed on thee.
From my sin, and the defiance
    Of the foolish, save thou me!
8 I, because it was thy pleasure,
    Murmured not, nor silence broke;

Yet remove thy plague: o'er measure
　　　　Grievous is thy heavy stroke.

9 When for sin or slighted duty
　　Man corrected is by thee,
　But a moth-worn robe his beauty,
　　And but vanity is he.
10 See my tears, regard my danger;
　　Be not deaf unto my prayer;
　For a sojourner and stranger
　　Am I, as my fathers were.

11 Spare me, yet a little spare me,
　　To recover strength, before
　Thy dread summons hence shall bear me
　　To be seen on earth no more!

PSALM XL. *Kilmarnock, 23.*

1 I WAITED for the Lord my God,
　　And patiently did bear;
　At length to me he did incline
　　My voice and cry to hear.
2 He took me from a fearful pit,
　　And from the miry clay,
　And on a rock he set my feet,
　　Establishing my way.

3 He put a new song in my mouth,
　　Our God to magnify:
　Many shall see it, and shall fear,
　　And on the Lord rely.
4 O blessed is the man whose trust
　　Upon the Lord relies;
　Respecting not the proud, nor such
　　As turn aside to lies.

5 O Lord my God, full many are
  The wonders thou hast done;
Thy gracious thoughts to us-ward far
  Above all thoughts are gone.
None can them reckon unto thee;
  If I would them declare,
If I would speak of them, they more
  Than can be numbered are.

6 No sacrifice nor offering
  Didst thou at all desire;
Mine ears thou op'st; sin-offering thou
  And burnt didst not require:
7 Then to the Lord these were my words,
  I come, behold and see;
Within the volume of the book
  It written is of me;

8 To do thy will I take delight,
  O thou my God that art:
Yea, that most holy law of thine
  I have within my heart.
9 Within the congregation great
  I righteousness did preach:
Lo, thou dost know, O Lord, that I
  Refrained not my speech.

10 I never did within my heart
  Conceal thy righteousness;
I thy salvation have declared,
  And shown thy faithfulness:
Thy kindness, which most loving is,
  Concealed have not I,
Nor from the congregation great
  Have hid thy verity.

11 Thy tender mercies, Lord, from me
   O do thou not restrain;
   Thy loving-kindness, and thy truth,
   Let them me still maintain.
12 For ills past reckoning compass me,
   And mine iniquities
   Such hold upon me taken have,
   I cannot lift mine eyes:

   More they than hairs upon my head,
   Thence is my heart dismayed;
13 Be pleased, O Lord, to rescue me;
   Lord, hasten to mine aid.
14 Shamed and confounded be they all
   That seek my soul to kill;
   Yea, let them backward driven be
   And sham'd, that wish me ill.

15 For a reward of this their shame
   Confounded let them be,
   Who in this manner scoffing say,
   Aha, aha! to me.
16 Let all who seek thy face rejoice,
   And still be glad in thee;
   Who thy salvation love, say still,
   The Lord exalted be.

17 I'm poor and needy, yet the Lord
   Of me a care doth take;
   Thou art my Saviour and my help;
   My God, no tarrying make.

PSALM XLI. *Jackson, 26.*

1 BLESSED is he that carefully
   Considereth the poor;

  The Lord in time of trouble him
   Deliverance will secure.
2 He will him keep, yea save alive;
   On earth he blessed shall live;
  And to his enemies' desire
   Thou wilt him never give.
3 The Lord will strengthen when on bed
   Of weakness he doth mourn;
  And in his sickness sore, O Lord,
   Thou all his bed wilt turn.
4 I said, O Lord, do thou extend
   Thy mercy unto me;
  O do thou heal my soul, because
   I have offended thee.
5 Those that to me are enemies
   Of me do evil say,
  When shall he die, that so his name
   May perish quite away?
6 To see me if he comes, he speaks
   Vain words: but then his heart
  Doth gather mischief, which he tells,
   When forth he doth depart.
7 My haters jointly whispering
   Against me hurt devise;
8 Mischief, say they, cleaves fast to him;
   He lies and shall not rise.
9 Yea, even mine own familiar friend,
   On whom I did rely,
  Who ate my bread, even he his heel
   Against me lifted high.
10 But, Lord, be merciful to me,
   And up again me raise,

      That I may justly them requite
        According to their ways.
11 By this I know that certainly
     I favoured am by thee;
   Because my hateful enemy
     Doth not exult o'er me.

12 But as for me, thou me uphold'st
     In mine integrity;
   And me before thy countenance
     Thou sett'st continually.
13 The Lord, the God of Israel,
     Be blest for ever then,
   From age to age eternally.
     Amen, yea, and amen.

PSALM XLII.   Farrant, 21.

1 AS pants the hart for water-brooks,
     My soul pants, Lord, for thee;
2 For God, the living God, I thirst;
   God's courts when shall I see?
3 My tears have unto me been meat
     Both in the night and day,
While unto me continually,
     Where is thy God? they say.

4 My soul is poured out in me,
     When this I think upon;
Because that with the multitude
   I heretofore had gone;
With them into God's house I went,
     With voice of joy and praise;
Yea, with the multitude that kept
     The solemn holy days.

5 O why art thou cast down, my soul?
    Why in me so dismayed?
  Trust God, for I shall praise him yet;
    His countenance is mine aid.
6 My God, my soul's cast down in me;
    Remember thee I will
  From Jordan's land, and Hermon's heights,
    Even from Mizar hill.

7 At voice of thy great water-spouts
    Deep unto deep doth call;
  Thy breaking waves pass over me,
    Yea, and thy billows all.
8 His loving-kindness yet the Lord
    Command will in the day;
  His song is with me in the night;
    To God, my life, I'll pray.

9 I'll say to God my rock, O why
    Dost thou forget me so?
  For the oppression of my foes
    Why do I mourning go?
10 'Tis as a sword within my bones,
    When me my foes upbraid;
  Even when by them, Where is thy God?
    Is daily to me said.

11 O why art thou cast down, my soul?
    Why thus with grief opprest
  Art thou disquieted in me?
    In God still hope and rest:
  For yet I know I shall him praise,
    Who graciously to me
  The health is of my countenance,
    Yea, mine own God is he.

PSALM XLIII.
Farrant, 21.

1 AGAINST a wicked race, O God,
    Plead thou my cause, judge me;
From the unjust and crafty man
    O do thou set me free.
2 For thou the God art of my strength;
    Why thrust me then away?
And for the oppression of the foe
    Why mourn I all the day?

3 O send thy light forth and thy truth;
    Let them be guides to me,
And bring me to thine holy hill,
    Even where thy dwellings be.
4 Then will I to God's altar go,
    To God my chiefest joy:
Yea, God, my God, thy name to praise
    My harp I will employ.

5 Why art thou then cast down, my soul?
    What should discourage thee?
And why with vexing thoughts art thou
    Disquieted in me?
Still trust in God; for him to praise
    Good cause I yet shall have:
He of my countenance is the health,
    My God that doth me save.

PSALM XLIV.
York, 54.

1 O GOD, we with our ears have heard,
    Our fathers have us told,
The work that in their days thou didst,
    Even in the days of old.

2 Thy hand did drive the heathen out,
    And plant them in their place;
  The nations all thou didst afflict,
    But them thou didst increase.

3 For neither got their sword the land,
    Nor did their arm them save;
  But thy right hand, arm, countenance;
    For God them favour gave.
4 Thou art my King: for Jacob, Lord,
    Deliverances command.
5 Through thee we shall push down our foes,
    That do against us stand:

  We, through thy name, shall tread down
    That risen against us have.   [those
6 For in my bow I shall not trust,
    Nor shall my sword me save.
7 But from our foes thou hast us saved,
    Our haters put to shame.
8 In God we all the day do boast,
    And ever praise thy name.

9 But now we are cast off by thee;
    Thou puttest us to shame;
  And when our armies forth do go,
    Thou goest not with them.
10 Thou mak'st us from the enemy
    To turn back in dismay;
  And they, who hate us, for themselves
    Our spoils do take away.

11 Like sheep for meat thou gavest us;
    'Mong heathen cast we be.
12 Thou didst for nought thy people sell;
    Their price enriched not thee.

13 Unto our neighbours a reproach
   We have been made by thee;
Derision and a scorn to those
   That round about us be.

14 A by-word also thou dost us
   Among the heathen make;
The people, in contempt and spite,
   At us their heads do shake.
15 Before me my confusion doth
   Abide continually,
And of my countenance the shame
   Doth wholly cover me.

16 For voice of him that doth reproach,
   And speaketh blasphemy;
Because of the avenging foe,
   And cruel enemy.
17 All this is come on us, yet we
   Have not forgotten thee;
Nor falsely in thy covenant
   Behaved ourselves have we.

18 Back from thy way turned not our hearts,
   From thee we have not strayed;
19 Though crushed by thee in dragons' haunts,
   And covered with death's shade.
20 If we God's name forgot, or stretched
   To a strange god our hands,
21 Shall not God search this out? for he
   Heart's secrets understands.

22 Yea, for thy sake we're killed all day,
   Counted as slaughter-sheep.
23 Rise, Lord, cast us not ever off;
   Awake, why dost thou sleep?

24 O wherefore hidest thou thy face?
    Forgett'st our cause distressed,
25 And our oppression? For our soul
    Down to the dust is pressed:

Our body also on the earth
    Fast cleaving hold doth take.
26 Rise for our help, and us redeem,
    Even for thy mercies' sake.

PSALM XLV.—1st Version.   Smart, 51.

1 MY heart brings forth a goodly thing;
    My words that I indite
Concern the King: my tongue's a pen
    Of one that swift doth write.
2 Thou fairer art than sons of men:
    Into thy lips is store
Of grace infused; God therefore thee
    Hath blessed for evermore.

3 O thou that art the mighty One,
    Thy sword gird on thy thigh;
Even with thy glory excellent,
    And with thy majesty.
4 For meekness, truth, and righteousness,
    Ride prosperously in state;
And thee thine own right hand shall teach
    Things terrible and great.

5 Thine arrows sharply pierce the heart
    Of the enemies of the King;
And under thy dominion they
    The people down do bring.
6 For ever and for ever is,
    O God, thy throne of might;

    The sceptre of thy kingdom is
      A sceptre that is right.
7 Thou lovest right and hatest ill;
      Hence God, thy God, even he
    Above thy fellows hath with oil
      Of joy anointed thee.
8 Of aloes, myrrh, and cassia
      A smell thy garments had,
    Out of the ivory palaces,
      Whereby they made thee glad.
9 Among thy women honourable
      Kings' daughters were at hand:
    Upon thy right hand did the queen
      In gold of Ophir stand.
10 O daughter, hearken and regard,
      And do thine ear incline;
    Likewise forget thy father's house,
      And people that are thine.
11 And so thy beauty by the King
      Greatly desired shall be;
    Because he is thy Lord, do thou
      Him worship reverently.
12 The daughter there of Tyre shall be
      With gifts and offerings great:
    Those of the people that are rich
      Thy favour shall entreat.
13 Behold, the daughter of the King
      All glorious is within;
    And with embroideries of gold
      Her garments wrought have been.
14 She shall be brought unto the King
      In robes with needle wrought;

  Her fellow-virgins following
   Shall unto thee be brought.

15 They shall be brought with gladness great,
   And mirth on every side,
  Into the palace of the King,
   And there they shall abide.
16 Thy fathers' place thy sons shall fill,
   Whom thou to thee shalt take,
  And in all places of the earth
   Them noble princes make.
17 Thy name remembered I will make
   Through ages all to be:
  The people therefore evermore
   Shall praises give to thee.

PSALM XLV.—2nd Version. Narenza, '.

1 MY heart inditing is
   Good matter in a song:
  I speak the things that I have made,
   Which to the King belong:
  My tongue shall be as quick,
   His honour to indite,
  As is the pen of any scribe
   That useth fast to write.

2 Thou fairer art than men;
   Grace in thy lips doth flow:
  And therefore blessings evermore
   On thee doth God bestow.
3 Thy sword gird on thy thigh,
   Thou that art great in might:
  Appear in dreadful majesty,
   And in thy glory bright.

4 For meekness, truth, and right,
　　Ride prosperously in state;
　And thy right hand shall teach to thee
　　Things terrible and great.
5 Thy shafts shall pierce their hearts
　　That foes are to the King;
　Whereby into subjection thou
　　The people down shalt bring.

6 Thy royal seat, O Lord,
　　For ever shall remain:
　The sceptre of thy kingdom doth
　　All righteousness maintain.
7 Thou lovest right, hat'st ill;
　　Hence God, thy God, even he
　Above thy fellows hath with oil
　　Of joy anointed thee.

8 Of myrrh and spices sweet
　　A smell thy garments had,
　Out of the ivory palaces,
　　Whereby they made thee glad.
9 And in thy glorious train
　　Kings' daughters waiting stand;
　And thy fair queen in Ophir gold
　　Doth stand at thy right hand.

10 O daughter, take good heed,
　　Incline, and give good ear;
　Thou must forget thy kindred all,
　　And father's house most dear.
11 Thy beauty by the King
　　Shall then desired be;
　And do thou humbly worship him,
　　Because thy Lord is he.

12 The daughter then of Tyre
    There with a gift shall be;
And all the wealthy of the land
    Shall make their suit to thee.
13 The daughter of the King
    All glorious is within;
And with embroideries of gold
    Her garments wrought have been.

14 She cometh to the King
    In robes with needle wrought;
The virgins that do follow her
    Shall unto thee be brought.
15 They shall be brought with joy,
    And mirth on every side,
Into the palace of the King,
    And there they shall abide.

16 And in thy fathers' stead,
    Thy children thou shalt take,
And in all places of the earth
    Them noble princes make.
17 I will show forth thy name
    To generations all:
Therefore the people evermore
    To thee give praises shall.

PSALM XLVI.—1st Version. St. David, 45.

1 GOD is our refuge and our strength,
    In straits a present aid;
2 Therefore, although the earth remove,
    We will not be afraid:
Though hills amidst the seas be cast;
3   Though waters roaring make,

And troubled be; yea, though the hills
  By swelling seas do shake.
4 A river is, whose streams make glad
  The city of our God,
The holy place, wherein the Lord
  Most high hath his abode.
5 God in the midst of her doth dwell;
  Nothing shall her remove:
God unto her an helper will,
  And that right early, prove.

6 The heathen raged tumultuously,
  The kingdoms moved were:
The Lord God uttered his voice,
  The earth did melt for fear.
7 The Lord of hosts is on our side
  Our safety to maintain:
The God of Jacob doth for us
  A refuge high remain.

8 Come, and behold what wondrous works
  Have by the Lord been wrought;
Come, see what desolations he
  Upon the earth hath brought.
9 Unto the ends of all the earth
  Wars into peace he turns:
The bow he breaks, the spear he cuts,
  In fire the chariot burns.

10 Be still, and know that I am God;
  Among the heathen I
Will be exalted; I on earth
  Will be exalted high.
11 The Lord of hosts is on our side
  Our safety to maintain;

The God of Jacob doth for us
A refuge high remain.

PSALM XLVI.—2nd Version. Zoheleth, 84.

1 GOD is our sure defence, our aid
    In time of tribulation;
Our heart shall never be dismayed,
    Though fail the earth's foundation,
O'er hills though foaming floods ascend,
Though billows roar, and ocean rend
    The mountain-peaks asunder.

2 A river by the holy shrine,
    A pure and peaceful river,
Makes glad the seat of power divine:
    She stands unmoved for ever;
For God is in the midst of her,
A help, a stay, a comforter;
    He comes at break of morning.

3 In Jacob's God our strength is found,
    When heathen hosts assemble;
He speaks in thunder; at the sound
    Earth melts and nations tremble:
The Lord of hosts a refuge stands.
And lo! the wonders of his hands,
    The wrath, the desolation!

4 He lulls the war, he burns the car,
    The bow and spear he breaketh;
Be still, he cries, for I arise;
    The Lord, the Lord awaketh,
O'er all the earth a God most high:
The Lord of hosts, our help, is nigh,
    Our strength, the God of Jacob.

PSALM XLVII.   Kaltenthal, 27

1 ALL people, clap your hands; to God
     With voice of triumph shout:
2 For dreadful is the Lord most high,
     Great King the earth throughout.
3 Subdue the people under us
     Assuredly shall he;
  Under our feet the nations all
     Brought down by him shall be.

4 The lot of our inheritance
     Choose out for us doth he,
  Even Jacob's glory, whom he loved,
     And called his own to be.
5 God is with shouts gone up, the Lord
     With trumpets sounding high.
6 Sing praise to God, sing praise, sing praise,
     Praise to our King sing ye.

7 For God is King of all the earth;
     With knowledge praise express.
8 God rules the nations; God sits on
     His throne of holiness.
9 The princes of the people are
     Assembled willingly;
  Even of the God of Abraham
     They who the people be.

  Because the shields that do defend
     The earth are only his:
  They unto God belong, and he
     Exalted greatly is.

PSALM XLVIII. Bedford, 10.

1 GREAT is the Lord, and greatly he
  Is to be praised still,
Within the city of our God,
  Upon his holy hill.
2 Mount Zion stands most beautiful,
  The joy of all the land;
The city of the mighty King
  Upon the north doth stand.

3 The Lord within her palaces
  Is for a refuge known.
4 For, lo, the kings that gathered were
  Together by have gone.
5 For when they did behold the same,
  They wondering would not stay;
But, being troubled at the sight,
  They thence did haste away.

6 Great terror there took hold on them,
  With fear possessed they were;
Their grief came like a woman's pain,
  When she a child doth bear.
7 Thou Tarshish ships with east wind break'st:
8 As we have heard it told,
So, in the city of the Lord,
  Our eyes did it behold;

In our God's city, which his hand
  For ever stablish will.
9 We of thy loving-kindness thought,
  Lord, in thy temple still.
10 O God, according to thy name,
  Through all the earth's thy praise;

And thy right hand, O God, is full
  Of righteousness always.

11 Because thy judgments are made known,
    Let Zion mount rejoice;
  Of Judah let the daughters all
    Send forth a cheerful voice.
12 Walk about Zion, and go round;
    The high towers thereof tell:
13 Consider ye her palaces,
    And mark her bulwarks well;

  That ye may tell posterity.
14   For this God doth abide
  Our God for evermore; he will
    Even unto death us guide.

PSALM XLIX.—1st Version.   Abbey, 8.

1 HEAR this, all people, and give ear,
    All in the world that dwell,
2 Both low and high, both rich and poor;
3   My mouth shall wisdom tell:
  My heart shall knowledge meditate.
4   I will incline mine ear
  To parables, and on the harp
    My sayings dark declare.

5 Amidst those days that evil be,
    Why should I fearing doubt?
  When my pursuers' wickedness
    Doth compass me about.
6 Whoe'er they be that in their wealth
    Their confidence do place,
  And who do boast themselves because
    Their riches grow apace;

7 Yet none of these his brother can
    Redeem by any way;
  Nor can he unto God for him
    Sufficient ransom pay;
8 That he should still for ever live
    And not corruption see:
9 Their soul's redemption costly is,
    Nor can it ever be.

10 Because he sees that wise men die,
    That fools and brutish all
  Do perish, and, when dead, their wealth
    Doth unto others fall.
11 Their inward thought is that their homes
    And dwelling places all
  Shall stand for evermore; their lands
    By their own names they call.

12 But yet in honour shall not man
    Abide continually;
  But passing hence may be compared
    Unto the beasts that die.
13 Thus brutish folly plainly is
    Their wisdom and their way;
  Yet their posterity approve
    What they do fondly say.

14 Like sheep they in the grave are laid,
    And death shall them devour;
  And in the morning upright men
    Shall over them have power:
  Their beauty from their dwelling shall
    Consume within the grave.
15 But from death's hand God will me free,
    For he shall me receive.

16 Be not afraid then when a man
    Enriched thou dost see;
  Nor when the glory of his house
    Increaseth wondrously.
17 For he shall carry nothing hence,
    When death his days doth end;
  Nor shall his glory after him
    Into the grave descend.

18 Although he his own soul did bless,
    Whilst he on earth did live;
  (And when thou to thyself dost well,
    Men will thee praises give;)
19 He to his fathers' race shall go;
    They never shall see light.
20 Man honoured wanting knowledge is
    Like beasts that perish quite.

PSALM XLIX.—2nd Version. Eisenach, 60.

1 YE dwellers all on earth, give ear,
    Both rich and poor, and high and low!
  For musings deep I will declare,
    And wisdom from my tongue shall flow.
  Mine ear I bend to mystic lays;
    Dark sayings on my harp expound.
  Why should I fear in evil days,
    When sinners hem me in around?

2 Mark those who on their wealth rely,
    And glory in their store's increase;
  Not one a brother's life can buy,
    Nor from his God procure him peace.
  The soul's redemption is so dear,
    That no man can sufficient have

> To purchase life for ever here,
> Or 'scape corruption in the grave.

3 Men see the fool and wise man fall,
  And all their hoards to others passed;
Yet by their names their lands they call,
  And think their house will ever last.
But man's vain honour soon decays,
  Even as the brutish herd they die;
And though their seed their sayings praise,
  Their way is only vanity.

4 Like sheep they in the grave are laid,
  Where hungry death shall on them prey;
Their glories in the dust shall fade,
  And just men rise more blest than they.
But God my soul from death will free,
  And home receive me to himself:
Then fear thou not, if one thou see
  Surpassing thee in place or pelf:

5 For though his life more blest he thought,
  And others did his path commend,
He to his grave shall carry nought,
  Nor shall his pomp to him descend.
No; to his fathers he must pass,
  And lie in darkness out of sight.
Man, foolish man, in honoured place,
  Is like the beasts, which perish quite.

PSALM L.—1st Version. *Swabia, 5.*

1 THE mighty God, the Lord,
    Speaks, and to earth doth call
  Even from the rising of the sun
    To where he hath his fall.

2 From out of Zion hill,
    Where beauty dwells enshrined,
  God in his glorious majesty
    And mighty power hath shined.

3 Our God shall surely come,
    Keep silence shall not he:
  Before him fire shall waste, great storms
    Shall round about him be.
4 Unto the heavens above
    He shall send forth his call,
  And likewise to the earth, that he
    May judge his people all.

5 Together let my saints
    Unto me gathered be,
  Those that by sacrifice have made
    A covenant with me.
6 And then the heavens shall
    His righteousness declare:
  Because the Lord himself is he
    By whom men judged are.

7 My people Israel, hear:
    Speak will I from on high;
  Against thee I will testify;
    God, even thy God, am I.
8 I for thy sacrifice
    No blame on thee will lay:
  Nor for burnt-offerings, which to me
    Thou offeredst every day.

9 I'll take no calf nor goats
    From house or fold of thine:
10 Beasts of the forest, cattle all
    On thousand hills, are mine.

11 The fowls on mountains high
    Are all to me well known;
Wild beasts which in the fields do lie,
    Even they are all mine own.

12 Then, if I hungry were,
    I would not tell it thee;
Because the world, and fulness all
    Thereof, belongs to me.
13 Will I eat flesh of bulls?
    Or goats' blood drink will I?
14 Thanks offer thou to God, and pay
    Thy vows to the Most High.

15 And call upon me when
    In trouble thou shalt be;
I will deliver thee, and thou
    Shalt glory give to me.
16 But to the wicked man
    God saith, Why dost thou dare
My covenant in thy mouth to take,
    My statutes to declare?

17 Yet thou instruction wise
    Perversely hated hast,
Likewise my words behind thy back
    Thou in contempt dost cast.
18 Thou didst to him consent,
    When thou a thief hast seen;
And with the vile adulterers
    Thou hast partaker been.

19 Thou giv'st thy mouth to ill;
    Thy tongue deceit doth frame;
20 Thou sitt'st, and 'gainst thy brother speak'st,
    Thy mother's son dost shame.

21 Because I silence kept,
   While thou these things hast wrought;
That I was altogether like
   Thyself hath been thy thought:

Yet I will thee reprove,
   And set before thine eyes,
Arrayed in order, thy misdeeds,
   And thine iniquities.
22 Now, ye that God forget,
   Consider this with care;
Lest I, when there is none to save,
   Do you in pieces tear.

23 He doth me glorify
   Who offers to me praise;
And him I'll God's salvation show
   That orders right his ways.

PSALM L.—2nd Version. St. Anne, 43.

1 THE mighty God, the Lord, doth speak,
   And to the earth doth call,
Even from the rising of the sun
   To where he hath his fall.
2 From out of Zion, his own hill,
   Where beauty dwells enshrined,
God in his glorious majesty
   And mighty power hath shined.

3 Our God assuredly shall come,
   Keep silence shall not he;
Before him fire shall waste, great storms
   Shall round about him be.
4 He to the heavens above shall call,
   And to the earth below,

> That of his people he to all
>   His judgment just may show.

5 Let all my saints together now
    Unto me gathered be,
  Those that by sacrifice have made
    A covenant with me.
6 And then the heavens shall declare
    His righteousness abroad;
  Because the Lord himself doth come;
    None else is judge but God.

7 Hear, O my people, I will speak,
    And I will testify
  Against thee, O mine Israel;
    God, even thy God, am I.
8 Not for thy sacrifices I
    Reprove thee ever will,
  Nor for burnt-offerings, which have been
    Before me offered still.

9 I'll take no bullock nor he-goats
    From house nor folds of thine:
10 Beasts of the forest, cattle all
    On thousand hills, are mine.
11 The fowls are all to me well known
    That mountains high do yield;
  And I do challenge as mine own
    The wild beasts of the field.

12 If I were hungry, I would not
    To thee for need complain;
  For earth, with all its fulness, doth
    To me of right pertain.
13 That I to eat the flesh of bulls
    Take pleasure dost thou think?

  Or that I need, to quench my thirst,
   The blood of goats to drink?
14 Nay, rather unto me, thy God,
   Thanksgiving offer thou;
  To the Most High perform thy word,
   And fully pay thy vow:
15 And in the day of thy distress
   Do thou unto me cry;
  I will deliver thee, and thou
   My name shalt glorify.

16 But to the wicked man God saith,
   How is it thou dost dare
  My covenant in thy mouth to take,
   My statutes to declare?
17 And yet all good instruction thou
   Perversely hated hast,
  Likewise my words behind thy back
   Thou in contempt dost cast.

18 When thou a thief didst see, with him
   Thou didst consent to sin,
  And with the vile adulterers
   Thou hast partaker been.
19 Thy mouth to evil thou dost give,
   Thy tongue deceit doth frame.
20 Thou sitt'st, and 'gainst thy brother speak'st,
   Thy mother's son to shame.

21 These things thou wickedly hast done,
   And I have silent been;
  Thou thought'st that I was like thyself,
   And did approve thy sin:
  But I will sharply thee reprove,
   And set before thine eyes,

Arrayed in order, thy misdeeds
And thine iniquities.

22 Consider this, and be afraid,
Ye that forget the Lord,
Lest I in pieces tear you all,
When none can help afford.
23 He truly doth me glorify
Who offers to me praise;
And him I'll God's salvation show
That orders right his ways.

PSALM LI. St. Mary, 47.

1 AFTER thy loving-kindness, Lord,
Have mercy upon me:
For thy compassions great, blot out
All mine iniquity.
2 Me cleanse from sin, and throughly wash
From mine iniquity;
3 For my transgressions I confess;
My sin I ever see.

4 'Gainst thee, thee only, have I sinned,
In thy sight done this ill;
That when thou speak'st thou may'st be
And clear in judging still.   [just,
5 Behold, I in iniquity
Was formed the womb within;
My mother also me conceived
In guiltiness and sin.

6 Behold, thou in the inward parts
With truth delighted art;
And wisdom thou shalt make me know
Within the hidden part.

7 Do thou with hyssop sprinkle me,
   I shall be cleansed so;
  Yea, wash thou me, and then I shall
   Be whiter than the snow.

8 Of gladness and of joyfulness
   Make me to hear the voice,
  That so these very bones which thou
   Hast broken may rejoice.
9 All mine iniquities blot out,
   Thy face hide from my sin.
10 Create a clean heart, Lord, renew
   A right spirit me within.

11 Cast me not from thy sight, nor take
   Thy Holy Spirit away.
12 Restore me thy salvation's joy;
   With thy free Spirit me stay.
13 Then will I teach thy ways unto
   Those that trangressors be;
  And those that sinners are shall then
   Be turned unto thee.

14 O God, of my salvation God,
   From guilt of blood me free:
  Then of thy righteousness my tongue
   Shall sing aloud to thee.
15 My closed lips, O Lord, by thee
   Let them be opened;
  Then shall thy praises by my mouth
   Abroad be published.

16 Thou sacrifice desirest not,
   Else would I give it thee;
  Nor wilt thou with burnt-offering
   At all delighted be.

17 A broken spirit is to God
    A pleasing sacrifice:
  A broken and a contrite heart,
    Lord, thou wilt not despise.

18 In thy good pleasure do thou good
    To Zion, thine own hill:
  The walls of thy Jerusalem
    Build up of thy good will.
19 Then righteous offerings shall thee please,
    And offerings burnt which they,
  With whole burnt-offerings, and with
    Shall on thine altar lay.   [calves,

PSALM LII. York, 54.

1 WHY boast thyself, O mighty man,
    Of mischief and of wrong?
  The goodness of Almighty God
    Endureth all day long.
2 Thy tongue doth mischief still devise,
    And falsely doth revile;
  Like to a razor whetted sharp,
    For ever working guile.

3 Ill more than good thou lov'st, lies more
    Than speaking righteousness:
4 Thou lovest all-devouring words,
    Tongue of deceitfulness.
5 So God shall thee destroy for aye,
    Remove thee, pluck thee out
  Quite from thy tent, and from the land
    Of living men thee root.

6 The righteous shall it see and fear,
    And laugh at him they shall:

7 Lo, this the man is that did not
    Make God his strength at all:
But he in his abundant wealth
    His confidence did place;
And he took strength unto himself
    From his own wickedness.

8 But I am in the house of God
    Like a green olive tree;
I in God's mercy put my trust
    Unto eternity.
9 And I for ever will thee praise,
    Because thou hast done this;
Before thy saints I on thy name
    Will wait, for good it is.

PSALM LIII. Moravia, 32.

1 THAT there is not a God, the fool
    Doth in his heart conclude:
They are corrupt, their works are vile,
    Not one of them doth good.
2 Upon the sons of men did God
    From heaven cast his eyes,
To see if any one there was
    That sought God, and was wise.

3 Corrupt they altogether are,
    They all are backward gone;
And there is none that doeth good,
    No, not so much as one.
4 These workers of iniquity,
    Do they not know at all,
That they my people eat as bread,
    And on God do not call?

5 Even there they were afraid, and stood
    With trembling all dismayed,
Whereas there was no cause at all
    Why they should be afraid.
For God his bones that thee besieged
    Hath scattered all abroad;
Thou hast confounded them, for they
    Despised are of God.

6 Let Israel's help from Zion come:
    When back the Lord shall bring
His captives, Jacob shall rejoice,
    And Israel shall sing.

PSALM LIV. Parry, 40.

1 SAVE me, O God, by thy great name,
    And judge me by thy strength:
2 Hear thou my prayer, O God; give ear
    Unto my words at length.
3 For they that strangers are to me
    Do up against me rise;
Oppressors seek my soul, and God
    Set not before their eyes.

4 Lo, God an helper is to me,
    And therefore I am bold;
The Lord hath taken part with those
    That do my soul uphold.
5 Unto my foes their wickedness
    He surely shall repay:
O for thy truth's sake cut them off,
    And sweep them clean away.

6 I with a willing mind will give
    A sacrifice to thee;

Thy name, O Lord, because 'tis good,
　　Shall be extolled by me.
7 Because he hath delivered me
　　From all adversities;
　And its desire mine eye hath seen
　　Upon mine enemies.

PSALM LV. Martyrs, 31.

1 HEAR thou my prayer, O God, hide not
　　From my entreating voice:
2 Attend and hear me, in my plaint
　　I mourn and make a noise;
3 For voice of enemies, and for
　　Vile men's oppression great:
　On me they cast iniquity,
　　And they in wrath me hate.

4 Sore pained within me is my heart:
　　Death's terrors on me fall.
5 On me comes trembling, fear and dread
　　Me overwhelmed withal.
6 O that I like a dove had wings,
　　Said I, then would I flee
　Far hence, that I might find a place
　　Where I in rest might be.

7 Lo, then far off I wander would,
　　And in the desert stay;
8 From stormy wind, and tempest I
　　Would haste to 'scape away.
9 O Lord, on them destruction bring,
　　Do thou their tongues divide;
　For in the city violence
　　And strife have I descried.

10 They day and night upon the walls
　　Do compass it around:
　There mischief is, and sorrow there
　　In midst of it is found.
11 Abundant wickedness there is
　　Within its inward part;
　And from its streets deceitfulness
　　And guile do not depart.

12 He was no foe that me reproached,
　　For that I could abide;
　No hater that against me rose,
　　Else I from him might hide.
13 'Twas thou, a man, mine equal, guide,
　　Who mine acquaintance wast:
14 We joined sweet counsels: to God's house
　　Amidst the throng we passed.

15 Let death them seize, and to the grave
　　Alive let them depart;
　For wickedness is in their house
　　And evil in their heart.
16 I call on God; the Lord me saves.
17　　I make my plaint and sigh
　At evening, morning, and at noon;
　　And he regards my cry.

18 He hath my soul delivered,
　　That it in peace might be
　From battle that against me was;
　　For many were with me.
19 The Lord shall hear and them afflict
　　(Of old abideth he),
　Even them who have no fear of God,
　　And changes never see.

20 'Gainst those that were at peace with him
    He hath put forth his hand:
The covenant that he had made,
    By breaking he profaned.
21 More smooth than butter were his words,
    While in his heart was war:
His speeches were more soft than oil,
    And yet drawn swords they are.

22 Cast thou thy burden on the Lord,
    And he shall thee sustain;
Yea, he shall cause the righteous man
    Unmoved to remain.
23 But thou, O God, in judgment just
    Those men shalt overthrow,
And in destruction's dungeon dark
    At last shalt lay them low;

The bloody and deceitful men
    Shall not live half their days:
But upon thee with confidence
    I will depend always.

PSALM LVI.   Newington, 34

1 SHOW mercy, Lord, to me, for man
    Would swallow me outright;
He me oppresseth, while he doth
    All day against me fight.
2 All day they would me swallow up
    Who hate me spitefully;
For they be many that do fight
    Against me, O Most High.

3 When I'm afraid I'll trust in thee:
4   In God I'll praise his word;

  I will not fear what flesh can do,
   My trust is in the Lord.
5 All day they wrest my words; their thoughts
  'Gainst me are all for ill.
6 They meet, they lurk, they mark my steps,
  Waiting my soul to kill.

7 But shall they by iniquity
  Escape thy judgments so?
  O God, with indignation down
  Do thou the people throw.
8 Thou tellest all my wanderings,
  Not one dost overlook;
 Into thy bottle put my tears:
  Are they not in thy book?

9 My foes shall, when I cry, turn back;
  I know God is for me.
10 In God his word I'll praise; his word
  In God shall praised be.
11 In God I trust; I will not fear
  What man can do to me.
12 Thy vows upon me are, O God:
  I'll render thanks to thee.

13 Thou, who from death didst save my soul,
  My feet from falling free,
 To walk before God in the light
  Of those that living be.

   PSALM LVII.—1st Version. Martyrdom, 30.

1 BE merciful to me, O God;
  Be merciful to me;
 Because my soul her confidence
  Doth wholly place in thee.

  Yea, in the shadow of thy wings
   My refuge I will place,
 Until these sad calamities
   Do wholly overpass.
2 My cry I will cause to ascend
   To God who is most high;
 To God, who doth all things for me
   Perform most perfectly.
3 From heaven he shall send down, and me
   From his reproach defend
 That would devour me: God his truth
   And mercy forth shall send.

4 My soul among fierce lions is,
   I firebrands live among,
 Men's sons, whose teeth are spears and darts,
   A sharp sword is their tongue.
5 Be thou exalted very high
   Above the heavens, O God;
 Let thou thy glory be advanced
   O'er all the earth abroad.

6 My soul's bowed down; for they a net
   Have laid, my steps to snare:
 Into the pit which they have digged
   For me, they fallen are.
7 My heart is fixed, my heart is fixed,
   O God; I'll sing and praise.
8 My glory wake; wake psaltery, harp:
   Myself I'll early raise.

9 I'll praise thee 'mong the people, Lord;
   'Mong nations sing will I:
10 For great to heaven thy mercy is,
   Thy truth is to the sky.

11 O Lord, exalted be thy name
    Above the heavens to stand:
Do thou thy glory far advance
    Above both sea and land.

PSALM LVII.—2nd Version.   Melcombe, 62.

1 THY mercy, Lord, to me extend;
    On thy protection I depend,
And to thy wings for shelter haste
Until this storm be overpast.
2 To him I will in trouble cry,
The sovereign Judge and God most high,
Who wonders hath for me begun,
And will not leave his work undone.

3 For he from heaven shall quell the power
Of him who would my life devour;
Forth shall his truth and mercy send,
And my distracted soul defend.
4 For I with cruel men converse,
Like hungry lions wild and fierce;
With men whose teeth are spears, their words
Envenomed darts and two-edged swords.

5 Be thou, O God, exalted high:
And, as thy glory fills the sky,
So be it o'er the earth displayed,
And thou, as there, be here obeyed!
6 To take me they their net prepared;
My sinking soul almost despaired;
But they are fallen, by thy decree,
Into the pit they dug for me.

7 O God, my heart is fixed, 'tis bent,
Its thankful tribute to present;

    And with my heart my voice I'll raise
    To thee, my God, in songs of praise.
8 Awake my glory; harp and lute,
    No longer let your strings be mute;
    And I, my tuneful part to take,
    Will with the early dawn awake.

9 Thy praises, Lord, I will resound
    To all the listening nations round;
    Thy mercy highest heaven transcends,
    Thy truth beyond the clouds extends.
10 Be thou, O God, exalted high!
    And, as thy glory fills the sky,
    So be it o'er the earth displayed,
    And thou, as there, be here obeyed.

PSALM LVIII.   Chester, 12.

1 Do ye, O congregation, then,
    Indeed speak righteousness?
  O ye that are the sons of men,
    Judge ye with uprightness?
2 Yea, even within your very hearts
    Ye wickedness have done;
  Ye of your hands the violence
    Weigh out the earth upon.

3 Estranged the ungodly are,
    Even from the very womb;
  They, speaking falsehood, stray as soon
    As to the world they come.
4 Unto a serpent's poison like
    Their poison doth appear;
  Yea, they are like the adder deaf,
    That closely stops her ear;

5 That so she may not hear the voice
    Of one that charm her would,
  No, not though he most cunning were,
    And charm most wisely could.
6 Their teeth, O God, within their mouth
    Break thou in pieces small;
  The great teeth break thou out, O Lord,
    Of these young lions all.

7 Let them like waters melt away,
    Which downward still do flow:
  In pieces cut his arrows all,
    When he shall bend his bow.
8 Like to a snail that melts away,
    Let each of them be gone:
  Like woman's birth untimely, that
    Hath never seen the sun.

9 He shall them take away before
    Your pots the thorns can find,
  Both living, and in fury great,
    As with a stormy wind.
10 The righteous when he vengeance sees
    Shall be most joyful then;
  The righteous one shall wash his feet
    In blood of wicked men.

11 So men shall say, The righteous man
    Reward shall never miss:
  And verily upon the earth
    A God to judge there is.

PSALM LIX. Bangor, 9.

1 MY God, deliver me from those
    That are mine enemies;

And be thou my defence from those
  That up against me rise.
2 From workers of iniquity
  Do thou deliver me;
And give me safety from the men
  Of blood and cruelty.

3 For, lo, they for my soul lay wait:
  The mighty do combine
Against me, Lord; not for my fault,
  Nor any sin of mine.
4 They run, and, without fault in me,
  Themselves do ready make:
Awake to meet me with thy help;
  And do thou notice take.

5 Awake, Jehovah, God of hosts,
  Thou God of Israel,
To visit heathen all: spare none
  That wickedly rebel.
6 At eventide they come again;
  They make great noise and sound,
Like to a dog, and often walk
  The city all around.

7 Behold, they belch out with their mouth,
  And in their lips are swords:
For thus they say, Who now is he
  That heareth these our words?
8 But thou, O Lord, shalt laugh at them,
  And all the heathen mock.
9 While he's in power I'll wait on thee;
  For God is my high rock.

10 He of my mercy that is God
  Betimes shall me prevent;

Upon mine enemies God shall let
　Me see mine heart's content.
11 Them slay not, lest my folk forget;
　But scatter them abroad
By thy strong power; and bring them down,
　O thou our shield and God.

12 For their mouth's sin, and for the words
　That from their lips do fly,
Let them be taken in their pride;
　Because they curse and lie.
13 In wrath consume them, them consume,
　That so they may not be:
And that in Jacob God doth rule
　To earth's ends let them see.

14 At eventide they come again,
　They make great noise and sound
Like to a dog, and often walk
　The city all around.
15 They also wander up and down,
　That food they may obtain;
And if they are not satisfied,
　They all night long remain.

16 But of thy power I'll sing aloud;
　At morn thy mercy praise:
For thou to me my refuge wast,
　And tower, in troublous days.
17 O God, thou art my strength, I will
　Sing praises unto thee;
For God is my defence, a God
　Of mercy unto me.

PSALM LX. Gräfenberg, 25.

1 O GOD, thou hast rejected us,
    And scattered us abroad;
Thou justly hast displeased been;
    Return to us, O God.
2 The earth to tremble thou hast made;
    Therein didst breaches make:
Do thou thereof the breaches heal,
    Because the land doth shake.

3 Hard things thou hast thy people shown,
    Distress upon them sent;
And thou hast caused us to drink
    Wine of astonishment.
4 And yet a banner thou hast given
    To those who thee do fear;
That it by them, because of truth,
    Displayed may appear.

5 That thy beloved people may
    Delivered be from thrall,
Save with the power of thy right hand,
    And hear me when I call.
6 God in his holiness did speak,
    My joy shall be complete;
I Shechem will divide, by line
    The vale of Succoth mete.

7 Gilead I claim as mine by right;
    Manasseh mine shall be;
Ephraim is of mine head the strength;
    Judah gives laws for me;
8 Moab my washpot is; my shoe,
    Edom, I'll cast o'er thee;

    Philistia, through thy borders all
        Cry out because of me.
9 O who is he will bring me to
        The city fortified?
    O who is he that to the land
        Of Edom will me guide?
10 O God, who hast rejected us,
        Wilt thou not help us so?
    Even thou, O God, who dost no more
        Forth with our armies go?

11 Help us from trouble; for the help
        Is vain which man bestows:
12 Through God we shall do valiantly;
        He shall tread down our foes.

PSALM LXI.—1st Version.   Patton, 41.

1 O GOD, give ear unto my cry;
        Unto my prayer attend.
2 From the utmost corner of the land
        My cry to thee I'll send.
    What time my heart is overwhelmed,
        And in perplexity,
    Do thou me lead unto the Rock
        That higher is than I.

3 For thou hast for my refuge been
        A shelter by thy power;
    And for defence against my foes
        Thou hast been a strong tower.
4 Within thy tabernacle I
        For ever will abide;
    And under covert of thy wings
        With confidence me hide.

5 For thou the vows that I did make,
   O Lord, my God, didst hear:
Thou hast given me the heritage
   Of those thy name that fear.
6 A life prolonged for many days
   Thou to the king shalt give;
As many generations are
   The years which he shall live.

7 He in God's presence his abode
   For evermore shall have;
O do thou truth and mercy both
   Prepare, that may him save.
8 And so will I perpetually
   Sing praise unto thy name;
That having made my vows, I may
   Each day perform the same.

PSALM LXI.—2nd Version. Manna, 85.

1 LORD, hear my voice, my prayer attend;
   From earth's remotest bound I send
     My supplicating cry.
When troubles great o'erwhelm my breast,
Then lead me on the rock to rest
     That higher is than I.

2 In thee my soul has shelter found,
And thou hast been from foes around
     The tower of my defence.
My home shall thy pavilion be;
To covert of thy wings I'll flee,
     And find deliverance.

3 For thou, O Lord, my vows hast heard;
  On me the heritage conferred
    Of those that fear thy name.
  Long life thou to the king wilt give;
  Through generations he shall live,
    From age to age the same.

4 Before the Lord shall he abide;
  O do thou truth and grace provide
    To guard him in the way.
  So I thy praises will make known,
  And humbly bending at thy throne,
    My vows will daily pay.

PSALM LXII. French, 22.

1 MY soul with expectation doth
    Depend on God indeed:
  My strength and my salvation do
    From him alone proceed.
2 He only my salvation is,
    And my strong rock is he:
  He only is my sure defence;
    Much moved I shall not be.

3 How long rush ye upon a man,
    And him to slay seek all?
  To crush him like a tottering fence,
    And as a bowing wall?
4 Only to cast him down they plot;
    In lies they take delight;
  And while they with the mouth do bless,
    They curse with inward spite.

5 Only on God do thou, my soul,
    Still patiently attend;

My expectation and my hope
   On him alone depend.
6 He only my salvation is,
   And my strong rock is he;
  He only is my sure defence:
   I shall not moved be.

7 In God my glory placed is,
   And my salvation sure;
  In God the rock is of my strength,
   My refuge most secure.
8 Ye people, place your confidence
   In him continually;
  Before him pour ye out your heart;
   God is our refuge high.

9 Surely mean men are vanity,
   And great men are a lie;
  In balance laid, they wholly are
   More light than vanity.
10 Do ye not in oppression trust,
    In robbery be not vain;
   Set not your hearts on riches, when
    Increased is your gain.

11 God hath it spoken once to me,
    Yea, this I heard again,
   That power to Almighty God
    Alone doth appertain.
12 Yea, mercy also unto thee
    Belongs, O Lord, alone:
   For thou according to his work
    Rewardest every one.

PSALM LXIII. St. Bartholomew, 44.

1 LORD, thee my God, I'll early seek:
    My soul doth thirst for thee;
  My flesh longs in a dry parched land,
    Wherein no waters be:
2 That I thy power may behold,
    And brightness of thy face,
  As I have seen thee heretofore
    Within thy holy place.

3 Since better is thy love than life,
    My lips thee praise shall give.
4 I in thy name will lift my hands,
    And bless thee while I live.
5 Even as with marrow and with fat
    My soul shall filled be;
  Then shall my mouth with joyful lips
    Sing praises unto thee.

6 When I do thee upon my bed
    Remember with delight,
  I meditate on thee throughout
    The watches of the night.
7 In shadow of thy wings I'll joy;
    For thou my help hast been.
8 My soul thee follows hard; and me
    Thy right hand doth sustain.

9 To lowest depths of earth shall go
    Those who my soul would slay;
10 They by the sword shall perish all,
    Of foxes be the prey.
11 Yet shall the king in God rejoice,
    And each one glory shall

That swears by him; but stopped shall be
  The mouth of liars all.

PSALM LXIV. Gloucester, 24.

1 UNTO the voice of my complaint,
    O God, give thou an ear;
  My life save from the enemy,
    Of whom I stand in fear.
2 Me from their secret counsel hide
    Who evil-doers be;
  From noisy tumult of the men
    That work iniquity:

3 Who do their tongues with malice whet,
    And make them cut like swords;
  In whose bent bows are arrows set,
    Even sharp and bitter words:
4 That they may at the perfect man
    In secret aim their shot:
  Yea, suddenly they dare at him
    To shoot, and fear it not.

5 In ill encourage they themselves,
    And close their snares do lay:
  Together conference they have;
    Who shall them see? they say.
6 They have searched out iniquities
    A perfect search they keep:
  Of each of them the inward thought,
    And heart, is very deep.

7 God shall an arrow shoot at them,
    And wound them suddenly:
8 So their own tongue shall them confound;
    All who them see shall fly.

9 And on all men a fear shall fall,
   God's works they shall declare;
  For they shall wisely notice take
   What these his doings are.

10 The righteous in the Lord shall joy,
   And in him trust he shall;
  And they that upright are in heart
   Shall greatly glory all.

PSALM LXV. St. Peter, 49.

1 PRAISE waits for thee in Zion, Lord:
   To thee vows paid shall be.
2 O thou that hearer art of prayer,
   All flesh shall come to thee.
3 Iniquities, I must confess,
   Prevail against me do:
  But as for our transgressions all,
   Them purge away shalt thou.

4 Blessed is the man whom thou dost choose,
   And makest approach to thee,
  That he within thy courts, O Lord,
   May still a dweller be:
  We surely shall be satisfied
   With thy abundant grace,
  And with the goodness of thy house,
   Even of thy holy place.

5 O God, who our salvation art,
   Thou, in thy righteousness,
  By fearful works unto our prayers
   Thine answer dost express:
  Therefore the ends of all the earth,
   And those upon the sea

Who dwell afar, their confidence,
 O Lord, will place in thee.

6 Who, being girt with power, sets fast
 By his great strength the hills.
7 Who noise of seas, noise of their waves,
 And people's tumult, stills.
8 Those in the utmost parts that dwell
 Are at thy signs afraid:
The outgoings of morn and eve
 By thee are joyful made.

9 Earth thou dost visit, watering it;
 Thou mak'st it rich to grow
With God's full flood; their corn provid'st,
 When thou prepar'st it so.
10 Its ridges thou dost water well,
 Its furrows down dost press;
Thou mak'st it soft with plenteous rain,
 Its springing thou dost bless.

11 So thou the year most liberally
 Dost with thy goodness crown;
And all thy paths abundantly
 On us drop fatness down.
12 They drop upon the pastures wide,
 That in the desert lie;
The little hills on every side
 Rejoice right pleasantly.

13 With flocks the pastures clothed be,
 The vales with corn are clad;
And now they shout and sing to thee,
 For thou hast made them glad.

PSALM LXVI. Nottingham, 37.

1 ALL lands to God, in joyful sounds,
    Aloft your voices raise.
2 Sing forth the honour of his name,
    And glorious make his praise.
3 Say unto God, How terrible
    In all thy works art thou!
  Through thy great power thy foes to thee
    Shall be constrained to bow.

4 All on the earth shall worship thee,
    They shall thy praise proclaim
  In songs: they shall sing cheerfully
    Unto thy holy name.
5 Come, and the works that God hath wrought
    With admiration see:
  In dealing with the sons of men
    Most terrible is he.

6 Into dry land the sea he turned,
    And they a passage had;
  Even marching through the flood on foot,
    There we in him were glad.
7 He ruleth ever by his power;
    His eyes the nations see:
  O let not the rebellious ones
    In pride exalted be.

8 Ye people, bless our God; aloud
    The voice speak of his praise;
9 Our soul in life who safe preserves,
    Our foot from sliding stays.
10 For thou didst prove and try us, Lord,
    As men do silver try;

11 Brought'st us into the net, and mad'st
    Bands on our loins to lie.
12 Thou hast made men ride o'er our heads;
    Through fire and flood we passed;
  But yet into abundance great
    Thou hast us brought at last.
13 I'll bring burnt-offerings to thy house;
    To thee my vows I'll pay,
14 Which my lips uttered, my mouth spake,
    When trouble on me lay.

15 Burnt-sacrifices of fat sheep,
    Incense of rams I'll bring;
  Of bullocks and of goats I will
    Present an offering.
16 All that fear God, come, hear, I'll tell
    What he did for my soul.
17 I with my mouth unto him cried,
    My tongue did him extol.

18 If in my heart I sin regard,
    The Lord me will not hear:
19 But surely God me heard, and to
    My prayer's voice gave ear.
20 O let the Lord, our gracious God,
    For ever blessed be,
  Who turned not my prayer from him,
    Nor yet his grace from me.

PSALM LXVII.—1st Version. Pilgrim, 7.

1 LORD, bless and pity us,
    Shine on us with thy face:
2 That the earth thy way, and nations all
    May know thy saving grace.

3 Let people praise thee, Lord;
    Let people all thee praise.
4 O let the nations all be glad,
    In songs their voices raise:

Thou'lt justly people judge,
    On earth rule nations all.
5 Let people praise thee, Lord; let them
    Praise thee, both great and small.
6 The earth her fruit hath given;
    Our God shall blessing send.
7 God shall us bless; men shall him fear
    Unto earth's utmost end.

PSALM LXVII.—2nd Version. Paisley, 39.

1 O GOD, be merciful to us,
    And bless us, in thy grace;
And do thou cause to shine on us
    The brightness of thy face:
2 That so thy way upon the earth
    To all men may be known;
Also among the nations all
    Thy saving health be shown.

3 Let people give thee praise, O God;
    Let people all thee praise.
4 O let the nations joyful be,
    In songs their voices raise.
For justly thou shalt people judge,
    And nations rule on earth.
5 Let people give thee praise, O God;
    Let all praise thee with mirth.
6 The earth her increase yielded hath;
    God, our God, bless us shall.

7 God shall us bless; and of the earth
   The ends shall fear him all.

PSALM LXVIII. *Nottingham, 37.*

1 LET God arise, and scattered
     Let all his enemies be;
   And let all those that do him hate
     Before his presence flee.
2 As smoke is driven, so drive thou them;
     As fire melts wax away,
   Before God's face let wicked men
     So perish and decay.

3 But let the righteous all be glad,
     Exult before God's sight;
   Yea let them filled with gladness be,
     And joy with all their might.
4 Sing praise to God, prepare his way,
     Whose name is JAH adored,
   Who through the desert rideth forth;
     Exult before the Lord.

5 Because the Lord a father is
     Unto the fatherless;
   God is the widow's judge, within
     His place of holiness.
6 God sets the lonely in a home,
     And frees the chained from bands;
   But those against him who rebel
     Inhabit parched lands.

7 O God, what time thou didst go forth
     Before thy people's face;
   And when through the great wilderness
     Thy glorious marching was;

8 Then at God's presence shook the earth,
    Then drops from heaven fell;
This Sinai shook before the Lord,
    The God of Israel.

9 O God, thou to thine heritage
    Didst send a plenteous rain,
Whereby thou, when it weary was,
    Didst it refresh again.
10 Thy congregation then did make
    Their habitation there:
Of thine own goodness for the poor,
    O God, thou didst prepare.

11 The Lord himself did give the word,
    The word abroad did spread;
Great was the company of them
    The same who published.
12 Kings of great armies foiled were,
    And forced to flee away;
And women, who remained at home,
    Distributed the prey.

13 Though ye have lain among the pots,
    Like doves ye shall appear,
Whose wings with silver, and with gold
    Whose feathers covered are.
14 When there the Almighty scattered kings,
    Like Salmon's snow 'twas white.
15 A hill of God is Bashan hill,
    A towering hill for height.
16 Why do ye frown, ye mountains high,
    Upon the hill of God?
Here God desires to dwell, the Lord
    For aye will make abode.

17 God's chariots twenty thousand are,
    Thousands on thousands strong;
Sinai is in the holy place,
    The Lord is them among.

18 Thou hast, O Lord, most glorious,
    Ascended up on high;
And in triumph victorious led
    Captive captivity:
Thou hast received gifts for men,
    For such as did rebel;
Yea, even for them, that God the Lord
    In midst of them might dwell.

19 Blessed be the Lord, who is to us
    Of our salvation God;
Who daily with his benefits
    Us plenteously doth load.

20 He of salvation is the God,
    Who is our God most strong;
And unto God the Lord from death
    The issues do belong.

21 But surely God shall wound the head
    Of those that are his foes;
The hairy scalp of him that still
    On in his trespass goes.

22 The Lord hath said, I will bring back
    Again from Bashan hill;
Yea, from the dark depths of the sea
    Bring back again I will.

23 That in the blood of enemies
    Thy foot imbrued may be,
And of thy dogs dipped in the same
    The tongues thou mayest see.

24 Thy goings they have seen, O God;
  The steps of majesty
Of my God, and my mighty King,
  Within the sanctuary.

25 Before went singers, after them
  The players took their way;
In midst of damsels that with skill
  Did on the timbrels play.

26 Within the congregations great
  Bless God with one accord;
Ye who from Israel's fountain are,
  Bless ye the mighty Lord.

27 Their ruler, little Benjamin,
  And Judah's princes high,
The chiefs of Zabulon, are there,
  And chiefs of Naphtali.   [strong
28 Thy God commands thy strength; make
  What thou wrought'st for us, Lord.
29 For thy house at Jerusalem
  Kings shall thee gifts afford.

30 The beast that dwelleth in the reeds,
  The bulls that fiercely look,
With herd of calves, the people all,
  Do thou, O Lord, rebuke,
Till every one submit himself,
  And silver pieces bring:
The people that delight in war
  Disperse, O God and King.

31 Those that be princes great shall then
  Come from Egyptian lands;
And Ethiopia to God
  Shall soon stretch out her hands.

32 O all ye kingdoms of the earth,
      Sing praises to this King;
   For he is Lord that ruleth all,
      Unto him praises sing.

33 To him that rides on heavens of heavens,
      Which he of old did found;
   Lo, he sends out his voice, a voice
      In might that doth abound.
34 Strength unto God do ye ascribe;
      Because his majesty
   Is over Israel, his strength
      Is in the clouds most high.

35 Dread art thou from thy temple, Lord;
      Israel's own God is he,
   Who gives his people strength and power:
      O let God blessed be.

PSALM LXIX. Dundee, 14.

1 SAVE me, O God, because the floods
      Do so environ me,
   That even unto my very soul
      Come in the waters be.
2 I downward in deep mire do sink,
      Where standing there is none:
   Into deep waters I am come,
      Where floods have o'er me gone.

3 I weary with my crying am,
      My throat is also dried;
   Mine eyes do fail, while for my God
      I waiting do abide.
4 Those men who do without a cause
      Bear hatred unto me

Are more in number than the hairs
　　Upon my head that be:
Strong are they who without a cause
　　Me hate and would me slay;
And therefore what I never took
　　I forced am to repay.
5 Lord, thou my folly know'st, my sins
　　Not covered are from thee.
6 Let none who wait on thee be shamed,
　　Lord God of hosts, in me.

O thou who God of Israel art,
　　Let none that wait on thee
Confounded be at any time,
　　Or made ashamed in me.
7 For I have borne reproach for thee;
　　My face is clothed with shame.
8 To brethren strange, to mother's sons
　　An alien I became.

9 Because the zeal did eat me up
　　Which to thine house I bear;
And the reproaches cast at thee
　　Upon me fallen are.
10 With tears and fasting mourned my soul,
　　And that was made my shame:
11 I put on sackcloth, and to them
　　A byword I became.

12 The men that in the gate do sit
　　Against me evil spake;
They also that vile drunkards were
　　Of me their song did make.
13 But in a time of favour, Lord,
　　I make my prayer to thee;

>   In truth of thy salvation, Lord,
>   And mercy great, hear me.
> 14 Deliver me out of the mire,
>   From sinking do me keep;
>   Free me from those that do me hate,
>   And from the waters deep.
> 15 Let not the flood o'er me prevail,
>   Whose water overflows;
>   Nor deep me swallow, nor the pit
>   Her mouth upon me close.
>
> 16 Hear me, O Lord, because thy love
>   And kindness are most good;
>   Turn unto me, according to
>   Thy mercies' multitude.
> 17 Nor from thy servant hide thy face:
>   I'm troubled, soon attend.
> 18 Draw near my soul, and it redeem;
>   Me from my foes defend.
>
> 19 To thee is my reproach well known,
>   My shame, and my disgrace:
>   Those that mine adversaries be
>   Are all before thy face.
> 20 My heart is broken by reproach,
>   I'm full of grief and pain:
>   For pity and for comforters
>   I looked, but looked in vain.
>
> 21 They also bitter gall did give
>   Unto me for my meat:
>   They gave me vinegar to drink,
>   What time my thirst was great.
> 22 Before them let their table prove
>   A snare; and do thou make

Their welfare and prosperity
 A trap themselves to take.
23 Let thou their eyes so darkened be,
 That sight may them forsake;
 And let their loins be made by thee
 Continually to shake.
24 Thine anger pour thou out on them,
 Let thy wrath seize them all;
25 Be desolation in their tents,
 Their homes to ruin fall.

26 Because they persecute the man
 Whom thou didst smite before;
 And mocking tell the grief of those
 Whom thou hast wounded sore.
27 Do thou add sin unto their sin,
 And, for their wickedness,
 Do thou not let them come at all
 Into thy righteousness.

28 Out of the book of life let them
 Be razed and blotted quite;
 Among the righteous and the just
 Their names do thou not write.
29 But now become exceeding poor
 And sorrowful am I:
 By thy salvation, O my God,
 Let me be set on high.

30 The name of God I with a song
 Most cheerfully will praise;
 And I, in giving thanks to him,
 His name will highly raise.
31 This to the Lord a sacrifice
 More grateful far shall prove

Than bullock, ox, or any beast
  That hath both horn and hoof.

32 When this the humble men shall see,
    It joy to them shall give:
  All ye that after God do seek,
    Your heart shall ever live.
33 For God the poor hears, and will not
    His prisoners contemn.
34 Let heaven, and earth, and seas him praise,
    And all that move in them.

35 For God will Judah's cities build,
    And he will Zion save,
  That they may dwell therein, and it
    In sure possession have.
36 And they that are his servants' seed
    Inherit shall the same;
  And they shall have their dwelling there
    That love his blessed name.

PSALM LXX.—1st Version. _{Augustine, 6.}

1 O GOD, to save me haste;
    With speed, Lord, succour me.
2 Let them that for my soul do seek
    Shamed and confounded be:
  Turned back be they, and shamed,
    That in my hurt delight.
3 Turned back be they, Ha, ha! that say,
    Their shaming to requite.

4 In thee let all be glad,
    And joy that seek for thee:
  Let them who thy salvation love
    Say still, God praised be.

5 I poor and needy am;
   Come, Lord, and make no stay:
My help thou and deliverer art;
   O Lord, make no delay.

PSALM LXX.—2nd Version. Chester, 12.

1 MAKE haste, O God, me to preserve;
   With speed, Lord, succour me.
2 Let them that for my soul do seek
   Shamed and confounded be:
Let them be turned back, and shamed,
   That in my hurt delight.
3 Turned back be they, Ha, ha!. that say,
   Their shaming to requite.

4 O Lord, in thee let all be glad,
   And joy that seek for thee:
Let them who thy salvation love
   Say still, God praised be.
5 But I both poor and needy am;
   Come, Lord, and make no stay:
My help thou and deliverer art;
   O Lord, make no delay.

PSALM LXXI. Parry, 40.

1 O LORD, my hope and confidence
   Are placed alone in thee;
O never let thy servant then
   Put to confusion be.
2 And let me, in thy righteousness,
   From thee deliverance have;
And set me free, incline thine ear
   Unto me, and me save.

3 Be thou my dwelling-rock, to which
    I ever may resort:
  Thou gav'st commandment me to save,
    Thou art my rock and fort.
4 Free me, my God, from wicked hands,
    Hands cruel and unjust:
5 For thou, O Lord God, art my hope,
    And from my youth my trust.

6 Thou from my birth didst hold me up;
    Thou didst me safely bring
  Out of my mother's womb; and I
    Still praise to thee will sing.
7 To many I a wonder am:
    Thou art my refuge strong.
8 Filled let my mouth be with thy praise
    And honour all day long.

9 O do not cast me off, when me
    Old age doth overtake;
  And in the time of failing strength
    Do thou not me forsake.
10 For those that are mine enemies
    Against me speak with hate;
  And they together counsel take
    That for my soul lay wait.

11 They say, God leaves him; him pursue
    And take: none will him save.
12 Be thou not far from me, my God:
    Thy speedy help I crave.
13 Confound, consume them, that unto
    My soul are enemies:
  Clothed be they with reproach and shame
    That do my hurt devise.

14 But as for me, with confidence
    Still hope in thee will I;
  And yet with praises more and more
    I will thee magnify.
15 Thy justice and thy saving help
    My mouth abroad shall show,
  Even all the day; for I thereof
    The numbers do not know.

16 And I will constantly go on
    In strength of God the Lord;
  And thine own righteousness, even thine
    Alone, I will record.
17 For even from my youth, O God,
    By thee I have been taught;
  And hitherto I have declared
    The wonders thou hast wrought.

18 Forsake me not, O God, when I
    Old and gray-headed grow:
  Till to this age thy strength, thy power
    To all to come, I show.
19 And thy most perfect righteousness,
    O Lord, is very high,
  Who hast so great things done: O God,
    Who is like unto thee?

20 Thou, Lord, who great adversities,
    And sore, to me didst show,
  Shalt me revive, and bring again
    From depths of earth below.
21 My greatness and my power thou wilt
    Increase, and far extend:
  On every side against all grief
    Thou wilt me comfort send.

22 Thee, even thy truth, I'll also praise,
    My God, with psaltery:
Thou Holy One of Israel,
    With harp I'll sing to thee.
23 My lips shall much rejoice in thee,
    When I thy praises sound;
My soul, which thou redeemed hast,
    In joy shall much abound.

24 My tongue thy justice shall proclaim,
    Continuing all day long;
For they confounded are, and shamed,
    That seek to do me wrong.

PSALM LXXII. *Smart, 51.*

1 O LORD, thy judgments give the king,
    His son thy righteousness.
2 With right he shall thy people judge,
    Thy poor with uprightness.
3 The lofty mountains shall bring forth
    Unto the people peace;
Likewise the little hills the same
    Shall do by righteousness.

4 The people's poor ones he shall judge,
    The needy's children save;
And those shall he in pieces break
    Who them oppressed have.
5 They shall thee fear, while sun and moon
    Do last, through ages all.
6 Like rain on mown grass he shall come,
    Or showers on earth that fall.

7 The just shall flourish in his days,
    And prosper in his reign:

He shall, while doth the moon endure,
   Abundant peace maintain.
8 His large and great dominion shall
   From sea to sea extend:
It from the river shall reach forth
   Unto earth's utmost end.

9 They in the wilderness that dwell
   Bow down before him must;
And they that are his enemies
   Shall lick the very dust.
10 The kings of Tarshish, and the isles,
   To him shall presents bring;
And unto him shall offer gifts
   Sheba's and Seba's king.

11 Yea, all the mighty kings on earth
   Before him down shall fall;
And all the nations of the world
   Do service to him shall.
12 For he the needy shall preserve,
   When he to him doth call;
Also the poor, and him that hath
   No help of man at all.

13 The poor man and the indigent
   In mercy he shall spare;
He shall preserve alive the souls
   Of those that needy are.
14 Both from deceit and violence
   Their soul he shall set free;
And in his sight most precious
   And dear their blood shall be.

15 Yea, he shall live, and given to him
   Shall be of Sheba's gold:

For him still shall they pray, and he
All day shall be extolled.
16 Of corn an handful in the earth
On tops of mountains high,
With prosperous fruit shall shake, like trees
On Lebanon that be.

The city shall be flourishing,
Her citizens abound
In number shall, like to the grass
That grows upon the ground.
17 His name for ever shall endure;
Last like the sun it shall:
Men shall be blessed in him, and blessed
All nations shall him call.

18 Now blessed be the Lord our God,
The God of Israel,
For he alone doth wondrous works,
In glory that excel.
19 And blessed be his glorious name
To all eternity:
The whole earth let his glory fill.
Amen, so let it be.

PSALM LXXIII. St. James, 46.

1 YEA, God is good to Israel,
To each pure-hearted one.
2 But as for me, my steps nigh slipped,
My feet were almost gone.
3 For I was envious, and grudged
The foolish folk to see,
When I perceived wicked men
Enjoy prosperity.

4 For still their strength continues firm;
　　Their death of bands is free.
5 Not troubled they like other men,
　　Nor plagued, as others be.
6 Therefore their pride, like to a chain,
　　Them compasseth about;
　And, as a garment, violence
　　Doth cover them throughout.

7 Their eyes stand out with fat; they have
　　More than their hearts could seek;
8 They mock, and loftily of wrong
　　And of oppression speak.
9 They set their mouth even in the heavens
　　In proud and haughty talk;
　Their boastful and reviling tongue
　　Upon the earth doth walk.

10 His people oftentimes for this
　　Look back, and turn about;
　Since waters of so full a cup
　　To these are poured out.
11 And thus they say, How can it be
　　That God these things doth know?
　Or, Can there in the Highest be
　　Knowledge of things below?

12 Lo these the wicked are, and yet
　　They prosper at their will
　In worldly things; they do increase
　　In wealth and riches still.
13 I verily have done in vain
　　My heart to purify;
　To no effect in innocence
　　My hands made clean have I.

14 For daily, and all day throughout,
    Great plagues I suffered have;
Yea, every morning I anew
    Did chastisement receive.
15 If in this manner foolishly
    To speak I would intend,
The generation of thy sons,
    Behold, I should offend.

16 But when I thought this thing to know,
    It was too hard for me,
17 Till to God's sanctuary I went;
    Then I their end did see.
18 Upon a slippery place them set
    Assuredly thou hast;
And down into destruction thou
    Dost suddenly them cast.

19 How in a moment suddenly
    To ruin brought are they!
With fearful terrors utterly
    They are consumed away.
20 Even like unto a dream, when one
    From sleeping doth arise;
So thou, O Lord, when thou awak'st,
    Their image shalt despise.

21 Thus I was grieved in my heart,
    And in my reins oppressed.
22 So rude was I, and ignorant,
    And in thy sight a beast.
23 And yet, O Lord, I do abide
    Continually with thee:
Thou dost me take by my right hand,
    And still upholdest me.

24 Thou with thy counsel, while I live,
    Wilt me conduct and guide;
And to thy glory afterward
    Receive me to abide.
25 Whom have I in the heavens high
    But thee, O Lord, alone?
And in the earth whom I desire
    Besides thee there is none.

26 My flesh and heart do faint and fail;
    But God doth fail me never;
For of my heart God is the strength;
    My portion sure for ever.
27 For, lo, they that are far from thee
    For ever perish shall;
Them that forsake thee wantonly
    Thou hast destroyed all.

28 But surely it is good for me
    That I draw near to God;
In God I trust that all thy works
    I may declare abroad.

    PSALM LXXIV.—1st Version. Moravia, 32.

1 O GOD, why hast thou cast us off?
    Is it for evermore?
Against thy pasture-sheep why doth
    Thine anger smoke so sore?
2 The congregation of thy choice
    In thy remembrance hold,
The people who have purchased been
    By thee in days of old;

The tribe of thine inheritance,
    Which thou redeemed hast,

This Zion hill, wherein thou hadst
  Thy dwelling in the past.
3 To these long desolations, Lord,
  Thy feet lift, tarry not,
 For all the ill thy foes within
  Thy holy place have wrought.

4 In midst of thine own meeting-place
  Thine enemies do roar:
 Their ensigns they set up for signs
  Of triumph thee before.
5 It seemed as if one lifted up
  His axe thick trees upon—
6 And now with hammer and with axe
  They break its carvings down.

7 They fired have thy holy place,
  And have defiled the same,
 By casting down unto the ground
  The place where dwelt thy name.
8 Thus said they in their hearts, Let us
  Destroy them out of hand:
 They burnt up all the synagogues
  Of God within the land.

9 Our signs we do not now behold;
  There is not us among
 A prophet more, nor any one
  That knows the time how long.
10 How long then shall the foe, O God,
  Reproachfully exclaim?
 And shall the adversary thus
  Always blaspheme thy name?

11 Thy hand, even thy right hand of might,
  To stretch forth why delay?

O from thy bosom pluck it out,
    And sweep them quite away.
12 For certainly God is my king,
    Even from the times of old,
Working in midst of all the earth
    Salvation manifold.

13 The sea, by thy great power, to part
    Asunder thou didst make;
And thou the dragons' heads, O Lord,
    Didst in the waters break.
14 The heads of the leviathan
    Thou brakest, and didst give
Him to be meat unto the folk
    That in the desert live.

15 Thou clav'st the fountain and the flood;
    Didst dry the rivers great;
16 Both day and night are thine; thou didst
    The light and sun create.
17 By thee the borders of the earth
    Were settled everywhere:
The summer and the winter both
    By thee created were.

18 How that the foe hath thee reproached,
    O keep it in record;
And that the foolish people have
    Blasphemed thy name, O Lord.
19 Unto the multitude do not
    Thy turtle's soul deliver:
The congregation of thy poor
    Do not forget for ever.

20 Unto thy covenant have respect;
    For earth's dark places be

      Full of the habitations dread
        Of horrid cruelty.
21 O let not those that be oppressed
        Return again with shame:
      Let those that poor and needy are
        Give praise unto thy name.

22 Do thou, O God, arise and plead
        The cause that is thine own:
      Remember how thou art reproached
        Still by the foolish one.
23 Forget not thou the voice of them
        That foes are unto thee;
      The tumult of thine enemies
        Ascends continually.

PSALM LXXIV.—2nd Version. _{Olmutz, 79}

1 O GOD, why hast thou cast us off?
        Why doth for ever smoke
      Thy wrath against thy chosen race,
        Sheep of thy flock?
2 Thy church, by thee redeemed of old,
        In love remember still;
      The tribe of thy inheritance,
        This Zion hill.

3 Here thou hast dwelt; lift up thy feet,
        To these sad ruins haste,
      Thy holy place with wicked hands
        By foes laid waste.
4 Thy enemies in triumph shout,
        Where saints were wont to pray;
      Their ensigns on thy temple's walls
        For signs display.

5 It seemed as if one cut down trees,
　　But now the carved work falls;
　With axes and with hammers now
　　They break the walls.
6 They have thy temple set on fire,
　　In dust they have defiled
　Thy holy place, where dwelt thy name,
　　Thy house despoiled.

7 They, to destroy us all at once,
　　Did in their hearts conspire;
　Through all the land God's synagogues
　　They've burnt with fire.
8 Our signs we see not; there is now
　　No prophet us among;
　Nor is there any one who knows
　　The time how long.

9 O Lord, how long shall those blaspheme
　　Thy name who thee withstand?
　Why hide thyself? Make bare thy hand,
　　Even thy right hand.
10 Because God is my King of old;
　　Salvation worketh he
　Through all the earth, and by his strength
　　Divides the sea.

11 Thou broken hast the dragons' heads,
　　And as their meat didst give
　Leviathan to those who did
　　In deserts live.
12 Fountain and flood thou didst divide,
　　Mad'st mighty rivers dry;
　The day is thine, the night is thine,
　　The sun and sky.

13 Thou hast established by decree
    All borders of the earth;
  To summer and to winter thou
    Hast given birth.
14 O Lord, do thou this keep in mind,
    How enemies defame,
  And how the foolish people have
    Blasphemed thy name.

15 Thy turtle dove deliver not
    To crowds which it beset,
  And thy poor flock for evermore
    Do not forget.
16 Unto thy covenant have respect,
    For everywhere we see
  The earth's dark habitations filled
    With cruelty.

17 O let not those that are oppressed
    Return again with shame;
  But let the poor and needy ones
    Still praise thy name.
18 Arise, O God, plead thine own cause;
    Keep thou in memory
  How every day the foolish man
    Reproacheth thee.

19 Of them that up against thee rise
    The tumult ever grows;
  Forget not thou the voice of them
    That are thy foes.

PSALM LXXV. *York, 54.*

1 TO thee, O God, do we give thanks,
    We do give thanks to thee;

Because thy wondrous works declare
    Thy great name near to be.
2 I shall the time appointed take,
    The moment fixed upon;
  And I shall judgment uprightly
    Render to every one.

3 Dissolved is the land, with all
    That in the same do dwell;
  But I the pillars thereof do
    Bear up, and stablish well.
4 I to the foolish people said,
    Do not deal foolishly;
  And unto those that wicked are,
    Lift not your horn on high.

5 Lift not your horn on high, nor speak
6   With stubborn neck. But know
  That not from east, nor west, nor south,
    Doth exaltation flow.
7 But God is judge; he puts down one,
    And sets another up.
8 For in the hand of God most high
    Of red wine is a cup:

  'Tis full of mixture, he pours forth,
    And makes the wicked all
  Wring out the bitter dregs thereof;
    Yea, and they drink them shall.
9 But I for ever will declare,
    I Jacob's God will praise.
10 All horns of wicked men I'll break,
    But just men's horns will raise.

PSALM LXXVI. Tallis, 53.

1 IN Judah God is known, his name
    Is great in Israel;
2 In Salem is his holy place,
    In Zion he doth dwell.
3 There arrows of the bow he brake,
    The shield, the sword, the war.
4 More glorious thou than hills of prey,
    More excellent by far.

5 Those that were stout of heart are spoiled,
    They slept their sleep outright;
  And none of those their hands did find,
    That were the men of might.
6 When thy rebuke, O Jacob's God,
    Had forth against them passed,
  Their horses and their chariots were
    Into a dead sleep cast.

7 Thou, even thou, art to be feared,
    And what man then is he
  That may stand up before thy sight,
    If once thou angry be?
8 From heaven thou madest judgment heard,
    The earth was still with fear,
9 When God to judgment rose, to save
    All meek on earth that were.

10 Surely the very wrath of man
    Unto thy praise resounds:
  Thou to the remnant of his wrath
    Wilt set restraining bounds.
11 Vow to the Lord your God, and pay:
    All ye that near him be,

Bring gifts and presents unto him;
     For to be feared is he.

12 For he the spirit shall cut off
     Of those that princes be:
   Unto the kings that are on earth
     Most terrible is he.

PSALM LXXVII. Abbey, 8.

1 MY voice I will lift up to God,
     I'll cry to God nor spare;
   My voice I will lift up to God,
     And he will hear my prayer.
2 In day of woe I sought the Lord;
     By night in ceaseless grief
   My hand was stretched out to him;
     My soul refused relief.

3 I to remembrance God do call,
     And then I sigh and mourn;
   I with myself commune, my heart
     With grief is overborne.
4 Thou dost deny mine eyelids sleep,
     Withhold the rest I seek;
   My trouble is so great that I
     Unable am to speak.

5 I thought on days and years of old,
     Recalled my song by night;
6 I with my heart communed, my soul
     Made earnest search for light.
7 For ever will the Lord cast off,
     And gracious be no more?
8 For ever is his mercy gone?
     Fails his word evermore?

9 Is't so that to be gracious
    The Lord forgotten hath;
  And that his tender mercies he
    Hath shut up in his wrath?
10 Then said I, This my weakness is;
    But call to mind will I
  The years of the right hand of him
    Who is the Lord most high.

11 Yea, I remember will the works
    Performed by the Lord:
  The wonders done of old by thee
    I surely will record.
12 Upon thy doings I will muse,
    On thy works meditate;
13 Most holy is thy way, O God:
    What God like thee is great?

14 Thou art the God that wonders dost
    By thy right hand most strong:
  Thy mighty power thou hast declared
    The nations all among.
15 To thine own people with thine arm
    Thou didst redemption bring;
  To Jacob's sons, and to the tribes
    Of Joseph that do spring.

16 The waters did thee see, O God,
    The waters did thee see;
  The depths thereof were troubled all,
    For fear aside did flee.
17 The clouds in water forth were poured,
    Sound loudly did the sky;
  And swiftly through the world abroad
    Thine arrows fierce did fly.

18 Thy thunder's voice along the heaven
    A mighty noise did make;
  Thy lightnings lighten did the world,
    Earth trembled and did shake.
19 Thy way is in the sea, and in
    The waters great thy path;
  Thy footsteps hidden are, O Lord;
    None knowledge thereof hath.

20 Thy people thou didst safely lead,
    Like to a flock of sheep;
  By Moses' hand and Aaron's thou
    Didst them conduct and keep.

PSALM LXXVIII. St. James, 46.

1 ATTEND, my people, to my law;
    Thereto give thou an ear;
  The words that from my mouth proceed
    Attentively do hear.
2 My mouth shall speak a parable,
    And sayings dark of old;
3 The same which we have heard and known,
    And us our fathers told.

4 We also will them not conceal
    From their posterity;
  But to the race that is to come
    Declare them faithfully.
  The praises of the Lord our God,
    And his almighty strength,
  The wondrous works that he hath done,
    We will show forth at length.

5 His testimony and his law
    In Israel he did place,

And charged our fathers it to show
To their succeeding race;
6 That so the race which was to come
Might well them learn and know;
And sons unborn, who should arise,
Might to their sons them show:

7 That they might set their hope in God,
And suffer not to fall
His mighty works out of their mind,
But keep his precepts all:
8 And might not, like their fathers, be
A stiff rebellious race;
A race not right in heart; with God
Whose spirit faithless was.

9 The sons of Ephraim nor bows
Nor other arms did lack;
Yet, when the day of battle came,
Faint-hearted they turned back.
10 They brake God's covenant, and refused
In his commands to go;
11 His works and wonders they forgot,
Which he to them did show.

12 Things marvellous he brought to pass;
Their fathers them beheld
Within the land of Egypt done,
Yea, even in Zoan's field.
13 The sea asunder he did cleave,
He led them through the deep;
And made the waters stand on high,
As though they were an heap.

14 With cloud by day, with light of fire
All night, he did them guide.

15 He in the desert clave the rocks,
    And drink as floods supplied.
16 He from the rock brought streams, like
    Made waters down to run;   [floods
17 Yet sinned they still, in desert they
    Provoked the Highest One.
18 For in their heart they tempted God,
    And, speaking with mistrust,
They greedily did meat require
    To satisfy their lust.
19 Against the Lord himself they spake,
    And, murmuring, said thus,
A table in the wilderness
    Can God prepare for us?
20 Behold, he smote the rock, and streams
    Forth gushed and waters wide:
But can he give his people bread,
    And flesh for them provide?
21 The Lord did hear, and waxed wroth;
    So kindled was a flame
'Gainst Jacob, and 'gainst Israel
    Up indignation came.
22 For they believed not God, nor trust
    In his salvation had;
23 Though clouds above he did command,
    And heaven's doors open made,
24 And manna rained on them, and gave
    Them corn of heaven to eat.
25 Man angel's food did eat; to them
    He to the full sent meat.
26 And in the heaven he did cause
    An eastern wind to blow;

    And by his power he did direct
      The southern wind to go.
27 Then flesh as thick as dust he made
      To rain down them among;
    And feathered fowls, like to the sand
      Which lies the shore along.

28 At his command amidst their camp
      These showers of flesh down fell,
    All round about the tabernacles
      And tents where they did dwell.
29 So they did eat abundantly,
      And had of meat their fill;
    For he did give to them what was
      Their own desire and will.

30 They from their lust had not estranged
      Their heart and their desire;
    But while the meat was in their mouths.
      Which they did so require,
31 God's wrath upon them came, and slew
      The fattest of them all;
    So that the choice of Israel,
      O'erthrown by death, did fall.

32 Yet after all the Lord had done
      They still went on in sin;
    Nor did believe, although his works
      So wonderful had been.
33 Wherefore their days in vanity
      He did consume and waste;
    And by his wrath their wretched years
      Away in grief did haste.

34 But when he slew them, then they did
      To seek him show desire;

Yea, they returned, and after God
    Right early did inquire.
35 And thus that God had been their Rock
    They did remember then;
And that the high almighty God
    Had their Redeemer been.

36 Yet with their mouth they flattered him,
    And with their tongues they lied;
37 Their heart not steadfast was; they from
    His covenant turned aside.
38 But, full of pity, he forgave
    Their sin, them did not slay,
Nor stirred up all his wrath, but oft
    His anger turned away.

39 For that they were but fading flesh
    To mind he did recall;
A wind that passeth soon away,
    Nor doth return at all.
40 How often did they him provoke
    Within the wilderness!
And in the desert did him grieve
    With their rebelliousness!

41 Yea, turning back, they tempted God,
    And limits they did place
Upon the High and Holy One,
    The God of Israel's race.
42 They did not call to mind his power,
    Nor yet the day when he
Delivered them out of the hand
    Of their fierce enemy;

43 When wonders he in Egypt wrought,
    And signs in Zoan's field;

44 Their rivers turned he into blood,
    Their streams no drink did yield.
45 He sent the fly which them devoured,
    The frog which did them spoil;
46 He gave the worm their increase all,
    The locust all their toil.

47 Their vines with hail, their sycamores
    He with the frost did blast;
48 Hail on their beasts, hot thunderbolts
    Upon their flocks, he cast.
49 Fierce anger he let loose on them,
    And indignation strong,
  Distress and trouble, angels sent
    Of evil them among.

50 He for his wrath made way; their soul
    From death he did not save;
  But over to the pestilence
    Their life in judgment gave.
51 In Egypt he the first-born all
    Did smite down everywhere;
  Among the tents of Ham, even those
    Chief of their strength that were.

52 But his own people, like to sheep,
    Thence to go forth he made;
  And he, amidst the wilderness,
    Them, as a flock, did lead.
53 And he in safety led them on,
    So that they did not fear;
  Whereas their enemies by the sea
    Quite overwhelmed were.

54 Unto his holy border then
    The Lord his people led.

> Even to the mount which his right hand
> For them had purchased.
55 The nations, which in Canaan dwelt,
> By his almighty hand
> Before his people's face he drove
> Out of their native land;

> Which for inheritance to them
> By line he did divide,
> And made the tribes of Israel
> Within their tents abide.
56 Yet God most high they did provoke,
> And him they tempted still;
> His testimonies to observe
> Did not incline their will;

57 But like their fathers turned back,
> And dealt unfaithfully:
> Aside they turned, like a bow
> That shoots deceitfully.
58 For they to anger did provoke
> Him with their places high;
> And with their graven images
> Moved him to jealousy.

59 When God heard this he waxed wroth,
> And much loathed Israel then:
60 So Shiloh's tent he left, the tent
> Which he had pitched with men.
61 And he his strength delivered
> Into captivity;
> He left his glory in the hand
> Of his proud enemy.

62 His people also he gave o'er
> Unto the sword's fierce rage:

  And hotly did his anger burn
   Against his heritage.
63 The fire consumed their choice young men;
   Their maids no marriage had;
64 And when their priests fell by the sword,
   Their wives no mourning made.

65 But then the Lord arose, as one
   Who from his sleep awakes;
  And like a strong man who from wine
   A shout of triumph makes.
66 Upon his enemies' backs he made
   His heavy stroke to fall;
  To a perpetual reproach
   And shame he put them all.

67 Moreover, he the tabernacle
   Of Joseph did refuse;
  The mighty tribe of Ephraim
   He would in no wise choose:
68 But he the tribe of Judah chose
   To be the rest above;
  And of mount Zion he made choice,
   Which he so much did love.

69 He also like unto the heights
   Did build his sanctuary,
  Like to the earth which he did found
   To perpetuity.
70 Of David, that his servant was,
   He also choice did make,
  And even from the folds of sheep
   Was pleased him to take:

71 From waiting on the ewes with young,
   He brought him forth to feed

Israel, his inheritance,
   His people, Jacob's seed.
72 And so in his integrity
   Of heart he did them feed;
 And with a wise and skilful hand
   Them prudently did lead.

PSALM LXXIX. *Esslingen, 19.*

1 O GOD, into thy heritage
    The heathen entrance made;
  Thy holy place they have defiled;
    On heaps Jerusalem laid.
2 Thy servants' bodies they have cast
    To fowls of heaven for meat;
  And of thy saints have thrown the flesh
    To beasts of earth to eat.

3 Their blood about Jerusalem
    Like water they have shed;
  And there was none to bury them
    When they were slain and dead.
4 Unto our neighbours a reproach
    Most base become are we;
  A scorn and laughing-stock to those
    That round about us be.

5 How long, Lord, shall thine anger last?
    Wilt thou still keep the same?
  And shall thy fervent jealousy
    Burn like unto a flame?
6 Thy fury on the heathen pour
    That have thee never known,
  And on those kingdoms which thy name
    Have never called upon.

7 For these are they who have devoured
    Thy servant Jacob's race;
  And they all waste and desolate
    Have made his dwelling-place.
8 Against us count not former sins,
    Thy tender mercies show;
  Let them prevent us speedily:
    We are brought very low.

9 For thy name's glory help us, Lord,
    Who hast our Saviour been:
  Deliver us; for thy name's sake
    O purge away our sin.
10 Why say the heathen, Where's their God?
    Let him to them be known,
  When those who shed thy servants' blood
    Are in our sight o'erthrown.

11 O let the prisoner's sighs ascend
    Before thy sight on high;
  Preserve thou in thy mighty power
    Those that are doomed to die.
12 And to our neighbours' bosom let
    It sevenfold rendered be,
  Even the reproach wherewith they have,
    O Lord, reproached thee.

13 So we, thy folk, and pasture-sheep,
    Shall give thee thanks always;
  And unto generations all
    We will show forth thy praise.

PSALM LXXX. St. Bartholomew, 44.

1 HEAR, Israel's Shepherd! like a flock
    Thou that dost Joseph guide;

Shine forth, O thou that dost between
  The cherubim abide.
2 In Ephraim's, and Benjamin's,
    And in Manasseh's sight,
  Do thou for our salvation come;
    Stir up thy strength and might.
3 Turn us again, O Lord our God,
    And upon us vouchsafe
  To make thy countenance to shine,
    And so we shall be safe.
4 O Lord of hosts, almighty God,
    How long shall kindled be
  Thy wrath against the prayer made
    By thine own folk to thee?
5 Thou tears of sorrow givest them
    Instead of bread to eat;
  Yea, tears instead of drink thou giv'st
    To them in measure great.
6 Thou makest us a strife unto
    Our neighbours round about;
  Our enemies among themselves
    At us do laugh and flout.
7 Turn us again, O God of hosts,
    And upon us vouchsafe
  To make thy countenance to shine,
    And so we shall be safe.
8 A vine from Egypt thou didst bring
    By thine outstretched hand:
  And thou didst cast the heathen out
    And plant it in their land.
9 A place thou didst prepare for it,
    Where it might grow and stand;

Thou madest it deep root to take,
　　And cover all the land.
10 The mountains veiled were with its shade,
　　As with a covering;
　The goodly cedars with the boughs
　　Which out of it did spring.

11 Upon the one hand to the sea
　　Her boughs she forth did send;
　Upon the other to the flood
　　Her branches did extend.
12 Why hast thou then thus broken down
　　And torn her hedge away;
　So that all passers-by do pluck,
　　And make of her a prey?

13 The boar that from the forest comes
　　Treads down and wastes it still;
　The wild beast also of the field
　　Devours it at his will.
14 O God of hosts, we thee beseech,
　　Return now unto thine;
　Look down from heaven in love, behold,
　　And visit this thy vine:

15 This vine tree, which thine own right hand
　　Hath planted us among;
　And that same branch, which for thyself
　　Thou hast made to be strong.
16 Burnt up it is with flaming fire,
　　'Tis utterly cut down;
　They quickly to destruction go
　　When once thy face doth frown.

17 O let thy hand be still upon
　　The man of thy right hand,

  The Son of man, whom for thyself
   Thou madest strong to stand.
18 So henceforth we will not go back,
   Nor turn from thee at all:
  O do thou quicken us, and we
   Upon thy name will call.

19 Turn us again, Lord God of hosts,
   And upon us vouchsafe
  To make thy countenance to shine,
   And so we shall be safe.

PSALM LXXXI. Parry, 40.

1 SING loud to God our strength; with joy
   To Jacob's God do sing.
2 Take up a psalm, the pleasant harp,
   Timbrel and psaltery bring.
3 Blow trumpets at new moon, and when
   Our feast appointed is:
4 A charge to Israel, and a law
   Of Jacob's God, was this.

5 To Joseph this an ordinance
   He made, when Egypt's land
  He travelled through, where speech I heard
   I did not understand.
6 His shoulder I from burdens took,
   His hands from pots did free.
7 Thou didst in trouble on me call,
   And I delivered thee:

  In secret place of thunder I
   To thee did answer make;
  And at the streams of Meribah
   Of thee a proof did take.

8 O thou, my people, give an ear,
  I'll testify to thee;
 To thee, O Israel, if thou wilt
  But hearken unto me.

9 In midst of thee there shall not be
  Any strange god at all;
 Nor unto any god unknown
  Thou bowing down shalt fall.
10 I am the Lord thy God, who did
  From Egypt land thee guide;
 I'll fill thy mouth abundantly,
  Do thou it open wide.

11 My people would not hear my voice,
  Israel my counsel spurned;
12 I gave them up to their hard hearts,
  To their own ways they turned.
13 O that my people had me heard,
  Israel my ways had chose!
14 I had their enemies soon subdued,
  My hand turned on their foes.

15 The haters of the Lord to him
  Submission should have feigned;
 But as for them, their time should have
  For evermore remained.
16 He should have also fed them with
  The finest of the wheat;
 Of honey from the rock thy fill
  I should have made thee eat.

PSALM LXXXII.
Tallis, 53.

1 IN gods' assembly God doth judge;
   He judgeth gods among.

2 How long, accepting persons vile,
    Will ye give judgment wrong?
3 The fatherless and needy judge;
    The poor and suffering right;
4 The destitute and needy free;
    Them rid of ill men's might.

5 They know not, nor will understand,
    In darkness they walk on:
All the foundations of the earth
    Out of their course have gone.
6 I said that ye are gods, and are
    Sons of the Highest all:
7 But ye shall die like men, and as
    One of the princes fall.

8 O God, do thou raise up thyself,
    The earth to judgment call:
For thou, as thine inheritance,
    Shalt take the nations all.

PSALM LXXXIII.   Martyrs, 31.

1 KEEP not, O God, we thee entreat,
    O keep not silence now:
No longer hold thy peace, O God,
    At rest no more be thou.
2 For, lo, thine enemies a noise
    Tumultuously have made;
And they that haters are of thee
    Have lifted up the head.

3 Against thy chosen people they
    Do crafty counsel take;
And they against thy hidden ones
    Do consultations make.

4 Come, let us cut them off, said they,
    No nation let them be;
  Nor let the name of Israel
    Be held in memory.

5 For with joint heart they plot, in league
    Against thee they combine:
6 The tents of Edom, Ishmaelites,
    Moab's and Hagar's line;
7 Gebal, and Ammon, Amalek,
    Philistines, those of Tyre,
8 And Assur joined with them; to help
    Lot's children they conspire.

9 Do to them as to Midian,
    Jabin at Kison strand,
10 And Sis'ra, who at En-dor fell,
    As dung to fat the land.
11 Like Oreb and like Zeeb make
    Their noble men to fall;
  To Zeba and Zalmunna like
    Make thou their princes all;

12 Who said, For our inheritance
    God's dwellings let us take;
13 Like stubble whirled before the blast,
    My God, do thou them make.
14 As fire consumes the wood, as flame
    Doth mountains set on fire,
15 Chase and affright them with the storm
    And tempest of thine ire.

16 Their faces fill with shame, O Lord,
    That they may seek thy name.
17 Let them confounded be and vexed,
    And perish in their shame:

18 That men may know, that thou, to whom
  Alone doth appertain
The name Jehovah, dost most high
  O'er all the earth remain.

PSALM LXXXIV. Patton, 4:.

1 HOW lovely is thy dwelling-place,
    O Lord of hosts, to me!
  The tabernacles of thy grace
    How pleasant, Lord, they be!
2 My thirsty soul longs veh'mently,
    Yea faints, thy courts to see;
  My very heart and flesh cry out,
    O living God, for thee.

3 Behold, the sparrow findeth out
    An house wherein to rest;
  The swallow also for herself
    Provided hath a nest;
  Even thine own altars, where she safe
    Her young ones forth may bring,
  O thou almighty Lord of hosts,
    Who art my God and King.

4 Blest are they in thy house that dwell,
    They ever give thee praise.
5 Blest is the man whose strength thou art,
    In whose heart are thy ways:
6 Who as they pass through Baca's vale
    Make it a place of springs;
  Also the rain that falleth down
    Rich blessing to it brings.

7 So they from strength unwearied go
    Still forward unto strength,

      Until in Zion they appear
        Before the Lord at length.
8 Lord God of hosts, my prayer hear;
    O Jacob's God, give ear.
9 See, God our shield, look on the face
    Of thine anointed dear.

10 For in thy courts one day excels
     A thousand; rather in
  My God's house will I keep a door,
     Than dwell in tents of sin.
11 For God the Lord's a sun and shield:
     He'll grace and glory give;
  And will withhold no good from them
     That uprightly do live.

12 O thou that art the Lord of hosts,
     That man is truly blest,
  Who with assured confidence
     On thee alone doth rest.

PSALM LXXXV.—1st Version. _{Richardson, 42.}

1 THOU hast been favourable, Lord,
    To thy beloved land;
  Jacob's captivity thou hast
    Recalled with mighty hand.
2 Thou pardoned thy people hast
    All their iniquities;
  Thou all their trespasses and sins
    Hast covered from thine eyes.

3 Thou hast thine anger all withdrawn,
    Turned from thy furiousness;
4 O God of our salvation, turn,
    And cause thy wrath to cease.

5 Shall thy displeasure thus endure
    Against us without end?
Wilt thou to generations all
    Thine anger still extend?

6 That in thee may thy people joy,
    Wilt thou not us revive?
7 Show us thy mercy, Lord, to us
    Do thy salvation give.
8 I'll hear what God the Lord will speak:
    To his folk he'll speak peace,
And to his saints; but let them not
    Return to foolishness.

9 Surely to them that fear the Lord
    Is his salvation near;
That glory in our land again
    A dweller may appear.
10 Truth meets with mercy, righteousness
    And peace kiss mutually:
11 Truth springs from earth, and righteousness
    Looks down from heaven high.

12 Yea, what is good the Lord shall give;
    Our land shall yield increase:
13 Justice, to set us in his steps,
    Shall go before his face.

PSALM LXXXV.—2nd Version. _{Redhead, 77.}

1 LORD, thine heart in love hath yearned
    On thy lost and fallen land;
Israel's race is homeward turned,
    Thou hast freed thy captive band:
2 Thou hast borne thy people's sin,
    Covered all their deeds of ill;

All thy wrath is gathered in,
  And thy burning anger still.

3 Turn us, stay us, now once more,
    God of all our health and peace;
  Let thy cloud of wrath fleet o'er,
    From thine own thy fury cease.
4 Wilt thou ne'er the storm assuage
    On the realm of thy desire,
  Lengthening out from age to age
    Thy consuming jealous ire?

5 Wilt thou not in mercy turn?
    Turn, and be our life again,
  That thy people's heart may burn
    With the gladness of thy reign.
6 Show us now thy tender love;
    Thy salvation, Lord, impart;
  I the voice divine would prove,
    Listening in my silent heart:

7 Listening what the Lord will say—
    "Peace" to all that own his will:
  To his saints that love his way,
    "Peace," and "turn no more to ill."
8 Ye that fear him, nigh at hand
    Now his saving health ye find,
  That the glory in our land,
    As of old, may dwell enshrined.

9 Mercy now and justice meet,
    Peace and truth for aye embrace;
  Truth from earth is springing sweet,
    Justice looks from her high place.
10 Nor will God his goodness stay,
    Nor our land her bounteous store:

Marking out her Maker's way,
    Righteousness shall go before.

PSALM LXXXVI. <small>Eden, 17.</small>

1 O LORD, do thou bow down thine ear,
    And hear me graciously;
  Because I sore afflicted am,
    And am in poverty.
2 Because I'm holy, let my soul
    By thee preserved be:
  O thou, my God, thy servant save,
    That puts his trust in thee.

3 Since unto thee all day I cry,
    Be merciful to me.
4 Rejoice thy servant's soul; for, Lord,
    I lift my soul to thee.
5 For thou art very gracious, Lord,
    And ready to forgive;
  And rich in mercy, all that call
    Upon thee to relieve.

6 Hear, Lord, my prayer; unto the voice
    Of my request attend:
7 In troublous times I'll call on thee,
    For thou wilt answer send.
8 Lord, there is none among the gods
    That may compare with thee;
  And to the works which thou hast done
    No works can likened be.

9 All nations whom thou mad'st shall come
    And worship reverently
  Before thy face; and they, O Lord,
    Thy name shall glorify.

10 Because thou art exceeding great,
    And works by thee are done
Which are to be admired; and thou
    Art God thyself alone.

11 Teach me thy way, and in thy truth,
    O Lord, then walk will I;
Unite my heart, that I thy name
    May fear continually.
12 O Lord my God, with all my heart
    To thee I will give praise;
And I the glory will ascribe
    Unto thy name always:

13 Because thy mercy toward me
    In greatness doth excel;
And thou delivered hast my soul
    Out from the lowest hell.
14 O God, the proud against me rise,
    The violent have met,
Who for my soul have sought; and thee
    Before them have not set.

15 But thou, Lord, art a gracious God,
    And most compassionate;
Long-suffering, and slow to wrath,
    In truth and mercy great.
16 O turn to me thy countenance,
    And mercy on me have;
Thy servant strengthen, and the son
    Of thine own handmaid save.

17 Show me a sign for good, that they
    Who do me hate may see,
And be ashamed: because thou, Lord,
    Didst help and comfort me.

PSALM LXXXVII. Jackson, 2s.

1 UPON the hills of holiness
 He his foundation sets.
2 God, more than Jacob's dwellings all,
 Delights in Zion's gates.
3 Things glorious are said of thee,
 Thou city of the Lord.
4 Rahab and Babel I as those
 That know me will record:

Lo, Tyrus, and with it the land
 Where dwells the Philistine,
And likewise Ethiopia;
 This one was born therein.
5 Of Zion shall be said, This man
 And that man born was there;
And he that is the Lord most high
 Himself shall stablish her.

6 When God the people writes, he'll count
 That this man born was there.
7 The singers as the players say,
 My well-springs in thee are.

PSALM LXXXVIII. Bangor, 9.

1 LORD God, my Saviour, day and night
 Before thee cried have I.
2 Before thee let my prayer come;
 Give ear unto my cry.
3 For troubles great do fill my soul;
 My life draws nigh the grave.
4 I'm counted with those that go down
 To death, and no strength have.

5 Free midst the dead, like to the slain
    That in the grave do lie;
  Cut off from thy hand, whom no more
    Thou hast in memory.
6 Thou hast me laid in lowest pit,
    In deeps and darksome caves;
7 Thy wrath lies hard on me, thou hast
    Me pressed with all thy waves.

8 Thou hast put far from me my friends,
    Made me their scorn to know;
  And I am so shut up that I
    No longer forth can go.
9 By reason of my deep distress,
    Mine eye doth waste away;
  To thee, O Lord, I call, and stretch
    My hands out every day.

10 Wilt thou show wonders to the dead?
    Shall they rise and thee bless?
11 Shall in the grave thy love be told?
    In death thy faithfulness?
12 Shall thy great wonders in the dark,
    Or shall thy righteousness
  Be known to any in the land
    Of deep forgetfulness?

13 But, Lord, to thee I cried; my prayer
    At morn shall come to thee.
14 Why, Lord, dost thou cast off my soul,
    And hide thy face from me?
15 Distressed am I, and from my youth
    I ready am to die;
  Thy terrors I have borne, and am
    Distracted fearfully.

16 By thy fierce wrath I'm overwhelmed,
    Cut off by dread of thee;
17 Like floods thy terrors round me close,
    All day they compass me.
18 My friends thou hast put far from me,
    And him that did me love;
  And those that mine acquaintance were
    To darkness didst remove.

PSALM LXXXIX. Old Winchester, 38.

1 GOD'S mercies I will ever sing;
    And with my mouth I shall
  Thy faithfulness make to be known
    To generations all.
2 For mercy shall be built, said I,
    For ever to endure;
  Thy faithfulness even in the heavens
    Thou wilt establish sure.

3 I with my chosen one have made
    A covenant graciously;
  And to my servant whom I loved,
    To David sworn have I;
4 That I thy seed establish shall
    For ever to remain,
  And will to generations all
    Thy throne build and maintain.

5 The praises of thy wonders, Lord,
    The heavens shall express;
  The assembly of the holy ones
    Shall praise thy faithfulness.
6 For who in heaven with the Lord
    May once himself compare?

    Who is like God among the sons
      Of those that mighty are?

7 Great fear in meeting of the saints
    Is due unto the Lord;
  And he above all round him should
    With reverence be adored.
8 O Lord, the God of hosts, who can
    To thee compared be?
  The mighty One, the Lord, whose truth
    Doth round encompass thee.
9 Even in the swelling of the sea
    Thou over it dost reign;
  And when the waves thereof do rise,
    Thou stillest them again.
10 Rahab in pieces thou didst break,
    Like one that slaughtered is;
  And with thy mighty arm thou hast
    Dispersed thine enemies.

11 The heavens are thine, thou for thine own
    The earth dost also take;
  The world, and fulness of the same,
    Thou by thy power didst make.
12 The north and south from thee alone
    Their first beginning had;
  Both Tabor mount and Hermon hill
    Shall in thy name be glad.
13 Thou hast an arm that's full of power:
    Thy hand is great in might;
  And thy right hand exceedingly
    Exalted is in height.
14 Justice and judgment of thy throne
    Are made the dwelling-place;

Mercy, accompanied with truth,
  Shall go before thy face.
15 O greatly blessed the people are
  The joyful sound that know;
  In brightness of thy face, O Lord,
  They ever on shall go.
16 They in thy name shall all the day
  Rejoice exceedingly;
  And in thy righteousness shall they
  Exalted be on high.

17 Because the glory of their strength
  Doth only stand in thee;
  And in thy favour shall our horn
  And power exalted be.
18 For to the Lord belongs our shield,
  That doth us safety bring;
  And unto Israel's Holy One
  The man that is our king.
19 In vision to thy holy one
  Thou saidst, I help upon
  A strong one laid; out of the folk
  I raised a chosen one;
20 Even David, I have found him out
  A servant unto me;
  And with my holy oil my King
  Anointed him to be.

21 With whom my hand shall stablished be;
  Mine arm shall make him strong.
22 From him the foe shall not exact,
  Nor son of mischief wrong.
23 I will beat down before his face
  All his malicious foes;

I will them greatly plague who do
With hatred him oppose.

24 My mercy and my faithfulness
With him yet still shall be;
And in my name his horn and power
Men shall exalted see.

25 His hand of might shall reach afar,
I'll set it in the sea;
And his right hand established
Shall in the rivers be.

26 Thou art my Father and my God,
He unto me shall cry;
The rock of my salvation thou
On whom I do rely.

27 I'll make him my first-born, more high
Than kings of any land.

28 My love I'll ever keep for him,
My covenant fast shall stand.

29 His seed I by my power will make
For ever to endure;
And, as the days of heaven, his throne
Shall stable be and sure.

St. Mary, 47.

30 But if his children shall forsake
My laws, and go astray,
And in my judgments shall not walk,
But wander from the way:

31 If they my statutes do profane,
My laws do not respect;

32 I'll visit then their faults with rods,
Their sins with stripes correct.

33 Yet I'll not take my love from him,
   Nor false my promise make.
34 My covenant I'll not break, nor change
   What with my mouth I spake.

35 Once by my holiness I sware,
   To David I'll not lie;
36 His seed and throne shall, as the sun,
   Before me last for aye.
37 Like to the moon established
   It shall for ever be:
   The witness which is in the heaven
   Doth witness faithfully.

38 But, wroth with thine anointed, thou
   Renounced and loathed him hast;
39 His covenant made void, his crown
   To earth profaned cast.
40 His hedges all hast broken down,
   His strong-holds down hast torn.
41 He is a spoil to passers-by,
   To neighbours all a scorn.

42 Thou hast set up his foes' right hand;
   Made all his enemies glad:
43 Turned his sword's edge, and him to stand
   In battle hast not made.
44 His glory thou hast made to cease,
   His throne to earth down cast;
45 Thou shortened hast his days of youth,
   With shame him covered hast.

46 How long, Lord, wilt thou hide thyself?
   For ever, in thine ire?
   And shall thine indignation hot
   Burn like unto a fire?

47 Remember, Lord, how short a time
   I shall on earth remain:
   O wherefore is it so that thou
   Hast made all men in vain?

48 What man is he that liveth here,
   And death shall never see?
   Or from the power of the grave
   What man his soul shall free?
49 Thy former loving-kindnesses,
   O Lord, where be they now?
   Those which in truth and faithfulness
   To David sworn hast thou?

50 Mind, Lord, thy servants' sad reproach:
   I in my bosom bear
   The scornings of the people all,
   Who strong and mighty are:
51 And that thine enemies, O Lord,
   Have cast reproach upon,
   Have cast reproach upon the steps
   Of thine anointed one.

52 All blessing to the Lord our God
   Let be ascribed then:
   For evermore so let it be.
   Amen, yea, and amen.

PSALM XC.—1st Version. Chester, 12.

1 LORD, thou hast been our dwelling-place
   In generations all.
2 Before thou ever hadst brought forth
   The mountains great or small;
   Ere ever thou hadst formed the earth,
   And all the world abroad;

Thou even from everlasting art
 To everlasting God.

3 Thou, Lord, unto destruction dost
 Man that is mortal turn;
 And unto them thou sayest, Again,
 Ye sons of men, return.
4 Because a thousand years appear
 No more before thy sight
 Than yesterday when it is past,
 Or than a watch by night.
5 As with an overflowing flood
 Thou carriest them away:
 They like a sleep are, like the grass
 That grows at morn are they.
6 At morn it flourishes and grows,
 Cut down at even doth fade.
7 For by thine anger we're consumed,
 Thy wrath makes us afraid.
8 Our sins thou and iniquities
 Dost in thy presence place,
 And sett'st our secret faults before
 The brightness of thy face.
9 For in thine anger all our days
 Do pass on to an end;
 And as a tale that hath been told,
 So we our years do spend.
10 Threescore and ten years do sum up
 Our days and years, we see;
 Or if, by reason of more strength,
 In some fourscore they be,
 Yet doth the strength of such old men
 But grief and labour prove;

For it is soon cut off, and we
    Fly hence and soon remove.

11 Who knows thine anger's power, and keeps
    Thy fear before his eyes?
12 To count our days so teach thou us
    That our hearts may be wise.
13 Turn yet again to us, O Lord,
    How long thus shall it be?
  Let it repent thee now for those
    That servants are to thee.

14 O with thy tender mercies, Lord,
    Us early satisfy;
  So we rejoice shall all our days,
    And still be glad in thee.
15 According as the days have been
    Wherein we grief have had,
  And years wherein we ill have seen,
    So do thou make us glad.

16 O let thy work and power appear
    Thy servants' face before;
  And show unto their children dear
    Thy glory evermore:
17 And let the beauty of the Lord
    Our God be us upon;
  And our hands' works establish thou,
    Establish them each one.

PSALM XC.—2nd Version. *Luther's Hymn, 83.*

1 LORD, thou hast been a dwelling-place,
    A rest in tribulations,
  To us, thine own redeemed race,
    Through all our generations.

Thou, ere the mountains sprang to birth,
Or ever thou hadst formed the earth,
  Art God from everlasting.

2 Thou turnest man again to clay;
  By thee that doom was spoken;
As with a torrent borne away,
  Gone like a sleep when broken.
A thousand years are in thy sight
But as a watch amid the night,
  Or yesterday departed.

3 At morn we flourish like the grass,
  When green and fresh it groweth;
Which, withered ere the evening pass,
  The sweeping sickle moweth.
Thus do thy chastisements consume
Our blasted hopes, our early bloom;
  We fade at thy displeasure.

4 Lo! thou hast set before thine eyes
  All our misdeeds and errors;
Our secret sins from darkness rise
  To thy confronting terrors.
At thy rebuke, cut short by death,
Our life is like the transient breath,
  That told a bygone story.

5 Our days are three-score years and ten;
  Ten more man's strength may borrow;
But if the span be lengthened then
  That strength is toil and sorrow;
For soon arrives the closing hour:
But who discerns thy fearful power,
  Proportioned to thine anger?

6 Lord, teach us so to count our days,
    That we may prize them duly,
And set our heart on wisdom's ways,
    That we may praise thee truly.
Return, thy servants' griefs behold,
And with thy mercy, as of old,
    O, satisfy us early!

7 Restore us comfort for our fears,
    Joy for our long affliction;
Our children give through changing years
    Increasing benediction.
Thy glorious beauty, Lord, reveal;
And with thy prospering favour seal
    Thy servants and their labours.

PSALM XCI. *St. David, 45.*

1 HE that doth in the secret place
    Of the Most High reside,
Under the shade of him that is
    The Almighty shall abide.
2 I of the Lord my God will say,
    He is my refuge still,
He is my fortress and my God,
    And in him trust I will.

3 Assuredly he shall thee save,
    And give deliverance
Both from the fowler's snare and from
    The noisome pestilence.
4 His feathers shall thee hide; thy trust
    Under his wings shall be:
His faithfulness shall be a shield
    And buckler unto thee.

5 Thou shalt not need to be afraid
    For terrors of the night;
  Nor for the arrow that doth fly
    By day, while it is light;
6 Nor for the pestilence that walks
    In darkness secretly;
  Nor for destruction that doth waste
    At noon-day openly.

7 A thousand at thy side shall fall,
    On thy right hand shall lie .
  Ten thousand dead; yet unto thee
    It shall not once come nigh.
8 Thou with thine eyes shalt only look,
    And a beholder be;
  And thou the merited reward
    Of wicked men shalt see.

9 For thou, O Lord, art constantly
    My refuge and mine aid;
  Thou hast the Lord who is most high
    Thy habitation made.
10 No plague shall near thy dwelling come;
    No ill shall thee befall:
11 For thee to keep in all thy ways
    His angels charge he shall.

12 They in their hands shall bear thee up,
    Still waiting thee upon;
  Lest thou at any time should'st dash
    Thy foot against a stone.
13 Upon the adder thou shalt tread,
    And on the lion strong;
  Thy feet on dragons trample shall,
    And on the lions young.

14 Because on me he set his love,
    Deliver him will I;
  Because my great name he hath known,
    I will him set on high.
15 He'll call on me, I'll answer him;
    I will be with him still
  In trouble, to deliver him,
    And honour him I will.

16 And length of days to his desire
    I will on him bestow;
  And, in my love, I unto him
    Will my salvation show.

PSALM XCII. Kaltenthal, 27.

1 TO render thanks unto the Lord
    It is a comely thing,
  And to thy name, O thou Most High,
    Due praise aloud to sing:
2 Thy loving-kindness to show forth
    When shines the morning light;
  And to declare thy faithfulness
    With pleasure every night,

3 Upon a ten-stringed instrument,
    And on the psaltery,
  Upon the harp with solemn sound
    And grave sweet melody.
4 For thou, Lord, by thy mighty deeds
    Hast gladness to me brought;
  And I will triumph in the works
    Which by thy hands are wrought.

5 How great and wondrous, Lord, thy works!
    Thy thought how deep it is!

6 A brutish man discerneth not,
    Fools understand not this.
7 When even like unto the grass
    Springs up the wicked race,
  And workers of iniquity
    Do flourish all apace;

  'Tis that cut off and quite destroyed
    They may for ever be:
8 But thou, O Lord, art throned on high,
    Unto eternity.
9 For, lo, thine enemies, O Lord,
    Thine enemies perish shall;
  The workers of iniquity
    Shall be dispersed all.

10 But, like the unicorn's, my horn
    Exalted is by thee:
  Anointed also with fresh oil
    I am abundantly.
11 Mine eye shall also my desire
    See on mine enemies;
  Mine ears shall of the wicked hear,
    That do against me rise.

12 But like the palm-tree flourishing
    Shall be the righteous one;
  He shall like to the cedar grow
    That is in Lebanon.
13 Those that within the house of God
    Are planted by his grace,
  They shall grow up, and flourish all
    In our God's holy place.

14 And in old age, when others fade,
    They fruit still forth shall bring;

They shall be fat and full of sap,
   And aye be flourishing;
15 To show that upright is the Lord:
   He is a rock to me;
   And he from all unrighteousness
   Is altogether free.

PSALM XCIII.—1st Version. Newlands, 35.

1 THE Lord doth reign, and clothed is he
     With majesty most bright;
   The Lord hath clothed himself, he hath
     Him girt about with might.
   The world is also stablished,
     That it cannot depart.
2 Thy throne is fixed of old, and thou
     From everlasting art.

3 The floods, O Lord, have lifted up,
     Have lifted up their voice;
   The floods have lifted up their waves,
     And made a mighty noise.
4 But yet the Lord, who is on high,
     Is more of might by far
   Than noise of many waters is,
     Than great sea-billows are.

5 Thy testimonies every one
     In faithfulness excel;
   And holiness for ever, Lord,
     Thine house becometh well.

PSALM XCIII.—2nd Version. Kocher, 75.

1 THE Lord is king and weareth
     A robe of glory bright,

He clothed with strength appeareth,
    And girt with powerful might.
2 The earth he hath so grounded
    That moved it cannot be;
His throne long since was founded,
    More old than time is he.

3 The waters highly flowing
    Have raised their voice, O Lord;
The seas their fury showing
    With billows loud have roared.
4 But God in strength excelleth
    Strong seas and powerful deeps;
With him still pureness dwelleth,
    And firm his truth he keeps.

PSALM XCIV.   Elgin, 18.

1 O LORD, the God to whom alone
    All vengeance doth belong;
Thou, who the God of vengeance art,
    Shine forth, avenging wrong.
2 Lift up thyself, thou of the earth
    The sovereign judge that art;
And unto those that haughty are
    A recompense impart.

3 How long, Jehovah, shall the men
    Who evil-doers be,
How long shall they who wicked are
    Thus triumph haughtily?
4 How long shall grievous things by them
    Be uttered and told?
And all that work iniquity
    To boast themselves be bold?

5 Thy folk they break in pieces, Lord,
　　Thine heritage oppress:
6 The widow and the stranger slay,
　　And kill the fatherless:
7 Yet say, The Lord shall not perceive,
　　Nor God of Jacob know.
8 Ye brutish people! understand;
　　Fools! when wise will ye grow?

9 Shall he who plants the ear of man
　　To hear unable be?
　And he who fashioneth the eye,
　　Shall he not clearly see?
10 He who the nations doth correct,
　　Shall he reproof not show?
　He that doth knowledge teach to man,
　　Shall he himself not know?

11 Man's thoughts to be but vanity
　　The Lord doth well discern.
12 Blessed is the man thou chastenest, Lord,
　　And mak'st thy law to learn:
13 That thou mayest give him rest from days
　　Of sad adversity,
　Until the pit be digged for those
　　That work iniquity.

14 Because the Lord will not cast off
　　Those that his people be,
　Nor yet his own inheritance
　　Forsake at all will he:
15 But judgment unto righteousness
　　Shall yet return again;
　And all shall follow after it
　　That are right-hearted men.

16 Who will rise up for me against
    Those that do wickedly?
  Who will stand up for me 'gainst those
    That work iniquity?
17 Unless the Lord had been my help,
    My soul in death had lain;
18 But if I say, My foot doth slip,
    Thy love doth me sustain.

19 Amidst the multitude of cares
    Whereby I am oppressed,
  Thy comforts, Lord, refresh my soul,
    Thy mercies give me rest.
20 Shall of iniquity the throne
    Have fellowship with thee,
  Which mischief, cunningly contrived,
    Doth by a law decree?

21 Against the righteous souls they join,
    They guiltless blood condemn.
22 But of my refuge God's the rock,
    And my defence from them.
23 On them their own iniquity
    The Lord shall cause to fall,
  And in their sin shall cut them off;
    Our God destroy them shall.

PSALM XCV.—1st Version. Gauntlett, 23.

1 O COME, and let us to the Lord
    In songs our voices raise,
  With joyful noise let us the rock
    Of our salvation praise.
2 Let us before his presence come
    With praise and thankful voice;

Let us sing psalms to him with grace,
  And make a joyful noise.

3 The Lord's a great God and great King,
   Above all gods he is.
4 Depths of the earth are in his hand,
   The strength of hills is his.
5 To him the spacious sea belongs,
   For he the same did make;
  The dry land also from his hands
   Its form at first did take.

6 O come and let us worship him,
   Let us bow down withal,
  And on our knees before the Lord
   Our Maker let us fall.
7 For he's our God, the people we
   Of his own pasture are,
  And of his hand the sheep; to-day,
   If ye his voice will hear;

8 Then harden not your hearts, as in
   The wilderness of old,
  When Meribah and Massah did
   Trial and strife behold.
9 When me your fathers tempted, proved,
   And did my working see.
10 Even for the space of forty years
   This race hath grieved me.

  I said, This people errs in heart,
   My ways they do not know;
11 So in my wrath I sware, that to
   My rest they should not go.

PSALM XCV.—2nd Version. <small>Fareham, 8c.</small>

1 O COME, let us sing to the Lord,
    In God our salvation rejoice,
In psalms of thanksgiving record
    His praise, with one spirit, one voice.
For Jehovah is king—and he reigns
    The God of all gods on his throne;
The strength of the hills he maintains,
    The ends of the earth are his own.

2 The sea is Jehovah's; he made
    The tide its dominion to know:
The land is Jehovah's; he laid
    Its solid foundations below.
O come let us worship and kneel
    Before our Creator, our God;
The people who serve him with zeal,
    The flock whom he guides with his rod.

3 To-day, if his voice ye will hear,
    He speaks from above to you still;
" O turn not aside; but forbear
    To harden your hearts to my will.
As once on the wilderness way
    Of old my long-suffering you tried;
The day of temptation, the day
    When God's righteous wrath ye defied.

4 " Your fathers against me rebelled;
    And forty years long was I grieved,
My works while they daily beheld,
    But, tempting their God, disbelieved.
Their heart had from me gone astray,
    And I sware in my wrath, that unblest

The people that knew not my way
　　Should ne'er enter into my rest."

PSALM XCVI. Old Winchester, 3S.

1 O SING a new song to the Lord:
　　Sing all the earth to God.
2 To God sing, bless his name, show still
　　His saving health abroad.
3 Among the nations of the earth
　　His glory do declare;
　And unto all the people show
　　His works that wondrous are.

4 For great's the Lord, and greatly he
　　Is to be magnified;
　Yea, worthy to be feared is he
　　Above all gods beside.
5 For all the gods are idols dumb
　　Which blinded nations fear;
　But our God is the Lord, by whom
　　The heavens created were.

6 Great honour is before his face,
　　And majesty divine;
　Strength is within his holy place,
　　And there doth beauty shine.
7 Do ye ascribe unto the Lord,
　　Of people every tribe,
　Glory do ye unto the Lord
　　And mighty power ascribe.

8 Give ye the glory to the Lord
　　That to his name is due;
　Come ye into his courts, and bring
　　An offering with you.

9 In beauty of his holiness
   O do the Lord adore;
   Likewise let all the earth throughout
   Tremble his face before.

10 'Mong heathen say, Jehovah reigns;
   The world shall steadfast be
   So that it move not; he shall judge
   The people righteously.
11 Let heavens be glad before the Lord,
   And let the earth rejoice;
   Let seas and all their fulness roar,
   And make a mighty noise.

12 Let fields rejoice, and everything
   That springeth of the earth;
   Then of the forest all the trees
   Shall shout aloud with mirth
13 Before the Lord; because he comes,
   To judge the earth comes he;
   He'll judge the world with righteousness,
   The people faithfully.

PSALM XCVII. St. Anne, 43.

1 GOD reigneth, let the earth be glad,
   And isles rejoice each one.
2 Dark clouds him compass; and in right
   And judgment dwells his throne.
3 Fire goes before him, and his foes
   It burns up round about:
4 His lightnings lighten did the world;
   Earth saw, and shook throughout.

5 Hills at the presence of the Lord,
   Like wax, did melt away;

    Even at the presence of the Lord
        Of all the earth, I say.
6 The heavens declare his righteousness,
        All men his glory see.
7 All who serve graven images,
        Confounded let them be.

    Who do of idols boast themselves,
        Let shame upon them fall:
    Ye that are called gods, see that
        Ye do him worship all.
8 Zion did hear, and joyful was,
        Glad Judah's daughters were;
    They much rejoiced, O Lord, because
        Thy judgments did appear.

9 For thou, O Lord, art high above
        All things on earth that are;
    Above all other gods thou art
        Exalted very far.
10 Hate ill, all ye that love the Lord:
        His saints' souls keepeth he;
    And from the hands of wicked men
        He sets them safe and free.

11 For every one that righteous is
        Sown is a joyful light,
    And gladness sown is for all those
        That are in heart upright.
12 Ye righteous, in the Lord rejoice;
        Express your thankfulness,
    When ye into your memory
        Do call his holiness.

PSALM XCVIII.—1st Version. <small>Old Winchester, 38.</small>

1 O SING a new song to the Lord,
　　For wonders he hath done:
　His right hand and his holy arm
　　Him victory have won.
2 Jehovah his salvation hath
　　Now caused to be known;
　His justice in the heathen's sight
　　He openly hath shown.

3 He mindful of his grace and truth
　　To Israel's house hath been;
　And the salvation of our God
　　All ends of the earth have seen.
4 Let all the earth unto the Lord
　　Send forth a joyful noise;
　Lift up your voice aloud to him,
　　Sing praises, and rejoice.

5 With harp, with harp, and voice of psalms,
　　Unto Jehovah sing:
6 With trumpets, cornets, gladly sound
　　Before the Lord the King.
7 Let seas and all their fulness roar;
　　The world, and dwellers there;
8 Let floods clap hands, and let the hills
　　Together joy declare

9 Before the Lord; because he comes,
　　To judge the earth comes he;
　He'll judge the world with righteousness,
　　The nations uprightly.

PSALM XCVIII.—2nd Version. <small>Stuttgart, 81.</small>

1 SING a new song to Jehovah,
    For he wondrous things hath wrought;
His right hand and arm most holy
    Victory to him have brought.
2 Lo! the Lord his great salvation
    Openly hath now made known;
In the sight of every nation
    He his righteousness has shown.

3 Mindful of his truth and mercy
    He to Israel's house hath been;
And the Lord our God's salvation
    All the ends of earth have seen.
4 All the earth sing to Jehovah!
    Shout aloud! sing and rejoice!
With the harp sing to Jehovah!
    With the harp and tuneful voice.

5 Sound the trumpet and the cornet,
    Shout before the Lord the King;
Sea, and all its fulness, thunder;
    Earth, and all its people, sing.
6 Let the rivers in their gladness
    Clap their hands with one accord;
Let the mountains sing together
    Joyfully before the Lord.

7 For to judge the earth he cometh;
    And with righteousness shall he
Judge the world, and all the nations
    With most perfect equity.

PSALM XCIX. New London, 3с.

1 JEHOVAH is enthroned as king,
    Let all the people quake;
  He sits between the cherubim,
    Let earth be moved and shake.
2 In Zion is Jehovah great,
    Above all people high;
3 Thy great dread name, which holy is,
    O let them magnify.

4 The king's strength also judgment loves;
    Thou settlest equity:
  Just judgment thou dost execute
    In Jacob righteously.
5 The Lord our God exalt on high,
    And reverently do ye
  Before his footstool bow yourselves:
    The Holy One is he.

6 Moses and Aaron 'mong his priests,
    Samuel 'mong those who prayed;
  These called upon the Lord, and he
    Unto them answer made.
7 Within the pillar of the cloud
    He to his people spake;
  His testimonies they observed,
    His statute did not break.

8 Thou answer'dst them, O Lord our God;
    Thou wast a God that gave
  Pardon to them, though on their deeds
    Thou wouldest vengeance have.
9 Do ye exalt the Lord our God,
    And at his holy hill

Do ye him worship: for the Lord
Our God is holy still.

PSALM C.—1st Version. Old Hundredth, 65.

1 ALL people that on earth do dwell,
   Sing to the Lord with cheerful voice;
2 Him serve with mirth, his praise forth tell,
   Come ye before him and rejoice.
3 Know that the Lord is God indeed;
   Without our aid he did us make:
   We are his flock, he doth us feed,
   And for his sheep he doth us take.

4 O enter then his gates with praise,
   Approach with joy his courts unto:
   Praise, laud, and bless his name always,
   For it is seemly so to do.
5 Because the Lord our God is good,
   His mercy is for ever sure;
   His truth at all times firmly stood,
   And shall from age to age endure.

PSALM C.—2nd Version. Nottingham, 37.

1 O ALL ye lands, unto the Lord
   Make ye a joyful noise.
2 Serve God with gladness, and before
   Him come with cheerful voice.
3 Know ye the Lord that he is God;
   Us for himself he made:
   We are his people, and the sheep
   Within his pasture fed.

4 O enter then his gates with thanks,
   His courts with voice of praise;

Give thanks to him with joyfulness,
    And bless his name always.
5 Because the Lord our God is good,
    His mercy faileth never;
And unto generations all
    His truth endureth ever.

PSALM CI. Esslingen, 19.

1 MERCY will and judgment sing,
    Lord, I will sing to thee.
2 With wisdom in a perfect way
    Shall my behaviour be.
O when in kindness unto me
    Wilt thou be pleased to come?
I with a perfect heart will walk
    Within my house at home.

3 I will endure no wicked thing
    Before mine eyes to be;
I hate their work that turn aside,
    It shall not cleave to me.
4 A stubborn and a froward heart
    Depart quite from me shall;
A person given to wickedness
    I will not know at all.

5 I'll cut him off that slandereth
    His neighbour privily:
The haughty heart I will not bear,
    Nor him whose look is high.
6 I'll mark the faithful of the land,
    That they may dwell with me;
Who walketh in a perfect way
    To me shall servant be.

7 Who of deceit a worker is
    In my house shall not dwell;
  And in my presence shall he not
    Remain that lies doth tell.
8 Each morn the wicked of the land
    Shall be cut off by me;
  To root out from God's city all
    That work iniquity.

PSALM CII.—1st Version. *Eden, 17.*

1 O LORD, unto my prayer give ear,
    My cry let come to thee;
2 And in the day of my distress
    Hide not thy face from me.
  Give ear to me; what time I call,
    To answer me make haste:
3 For, as an hearth, my bones are burnt,
    My days, like smoke, do waste.

4 My heart within me smitten is,
    Like grass is withered;
  Because for very grief I do
    Forget to eat my bread.
5 By reason of my cries and groans
    My bones cleave to my skin.
6 Like pelican in wilderness
    Forsaken I have been:

  I like an owl 'mid ruins am,
    That nightly there doth moan;
7 I watch, like sparrow that doth sit
    On the house-top alone.
8 My bitter enemies all the day
    Reproaches cast on me;

And, being mad at me, with rage
　　Against me sworn they be.

9 For I did ashes eat as bread,
　　And, in my sorrow deep,
　My drink I also mingled have
　　With tears that I did weep.
10 Thine indignation and thy wrath
　　Did cause this grief and pain;
　For thou hast lifted me on high,
　　And cast me down again.

11˙ My days are like unto a shade,
　　Which doth declining pass;
　And I am dried and withered,
　　Even like unto the grass.
12 But thou, O Lord, dost sit enthroned,
　　Eternal is thy sway;
　And thy remembrance shall endure
　　From age to age alway.

13 Thou shalt arise and mercy have
　　Upon thy Zion yet;
　The time to favour her is come,
　　The time that thou hast set.
14 For in her rubbish and her stones
　　Thy servants pleasure take;
　Yea, they the very dust thereof
　　Do favour for her sake.

15 So shall the heathen people fear
　　The Lord's most holy name;
　And all the kings upon the earth
　　Thy glory and thy fame.

16 For Zion by thy mighty Lord
    Built up again shall be,
And in his glorious majesty
    To men appear shall he.

17 The prayer of the destitute
    He surely will regard;
Their prayer he will not despise,
    By him it shall be heard.
18 For generations yet to come
    Shall men these things record;
So shall a people yet to be
    Created praise the Lord.

19 For from his holy height the Lord
    Hath downward cast his eye;
And he upon the earth beneath
    Hath looked from heaven high;
20 That of the mournful prisoner
    The groanings he might hear,
To set them free that unto death
    By men appointed are:

21 That they in Zion may declare
    The Lord's most holy name,
And publish in Jerusalem
    The praises of the same:
22 When all the people gathered are
    In troops with one accord,
And kingdoms are assembled all
    To serve the mighty Lord.

23 My wonted strength and force he hath
    Abated in the way,
My days he also shortened hath:
24   Thus therefore did I say,

My God, in mid-time of my days
　　Take thou me not away:
From age to age eternally
　　Thy years endure and stay.

25 The firm foundation of the earth
　　Of old time thou hast laid:
The heavens also are the work
　　Which thine own hands have made.
26 Thou shalt for evermore endure,
　　But they shall perish all;
Yea, every one of them wax old,
　　Like to a garment, shall:

Thou, as a vesture, shalt them change,
　　And they shall changed be;
27 But thou the same art, and thy years
　　Are to eternity.
28 The children of thy servants shall
　　Continually endure;
And in thy sight, O Lord, their seed
　　Shall be established sure.

PSALM CII.—2nd Version. <small>Calvary, 8S.</small>

1 LORD, hear my prayer, and let my cry
　　Have speedy access unto thee;
2 In day of my calamity
O hide not thou thy face from me.
Hear when I call to thee; that day
An answer speedily return:
3 My days, like smoke, consume away,
And, as an hearth, my bones do burn.

4 My heart is smitten like the grass
When withered by the scorching heat,

> Because in grief my days I pass,
> And quite forget my bread to eat.
> 5 By reason of my smart within,
> And my most bitter cries and groans,
> My flesh consumed is, my skin
> All parched doth cleave unto my bones.
>
> 6 The pelican of wilderness,
> The owl of ruins drear, I match;
> 7 And, like a bird companionless
> Upon the housetop, I keep watch.
> 8 I all day long am made a scorn,
> Reproached by my malicious foes;
> They mad with rage 'gainst me have sworn,
> The men against me that arose.
>
> 9 For I have ashes eaten up,
> As if to me they had been bread;
> And with my drink I in my cup
> Of bitter tears a mixture made.
> 10 Because thy wrath was not appeased,
> Nor thou thine anger didst restrain;
> For though thou hadst me high upraised,
> Thou hast me now cast down again.
>
> 11 My days are like a shade alway,
> Which doth declining swiftly pass;
> And I am withered away,
> Even like unto the fading grass.
> 12 But thou, O Lord, shalt still endure,
> And from all changes thou art free,
> And to all generations sure
> Shall thy remembrance ever be.

Mainzer, 61.

> 13 Thou shalt arise, and mercy yet
> Thou to mount Zion shalt extend:

The time is come for favour set,
The time when thou shalt blessing send.
14 Thy saints take pleasure in her stones,
Her very dust to them is dear.
15 All heathen lands and kingly thrones
On earth thy glorious name shall fear.
16 For God in glory shall appear,
To build up Zion and repair.
17 He shall regard and lend his ear
Unto the needy's humble prayer:
The afflicted's prayer he will not scorn.
18 All times shall this be on record:
And generations yet unborn
Shall praise and magnify the Lord.
19 He from his holy place looked down,
The earth he viewed from heaven on high;
20 To hear the prisoner's mourning groan,
And free them that are doomed to die;
21 That Zion, and Jerusalem too,
His name and praise may well record,
22 When people and the kingdoms do
Assemble all to praise the Lord.
23 My strength he weakened in the way,
My days of life he shortened.
24 My God, O take me not away
In mid-time of my days, I said:
Thy years throughout all ages last.
25 Of old thou hast established
The earth's foundations firm and fast:
Thy mighty hands the heavens have made.
26 They perish shall, as garments do,
But thou shalt evermore endure;

As vestures, thou shalt change them so;
And they shall all be changed sure:
27 But from all changes thou art free;
Thy countless years do last for aye.
28 Thy servants, and their seed who be,
Established shall before thee stay.

PSALM CIII. St. Peter, 49.

1 O THOU my soul, bless God the Lord;
 And all that in me is
Be stirred up his holy name
 To magnify and bless.
2 Bless, O my soul, the Lord thy God,
 And not forgetful be
Of all his gracious benefits
 He hath bestowed on thee.

3 All thine iniquities who doth
 Most graciously forgive:
Who thy diseases all and pains
 Doth heal, and thee relieve.
4 Who doth redeem thy life, that thou
 To death mayest not go down;
Who thee with loving-kindness doth
 And tender mercies crown:

5 Who with abundance of good things
 Doth satisfy thy mouth;
So that, even as the eagle's age,
 Renewed is thy youth.
6 God righteous judgment executes
 For all oppressed ones.
7 His ways to Moses he made known,
 His acts to Israel's sons.

8 The Lord our God is merciful,
    And he is gracious,
  Long-suffering, and slow to wrath,
    In mercy plenteous.
9 He will not chide continually,
    Nor keep his anger still.
10 With us he dealt not as we sinned,
    Nor did requite our ill.

11 For as the heaven in its height
    The earth surmounteth far,
  So great to those that do him fear
    His tender mercies are:
12 As far as east is distant from
    The west, so far hath he
  From us removed, in his love,
    All our iniquity.

13 Such pity as a father hath
    Unto his children dear,
  Like pity shows the Lord to such
    As worship him in fear.
14 For he remembers we are dust,
    And he our frame well knows.
15 Frail man, his days are like the grass,
    As flower in field he grows:

16 For over it the wind doth pass,
    And it away is gone;
  And of the place where once it was
    It shall no more be known.
17 But unto them that do him fear
    God's mercy never ends;
  And to their children's children still
    His righteousness extends:

18 To such as keep his covenant,
     And mindful are alway
  Of his commandments just and good,
     That they may them obey.
19 The Lord prepared hath his throne
     In heavens firm to stand;
  And every thing that being hath
     His kingdom doth command.

20 O ye his angels, that excel
     In strength, bless ye the Lord;
  Ye who obey what he commands,
     And hearken to his word.
21 O bless and magnify the Lord,
     Ye glorious hosts of his;
  Ye ministers that do fulfil
     Whate'er his pleasure is.

22 O bless the Lord, all ye his works,
     Wherewith the world is stored
  In his dominions every where.
     My soul, bless thou the Lord.

PSALM CIV.—1st Version. St. Matthew, 56.

1 BLESS God, my soul. O Lord my God,
     Thou art exceeding great;
  With honour and with majesty
     Thou clothed art in state.
2 With light, as with a robe, thyself
     Thou coverest about;
  And, like unto a curtain, thou
     The heavens stretchest out.

3 Who of his chambers doth the beams
     Within the waters lay;

  Who doth the clouds his chariot make,
   On wings of wind make way.
4 Who flaming fire his ministers,
   His angels spirits, doth make:
5 Who earth's foundations firm did lay,
   That it should never shake.

6 Thou didst it cover with the deep,
   As with a garment spread;
  The waters stood above the hills,
   Above the mountains' head.
7 But at the voice of thy rebuke
   They fled and would not stay;
  They at thy thunder's dreadful voice
   Did haste them fast away.

8 They by the hills ascend, their way
   Back by the vales they take,
  Descending to the very place
   Which thou for them didst make.
9 Thou hast a bound unto them set,
   O'er which they may not go,
  That they may not return again
   The earth to overflow.

10 He through the valley sendeth springs,
   'Mong hills their course they take:
11 Beasts of the field all drink of them,
   Their thirst wild asses slake.
12 The birds of heaven their dwelling make
   Where these do flow along,
  And from among the leafy boughs
   With joy give forth their song.

13 He from his chambers watereth
   The hills when they are dried:

With fruit and increase of thy works
  The earth is satisfied.
14 For cattle he makes grass to grow,
  Herb for man's use to spring,
That from the bosom of the earth
  He bread for him may bring;

15 And wine that to the heart of man
  Doth cheerfulness impart,
Oil that doth make his face to shine,
  Bread strengthening his heart.
16 The trees of God are full of sap;
  The cedars that do stand
On Lebanon, which planted were
  By his almighty hand.

17 Birds of the air upon their boughs
  Do choose their nests to make;
As for the stork, the fir tree she
  Doth for her dwelling take.
18 The lofty mountains for wild goats
  A place of refuge be:
The conies also to the rocks
  Do for their safety flee.

19 He sets the moon in heaven, thereby
  The seasons to discern:
From him the sun his certain time
  Of going down doth learn.
20 Thou darkness mak'st, 'tis night, then beasts
  Of forest creep abroad.
21 The lions young roar for their prey,
  And seek their meat from God.

22 The sun doth rise, and home they flock,
  Down in their dens they lie.

23 Man goeth to his work, and doth
  His toil till evening ply.
24 O Lord, how manifold thy works!
  In wisdom wonderful
 Thou every one of them hast made;
  Earth's of thy riches full:

25 So is this great and spacious sea,
  Wherein things creeping are,
 Which numbered cannot be; and beasts
  Both great and small are there.
26 There ships go, there leviathan,
  Which thou mad'st there to play;
27 All wait on thee, that in due time
  Their food receive they may.

28 That which thou givest unto them
  They gather for their food;
 Thy bounteous hand thou openest,
  They filled are with good.
29 Thou hid'st thy face, they troubled are;
  Their breath thou tak'st away,
 Then do they die, and to their dust
  Return again do they.

30 Thy quickening spirit thou send'st forth,
  And they created be;
 And then the earth's decayed face
  Renewed is by thee.
31 The glory of Jehovah shall
  Endure while ages run;
 The Lord Almighty shall rejoice
  In all that he hath done.

32 Earth, as affrighted, trembleth all,
  If he on it but look;

      And if the mountains he but touch,
        They presently do smoke.
33 I to the Lord most high will sing,
        So long as I shall live;
      And while I being have I shall
        To my God praises give.

34 Of him my meditation shall
        Sweet thoughts to me afford;
      And as for me, I will rejoice
        And triumph in the Lord.
35 From earth let sinners be consumed,
        Let ill men no more be.
      O thou my soul, bless thou the Lord.
        Praise to the Lord give ye.

PSALM CIV.—2nd Version. *Hanover, 67*

1 MY soul, praise the Lord;
        Thou, Lord, mine own God,
    Art glorious, enrobed
        In beauty and might;
2 The heavens, like a curtain,
        Thou spreadest abroad;
    As raiment, around thee
        Enfoldest the light.

3 For chamber-beams sure,
        Dark waters he binds;
    Of clouds dim and deep
        His chariot doth frame,
    On stormy blasts riding,
        On wings of all winds;
4 His angels are spirits,
        His servants a flame.

5 Foundations secure
    He laid for the globe,
That stable and firm
    It ever should last;
6 The waste ocean gathering
    O'er all as a robe:
O'er all the high mountains
    The surging waves passed.

7 At thy dread rebuke
    They flee and they fail;
Thy thunder is heard,
    They speed here and there;
8 They burst the ridge over,
    They rush down the vale;
Where thou hast appointed,
    They haste to repair.

9 Thine own word hath set
    Their border and bound;
They roar and they toss,
    But cannot pass o'er:
The word of Jehovah
    A sure fence is found;
The flood o'er the mountains
    Returneth no more.

10 He unto the vales
    The springs doth convey;
And onward they wind
    Their course through the hills;
11 Whereat the wild asses
    Their thirst oft allay,
And beasts of the forest
    Thereof drink their fills.

12 By these pleasant springs,
       The fowls of the air
    Inhabit the trees,
       The margin along;
    And, as in their gladness
       They move here and there
    Among the green branches,
       Praise God with their song.

13 His rain on the hills
       He pours from on high;
    With fruit of thy works
       The earth is replete;
14 His grass to the cattle
       He doth not deny,
    And gives for man's service
       The green herb as meat.

15 From earth, store of food
       He brings for man's sake;
    Rich oil, gladsome wine,
       Heart-strengthening bread.
16 His trees full of moisture
       The great God did make;
    His cedars he planted
       On Lebanon's head.

17 Secure in those shades
       The bird builds her nest;
    The firs to the stork
       A house have supplied;
18 The hills are a refuge
       For wild goats to rest;
    The crags of the rough rocks
       For conies to hide.

19 The moon he hath set
    For seasons to run;
The times he ordained
    Her change ever shows;
And so, his course circling,
    The glorious sun
His hour of descending
    As constantly knows.

20 When darkness doth come
    By thy will and power,
Then prowl forth abroad
    The beasts of the wood.
21 The lions range roaring
    Their prey to devour;
And yet it is thou, Lord,
    Who givest them food.

22 As riseth the sun,
    They all get them in;
Withdrawn from his light,
    To couch in their den;
23 But man forth proceedeth
    His toil to begin;
Till night come to call him
    To take rest again.

24 How manifold, Lord,
    The works of thy hand!
Surpassing our thoughts
    Their numbers are found!
Thy outspread creation
    In wisdom is planned,
And full of thy riches
    The wide world around.

25 So in the great sea
    Thy works are displayed,
Where creeping things move,
    Unnumbered in sort;
26 And there the ships wander,
    And there thou hast made
Leviathan, hugest
    Of monsters, to sport.

27 All these wait on thee
    Their food to receive;
That thou, in due time,
    Their portion may'st give:
28 And, when it doth please thee
    Their wants to relieve,
Full gladly they gather
    Thy bounty and live.

Thou openest thine hand;
    How full their supply!
29 Thou hidest thy face;
    Confounded they mourn:
When thou from them takest
    Their spirit, they die,
And to their dust, changing,
    Again they return.

30 Thou send'st forth thy breath,
    And they are new made;
And earth, as at first,
    Looks vernal and bright.
31 In glory for ever
    The Lord is arrayed;
And in his creation
    Our God will delight.

32 He looks on the earth,
　　It reels to and fro;
　　He touches the hills,
　　　With smoke they are crowned.
33 Through life to Jehovah
　　　Mine anthems shall flow;
　　While yet I have being
　　　His praise I will sound.

34 With dear thoughts of him
　　　My heart shall run o'er;
　　With God all my joy
　　　In treasure is stored.
35 The sinners are wasted;
　　　Earth sees them no more;
　　The rebels—where are they?
　　　My soul, praise the Lord.

PSALM CV. Smart, 51.

1 GIVE thanks to God, call on his name;
　　To men his deeds make known.
2 Sing ye to him, sing psalms; proclaim
　　His wondrous works each one.
3 To glory in his holy name,
　　Unite with one accord:
　And let the heart of every one
　　Rejoice that seeks the Lord.

4 The Lord Almighty and his strength
　　With steadfast hearts seek ye:
　His blessed and his gracious face
　　Seek ye continually.
5 Think on the works that he hath done,
　　Which admiration breed;

      His wonders, and the judgments all
        Which from his mouth proceed;

6 O ye that are of Abraham's race,
      His servant faithful known;
  And ye that Jacob's children are,
      Whom he chose for his own.

7 Because he, and he only, is
      The mighty Lord our God;
  And his most righteous judgments are
      In all the earth abroad.

8 His covenant he remembered hath,
      That it may ever stand:
  To thousand generations he
      His promise did command.

9 Which covenant he firmly made
      With faithful Abraham,
  And unto Isaac by his oath
      He did renew the same:

10 And unto Jacob, for a law,
      He made it firm and sure,
  A covenant to Israel,
      Which ever should endure:

11 He said, I will give Canaan's land
      For heritage to you;

12 While they were strangers there, and few,
      In number very few:

13 While yet they went from land to land
      Without a sure abode;
  And while through sundry kingdoms they
      Did wander far abroad;

14 Yet, notwithstanding, suffered he
      No man to do them wrong;

    Yea, for their sakes, he did reprove
      Kings, who were great and strong.
15 Thus did he say, Touch ye not those
      That mine anointed be,
    Nor do the prophets any harm
      That do pertain to me.
16 He called for famine on the land,
      He brake the staff of bread:
17 But yet he sent a man before,
      By whom they should be fed;
    Even Joseph, whom unnaturally
      Sell for a slave did they;
18 Whose feet with fetters they did hurt,
      And he in irons lay;
19 Until the time that his word came
      To give him liberty;
    The word and purpose of the Lord
      Did him in prison try.
20 Then sent the king and did command
      That he enlarged should be:
    He that the people's ruler was
      Did send to set him free.
21 To be the Lord of all his house
      He raised him as most fit;
    To him of all that he possessed
      He did the charge commit:
22 That he might at his pleasure bind
      The princes of the land;
    And also teach his senators
      Wisdom to understand.
23 And down into the land of Ham,
      To Egypt, Israel came;

    And for a season Jacob then
        Did sojourn in the same.

24 And he did greatly by his power
        Increase his people there;
    And stronger than their enemies
        They by his blessing were.
25 Their heart he turned then to hate
        His people bitterly,
    With those that his own servants were
        To deal in subtlety.

26 His servant Moses he did send,
        Aaron his chosen one:
27 By these his signs and wonders great
        In Ham's land were made known.
28 Darkness he sent, and made it dark;
        His word they did obey.
29 He turned their waters into blood,
        And he their fish did slay.

30 The land in plenty brought forth frogs
        In chambers of their kings.
31 His word all sorts of flies and lice
        In all their border brings.
32 For showers hail and flaming fire
        Into their land he sent:
33 And he their vines and fig-trees smote;
        Trees of their coast he rent.

34 He spake, and caterpillars came,
        Locusts did much abound;
35 Which in their land all herbs consumed,
        And all fruits of their ground.
36 He smote all first-born in their land,
        Chief of their strength each one.

37 With gold and silver brought them forth,
   Weak in their tribes were none.

38 Egypt was glad when forth they went,
   Their fear on them did light.
39 He spread a cloud for covering,
   And fire to shine by night.
40 They asked, he sent the quail, and bread
   Of heaven on them bestowed;
41 The rock he opened, waters gushed,
   Streams in the desert flowed.

42 For on his holy promise he,
   And servant Abraham, thought.
43 With joy his people, his elect
   With gladness, forth he brought.
44 And unto them the pleasant lands
   He of the heathen gave;
   That of the people's labour they
   Inheritance might have.

45 That they his statutes might observe
   According to his word;
   And that they might his laws obey.
   Give praise unto the Lord.

PSALM CVI. Leicester, 29.

1 GIVE praise and thanks unto the Lord,
   For bountiful is he;
   His tender mercy doth endure
   Unto eternity.
2 God's mighty works who can express?
   Or show forth all his praise?
3 Blessed are they that judgment keep,
   And justly do always.

4 Remember me, Lord, with that love
    Which thou to thine dost bear;
With thy salvation, O my God,
    To visit me draw near:
5 That I thy chosen's good may see,
    And in their joy rejoice;
And may with thine inheritance
    Triumph with cheerful voice.

6 We with our fathers sinned have,
    And of iniquity
Too long we have the workers been;
    We have done wickedly.
7 The wonders great, which thou, O Lord,
    Didst work in Egypt's land,
Our fathers, though they them beheld,
    Yet did not understand:

And they thy mercies' multitude
    Kept not in memory;
But at the sea, even the Red Sea,
    Rebelled most grievously.
8 Nevertheless he saved them,
    Even for his own name's sake;
That so he might to be well known
    His mighty power make.

9 The Red Sea also he rebuked,
    And then dried up it was:
Through depths, as through the wilderness,
    He safely made them pass.
10 From hands of those that hated them
    He did his people save;
And from the foeman's cruel hand
    To them redemption gave.

11 The waters overwhelmed their foes;
    Not one was left alive.
12 Then they believed his word, and praise
    To him in songs did give.
13 But soon did they his mighty works
    Forget unthankfully,
And on his counsel and his will
    Did not wait patiently;

14 They lusted in the wilderness,
    In desert God did tempt.
15 He gave them what they sought, but to
    Their soul he leanness sent.
16 They envied Moses in the camp,
    And grudged his rule to see;
Aaron, Jehovah's holy one,
    They viewed with jealousy.

17 Therefore the earth did open wide.
    And Dathan did devour,
And all Abiram's company
    Did cover in that hour.
18 Likewise among their company
    A fire was kindled then;
And so the hot consuming flame
    Burnt up these wicked men.

19 Upon the hill of Horeb they
    An idol-calf did frame,
A molten image they did make,
    And worshipped the same.
20 And changed the High and Holy One,
    Who all their glory was,
Into the likeness of an ox
    That feedeth upon grass.

21 They did forget the mighty God,
   Who had their saviour been,
 By whom such great things brought to pass
   They had in Egypt seen.
22 He in the land of Ham wrought signs,
   Things terrible did he,
 When he his mighty hand and arm
   Stretched out at the Red Sea.

23 Then said he, he would them destroy,
   Had not, his wrath to stay,
 His chosen Moses stood in breach,
   That them he should not slay.
24 Yea, they despised the pleasant land,
   Believed not his word:
25 But in their tents they murmured,
   Not hearkening to the Lord.

26 To slay them in the desert then
   He lifted up his hand:
27 'Mong nations to o'erthrow their seed,
   And scatter in each land.
28 They unto Baal-peor did
   Themselves associate;
 The sacrifices of the dead
   They impiously ate.

29 Thus by inventions of their own
   They did provoke his ire;
 And then upon them suddenly
   The plague brake in as fire.
30 Then Phinehas stood up and judged,
   And so the plague did cease;
31 To ages all this counted was
   To him for righteousness.

32 And at the waters, where they strove,
   They did him angry make,
 In such sort, that it fared ill
   With Moses for their sake:
33 Because against his spirit they
   Rebelled most grievously,
 So that he uttered with his lips
   Words unadvisedly.

34 Nor, as the Lord commanded them,
   Did they the nations slay:
35 But with the heathen mingled were,
   And learned of them their way.
36 Their idols they did serve, and these
   Became to them a snare;
37 They unto demons sacrificed
   Their sons and daughters there.

38 In their own children's guiltless blood
   Their hands they did imbrue,
 Whom unto Canaan's idols they
   For sacrifices slew:
 So was the land defiled with blood.
39   Stained by their works were they:
 And by inventions of their own
   They wantonly did stray.

40 For this against his people burned
   The anger of the Lord;
 And he his own inheritance
   In righteousness abhorred.
41 He gave them to the heathen's power;
   Their foes did them command:
42 Their enemies them oppressed, they were
   Made subject to their hand.

43 He many times delivered them,
    Yet still they did rebel
  With counsels vain, and by their sin
    Into destruction fell.
44 Yet their affliction he beheld,
    When he did hear their cry:
45 And he for them his covenant
    Did call to memory;

46 After his mercies' multitude
    He did repent, and make
  Them to be pitied of all those
    Who did them captive take.
47 Save, Lord our God, and gather us
    The heathen from among,
  That we thy holy name may praise
    In a triumphant song.

48 Blessed be Jehovah, Israel's God,
    To all eternity:
  Let all the people say, Amen.
    Praise to the Lord give ye.

PSALM CVII. Parry,

1 PRAISE ye the Lord, for he is good,
    His mercies lasting be;
2 Let his redeemed say so, whom he
    From hand of foes did free;
3 And gathered them out of the lands,
    From north, south, east, and west.
4 They strayed in desert's pathless way,
    No city found to rest.

5 Their soul with thirst and hunger faints:
  When troubles sore them press,

6 They cry unto the Lord, and he
    Them frees from their distress.
7 Them also in a way to walk
    That right is he did guide,
  That they might to a city go,
    Wherein they might abide.

8 O that men to the Lord would give
    Praise for his goodness then,
  And for his works of wonder done
    Unto the sons of men!
9 For he the soul that longing is
    Doth fully satisfy;
  With goodness he the hungry soul
    Doth fill abundantly.

10 Such as shut up in darkness deep,
    And in death's shade abide,
  Whom strongly hath affliction bound,
    And irons fast have tied:
11 Because against the words of God
    They wrought rebelliously;
  And they the counsel did contemn
    Of him that is most High:

12 With labour he brought down their hearts,
    They fell, and help none gave;
13 In trouble to the Lord they cried,
    From straits he did them save.
14 He out of darkness did them bring,
    And from death's shade them take;
  Their bands, wherewith they had been
    He did asunder break.   [bound,

15 O that men to the Lord would give
    Praise for his goodness then,

    And for his works of wonder done
      Unto the sons of men!
16 Because the mighty gates of brass
      In pieces he did tear,
    By him in sunder also cut
      The bars of iron were.

17 Fools, for their trespasses and sins,
      Do sore affliction bear;
18 All kinds of meat their soul abhors;
      They to death's gates draw near.
19 In grief they cry to God; he saves
      Them from their miseries.
20 He sends his word, them heals, and them
      From their destruction frees.

21 O that men to the Lord would give
      Praise for his goodness then,
    And for his works of wonder done
      Unto the sons of men!
22 And let them sacrifice to him
      Offerings of thankfulness;
    And let them show abroad his works
      In songs of joyfulness.

23 Who go to sea in ships, and in
      Great waters trading be,
24 The Lord's works these within the deep
      And his great wonders see.
25 For he commands, and forth in haste
      The stormy tempest flies,
    Which makes the sea with rolling waves
      Aloft to swell and rise.

26 They mount to heaven, then to the depths
      They do go down again;

Their soul doth faint and melt away
    With trouble and with pain.
27 They reel and stagger like one drunk,
    At their wit's end they be:
28 In trouble to the Lord they cry,
    From straits he sets them free.

29 The storm is changed into a calm
    At his command and will;
So that the waves, which raged before,
    Now quiet are and still.
30 Then are they glad, because at rest
    And quiet now they be:
So to the haven he them brings,
    Which they desired to see.

31 O that men to the Lord would give
    Praise for his goodness then,
And for his works of wonder done
    Unto the sons of men!
32 Among the people gathered
    Let them exalt his name;
Among assembled elders spread
    His most renowned fame.

33 He turneth springs to thirsty ground,
    Floods to a wilderness;
34 For sins of those that dwell therein,
    Fat land to barrenness.
35 He turns to pools the wilderness
    Long parched with drought and burned;
By him the ground dried up before
    To water-springs is turned.

36 And there, for dwelling, he a place
    Doth to the hungry give,

That they a city may prepare
   Where they in peace may live.
37 There sow they fields, and vineyards plant,
   Which yield fruits of increase;
38 His blessing makes them multiply,
   Lets not their herds decrease.

39 Again they are diminished,
   And brought to low estate,
By pressure of calamity,
   And by affliction great.
40 On princes he doth pour contempt,
   And causeth them to stray,
And wander in a wilderness,
   Wherein there is no way.

41 Yet setteth he the poor on high
   From all their miseries,
And even like unto a flock
   He maketh families.
42 They that are righteous shall rejoice,
   When they the same shall see;
And, as ashamed, stop her mouth
   Shall all iniquity.

43 Whoso is wise, and will these things
   Observe, and them record,
Even they shall understand the love
   And kindness of the Lord.

PSALM CVIII. Kaltenthal, 7.

1 MY heart is fixed, O God; I'll sing,
   And with my glory praise.
2 Awake up psaltery and harp;
   Myself I'll early raise.

3 I'll praise thee 'mong the people, Lord;
   'Mong nations sing will I:
4 For above heaven thy mercy's great,
   Thy truth doth reach the sky.

5 Be thou above the heavens, O God,
   Exalted gloriously;
  Thy glory all the earth above
   Be lifted up on high.
6 That those who thy beloved are
   Delivered may be,
  O do thou save with thy right hand,
   And answer give to me.

7 God in his holiness did speak,
   My joy shall be complete;
  Shechem I will divide, by line
   The vale of Succoth mete.
8 Gilead I claim as mine by right;
   Manasseh mine shall be;
  Ephraim is of my head the strength;
   Judah gives laws for me;

9 Moab my wash-pot is; my shoe
   I'll over Edom throw;
  Over Philistia my shout
   Of triumph forth shall go.
10 O who is he will bring me to
   The city fortified?
  O who is he that to the land
   Of Edom will me guide?

11 O God, who hast rejected us,
   Wilt thou not help us so?
  Even thou, O God, who dost no more
   Forth with our armies go.

12 From trouble help thou us, for vain
    The help from man that flows.
13 Through God we shall do valiantly;
    He shall tread down our foes.

PSALM CIX. Martyrs, 31.

1 O THOU the God of all my praise,
    Do thou not hold thy peace;
2 For mouths of wicked men to speak
    Against me do not cease:
  The mouths of vile deceitful men
    Against me opened be;
  And with a false and lying tongue
    They have accused me.

3 They did beset me round with words
    Of hatred and of spite;
  And, though to them no cause I gave,
    Against me they did fight.
4 They for my love became my foes:
    I set myself to pray.
5 Evil for good, hatred for love,
    To me they did repay.

6 Set thou the wicked over him;
    And upon his right hand
  Against him in the judgment let
    The adversary stand.
7 And when by thee he shall be judged,
    Let him condemned be;
  And let his prayer sin become,
    When he shall call on thee.

8 Few be his days, and in his room
    His charge another take.

9 His children let be fatherless,
    His wife a widow make.
10 His children let be vagabonds,
    And beg continually;
  And from their places desolate
    Seek bread for their supply.

11 Let covetous extortioners
    Catch all he hath away:
  Of all for which he laboured hath
    Let strangers make a prey.
12 Let there be none to pity him,
    Let there be none at all
  That on his children fatherless
    Will let his mercy fall.
13 Let his posterity from earth
    Cut off for ever be,
  And in the next age let their name
    Be blotted out by thee.
14 Let God his father's wickedness
    Still to remembrance call;
  And never let his mother's sin
    Be blotted out at all.
15 But let them all before the Lord
    Appear continually,
  That he may wholly from the earth
    Cut off their memory.
16 Because he mercy minded not,
    But persecuted still
  The poor and needy, that he might
    The broken-hearted kill.

17 As he in cursing pleasure took,
    So doth it to him fall;

As he delighted not to bless,
    He is not blest at all.
18 As cursing he like clothes puts on,
    Into his bowels so,
  Like water, and into his bones,
    Like oil, it down doth go.

19 Like to the garment let it be
    Which doth himself array,
  And for a girdle, wherewith he
    Is girt about alway.
20 From God let this be their reward
    That enemies are to me,
  And their reward that speak against
    My soul maliciously.

21 But for thine own name's sake, deal thou,
    O God the Lord, with me:
  Since good thy loving-kindness is,
    From trouble set me free.
22 For I am poor and indigent,
    Afflicted sore am I,
  My heart within me also is
    Wounded exceedingly.

23 I pass like a declining shade,
    I'm like the locust tossed:
24 My knees through fasting weakened are,
    My flesh hath fatness lost.
25 I also am a vile reproach
    Unto them made to be;
  And they that do upon me look
    Do shake their heads at me.

26 O thou, who art the Lord my God,
    An helper be to me;

And, for thy tender mercy's sake,
  Do thou my Saviour be.
27 That thereby they may know that this
    Is thy almighty hand;
  And that thou, Lord, hast done the same
    They may well understand.

28 Although they curse with spite, yet, Lord,
    Bless thou with loving voice:
  Let them asham'd be when they rise;
    Thy servant let rejoice.
29 Let thou mine adversaries fierce
    With shame be clothed all;
  And, as a mantle, over them
    Let their confusion fall.

30 But as for me, I with my mouth
    Will greatly praise the Lord;
  And I among the multitude
    His praises will record.
31 For at the right hand of the poor
    Shall stand the Lord most high,
  To save him from all those that would
    Condemn his soul to die.

PSALM CX.—1st Version. New London, 36.

1 JEHOVAH said unto my Lord,
    Sit thou at my right hand,
  Until I make thy foes a stool,
    Whereon thy feet may stand.
2 The Lord shall out of Zion send
    The rod of thy great power:
  In midst of all thine enemies
    Be thou the governor.

3 A willing people in thy day
    Of power shall come to thee,
  In holy beauties from morn's womb;
    Thy youth like dew shall be.
4 The Lord himself hath made an oath,
    And will repent him never,
  Of the order of Melchizedek
    Thou art a priest for ever.
5 The glorious and mighty Lord,
    That sits at thy right hand,
  Shall, in his day of wrath, strike through
    Kings that do him withstand.
6 Among the nations he shall judge,
    The places fill with dead;
  And over broad and spacious lands
    He shall strike down the head.
7 The brook that runneth in the way
    With drink shall him supply;
  And, for this cause, in triumph he
    Shall lift his head on high.

PSALM CX.—2nd Version. Zoheleth, 8

1 UNTO my Lord Jehovah said:
    At my right hand I throne thee,
  Till, at thy feet in triumph laid,
    Thy foes their ruler own thee.
  From Zion hill the Lord shall send
    Thy sceptre, till before thee bend
      The knees of proud rebellion.
2 Thy saints, to greet thy day of might,
    In holy raiment muster:
  As dewdrops in the morning light
    Thy youths around thee cluster.

The Lord hath sworn and made decree,
Thou, like Melchizedek, shalt be
  A kingly priest for ever.

3 The Lord at thy right hand shall bring
    On rulers desolation;
The Lord shall smite each heathen king,
    And judge each rebel nation.
He, swiftly marching in his wrath,
Shall quaff the brook upon his path.
And lift his head in glory.

PSALM CXI. St. Anne, 43

1 PRAISE ye the Lord: with my whole heart
    The Lord's praise I'll declare,
Where the assemblies of the just
    And congregations are.
2 The doings of Jehovah are
    Exceeding great in might;
Sought out they are of every one
    That doth therein delight.

3 His work most honourable is,
    Most glorious and pure,
And his untainted righteousness
    For ever doth endure.
4 His works most wondrous he hath made
    Remembered still to be;
The Lord is most compassionate,
    And merciful is he.

5 He giveth meat unto all those
    That truly do him fear;
And evermore his covenant
    He in his mind will bear.

6 He did the power of his works
　　Unto his people show,
When he the heathen's heritage
　　Upon them did bestow.

7 His hands' works all are truth and right,
　　All his commands are sure;
8 And, done in truth and uprightness,
　　They evermore endure.
9 He sent redemption to his folk,
　　His covenant set for aye:
Holy and reverend is his name,
　　To be adored alway.

10 Wisdom's beginning is God's fear:
　　And wise in heart are they
Who his most holy precepts keep:
　　His praise endures for aye.

PSALM CXII. *Gauntlett, 23.*

1 PRAISE ye the Lord. The man is blessed
　　That fears the Lord aright,
He who in his commandments all
　　Doth greatly take delight.
2 His seed shall power have on earth
　　And great prosperity:
The children of the upright man
　　Shall ever blessed be.

3 Riches and wealth shall ever be
　　Within his house in store;
And his unspotted righteousness
　　Endures for evermore.
4 Unto the upright light doth rise,
　　Though he in darkness be:

Compassionate, and merciful,
    And righteous is he.

5 A good man doth his favour show,
    And doth to others lend:
  He in the judgment will his cause
    Maintain unto the end.
6 Surely there is not anything
    That ever shall him move:
  The righteous man's memorial
    Shall everlasting prove.

7 When he shall evil tidings hear,
    He shall not be afraid:
  His heart is fixed, his confidence
    Upon the Lord is stay'd.
8 His heart is firmly stablished,
    Afraid he shall not be,
  Until upon his enemies
    He his desire shall see.

9 He hath dispersed his wealth abroad,
    And given to the poor;
  His horn in honour shall be raised,
    His righteousness endure.
10 The wicked shall it see, and fret,
    His teeth gnash, melt away:
  What wicked men do most desire
    Shall utterly decay.

PSALM CXIII. *Dunfermline, 15.*

1 PRAISE ye the Lord: who serve the Lord,
    O praise, the Lord's name praise.
2 The Lord's name, blessed let it be
    From this time forth always.

3 From rising sun to where he sets
   The Lord's name's to be praised.
4 'Bove nations all the Lord is high,
   'Bove heavens his glory raised.

5 Unto the Lord our God that dwells
   On high, who can compare?
6 Himself that humbleth things to see
   In heaven and earth that are.
7 He lifts the helpless from the dust,
   The poor from low estate;
8 That he may him with princes set,
   His people's princes great.

9 The barren woman house to keep
   He maketh, and to be
 Of sons a mother full of joy.
   Praise to the Lord give ye.

PSALM CXIV.—1st Version. Nativity, 33.

1 WHEN Israel out of Egypt went,
     And did his dwelling change,
 When Jacob's house went out from those
   That were of language strange,
2 Judah became his holy place,
   Israel his own domain;
3 The sea beheld, and quickly fled,
   Jordan turned back again.

4 Like rams the mountains, and like lambs
   The hills skipped to and fro.
5 O sea, why fledd'st thou? Jordan, back
   Why wast thou driven so?
6 Ye mountains great, wherefore was it
   That ye did skip like rams?

And wherefore was it, little hills,
  That ye did leap like lambs?

7 O at the presence of the Lord,
    Earth, tremble thou for fear,
  What time the presence of the God
    Of Jacob doth appear:
8 Who in the desert from the rock
    Did pools of water bring;
  And by his power did turn the flint
    Into a water-spring.

PSALM CXIV.—2nd Version. <small>New Peterborough, 63.</small>

1 WHEN Israel had from Egypt gone,
    Jacob from men of speech unknown;
  Then Judah was his holy place,
  And his dominion Israel's race.
2 The sea, affrighted, saw and fled;
  Back Jordan driven was with dread;
  The lofty mountains skipped like rams,
  And all the little hills like lambs.
3 What ailed thee, that thou fledd'st, O sea?
  Thou, Jordan, that thou back didst flee?
  Ye mountains, that ye skipped like rams?
  And all ye little hills like lambs?
4 Earth, tremble, for the Lord is near:
  Before the God of Jacob, fear;
  Who from the rock did water bring,
  And made the flint a water-spring.

PSALM CXV.—1st Version. <small>Newlands, 35.</small>

1 NOT unto us, Lord, not to us,
    But do thou glory take

Unto thy name, even for thy truth,
   And for thy mercy's sake.
2 O wherefore should the heathen say,
   Where is their God now gone?
3 But our God in the heavens is,
   What pleased him he hath done.

4 Their idols silver are and gold,
   Work of men's hands they be.
5 Mouths have they, but they do not speak;
   And eyes, but do not see;
6 Ears have they, but they do not hear;
   Noses, yet smell they not;
7 Hands, feet, but handle not, nor walk;
   Nor speak they through their throat.

8 Like them their makers are, and all
   On them their trust that build.
9 O Israel, trust thou in the Lord,
   He is their help and shield.
10 O Aaron's house, trust in the Lord,
   Their help and shield is he.
11 Who fear the Lord, trust in the Lord,
   Their help and shield is he.

12 The Lord of us hath mindful been,
   And he will bless us still:
   He will the house of Israel bless,
   Bless Aaron's house he will.
13 Both small and great, that fear the Lord,
   He will them surely bless.
14 The Lord will you, you and your seed,
   Yet more and more increase.

15 O blessed are ye of the Lord,
   Who made the earth and heaven.

16 The heavens are for the Lord, but earth
    He to men's sons hath given.
17 The dead praise not the Lord, nor those
    In grave that silent be;
18 Him praise will we henceforth for aye.
    Praise to the Lord give ye.

PSALM CXV.—2nd Version. Potsdam, 2.

1 NOT ours the glory make,
    Lord, give not us the fame;
But for thy truth and mercy's sake
    Ascribe it to thy name!
2 To say, Where is their God,
    Why should the heathen dare?
Since he in heaven hath his abode,
    And works his pleasure there.

3 Men's hands their idols make
    Of silver and of gold;
Mouths have they, but they cannot speak;
    Eyes, but they nought behold.
4 Their ears are senseless too;
    Their nostrils smelling not;
Their hands and feet nor feel nor go,
    Nor speak they through their throat.

5 All those who them adore,
    Or form them, like them be;
O Israel, trust God evermore,
    For our defence is he.
6 On God, who shields the just,
    Let Aaron's house depend;
Let those who fear him in him trust,
    For he will such defend.

7 God hath remembered us,
    And will his mercy show;
  On Israel, and on Aaron's house,
    He blessings will bestow.
8 Of high and low degree,
    All those that him adore
  He keeps; and you and yours shall he
    Increase yet more and more.

9 Blest of the Lord are ye,
    Who made both earth and heaven;
  Heaven for himself created he,
    But earth to men hath given.
10 Their voice they cannot raise,
    Who down to silence go;
  But we, from this time forth, his praise
    For evermore will show.

PSALM CXVI. St. Paul, 48.

1 I LOVE the Lord, because my voice
    And prayers he did hear.
2 I, while I live, will call on him,
    Who bowed to me his ear.
3 The cords of death on every side
    Encompassed me around;
  The sorrows of the grave me seized,
    I grief and trouble found.

4 Then on the Lord's name did I call,
    And unto him did say,
  Deliver thou my soul, O Lord,
    I do thee humbly pray.
5 Our God is very merciful,
    Gracious and just the Lord:

6 He saves the meek: I was brought low,
    He did me help afford.
7 O thou my soul, do thou return
    Unto thy quiet rest;
  For largely unto thee the Lord
    His bounty hath expressed.
8 For my distressed soul from death
    Delivered was by thee;
  Thou didst my mourning eyes from tears,
    My feet from falling, free.
9 I in the land of those that live
    Will walk the Lord before.
10 I did believe, I therefore spake:
    I was afflicted sore.
11 I said, when I was in my haste,
    That all men liars be.
12 What shall I render to the Lord
    For all his gifts to me?
13 I'll of salvation take the cup,
    And on the Lord's name call;
14 I'll pay my vows unto the Lord
    Before his people all.
15 Dear in his sight is his saints' death.
16   Thy servant, Lord, am I;
  Thy servant sure, thine handmaid's son:
    My bands thou didst untie.
17 Thank-offerings I to thee will give,
    And on the Lord's name call.
18 I'll pay my vows now to the Lord
    Before his people all,
19 Within the courts of the Lord's house,
    Within the midst of thee,

O city of Jerusalem.
Praise to the Lord give ye.

PSALM CXVII.—1st Version. Paisley, 39.

1 O ALL ye nations of the earth
    Give praise unto the Lord;
And all ye people magnify
    His name with one accord.
2 For great to us-ward ever are
    His loving-kindnesses:
His truth endures for evermore.
    The Lord O do ye bless.

PSALM CXVII.—2nd Version. Old Hundredth, 65.

1 FROM all that dwell below the skies,
    O let Jehovah's praise arise!
And let his glorious name be sung
    In every land, by every tongue!

2 Great are the mercies of the Lord,
    And truth eternal is his word;
Ye nations, sound from shore to shore
    Jehovah's praise for evermore!

PSALM CXVIII. Old Winchester, 38.

1 O PRAISE the Lord, for he is good;
    His mercy lasteth ever.
2 Let those who are of Israel say,
    His mercy faileth never.
3 Now let the house of Aaron say,
    His mercy lasteth ever.
4 Let those that fear the Lord now say,
    His mercy faileth never.

5 I in distress called on the Lord;
  The Lord did answer me:
 He in a large place did me set,
  From trouble made me free.
6 The Lord himself is on my side,
  I will not be afraid;
 For anything that man can do
  I shall not be dismayed.

7 The Lord doth take my part with them
   That help to succour me;
  Therefore on those that do me hate
   I my desire shall see.
8 'Tis better in the Lord to trust
   Than trust in man's defence;
9 Better trust in the Lord than make
   Princes our confidence.

10 The nations, joining all in one,
    Did compass me about:
   But in the Lord's most holy name
    I shall them all root out.
11 They compassed me about; I say,
    They compassed me about:
   But in the Lord's most holy name
    I shall them all root out.

12 Like bees they compassed me about;
    They're quenched like thorns that flame:
   For I will surely them destroy,
    In the Lord's holy name.
13 Thou hast sore thrust that I might fall,
    The Lord hath succoured me:
14 The Lord my Saviour is become,
    My strength and song is he.

15 In dwellings of the just the voice
    Of joy and health shall be;
  The right hand of the mighty Lord
    Doth ever valiantly.
16 The right hand of the mighty Lord
    Exalted is on high;
  The right hand of the mighty Lord
    Doth ever valiantly.

17 I shall not die, but live, and shall
    Jehovah's works make known.
18 The Lord hath me chastised sore,
    But not to death brought down.
19 O set ye open unto me
    The gates of righteousness;
  Then will I enter into them,
    And I the Lord will bless.

20 This is the gate of God, by it
    The just shall enter in.
21 Thee will I praise, for thou me heard'st,
    And hast my safety been.
22 That stone is made head corner-stone,
    Which builders did despise:
23 This is the doing of the Lord,
    And wondrous in our eyes.

24 This day the Lord hath made, in it
    We'll joy triumphantly.
25 Save, Lord, I pray thee; Lord, I pray
    Send thou prosperity.
26 Blest in the Lord's great name is he
    That cometh us among;
  We bless you from the house which doth
    Unto the Lord belong.

27 God is the Lord, who unto us
   Hath made light to arise:
Bind ye unto the altar's horns
   With cords the sacrifice.
28 Thou art my God, I'll thee exalt;
   My God, I will thee praise.
29 Praise ye the Lord, for he is good:
   His mercy lasts always.

PSALM CXIX.

ALEPH. The 1st Part. Martyrdom, 30.

1 BLESSED are they that undefiled,
   And straight are in the way;
Who in the Lord's most holy law
   Do walk, and do not stray.
2 Blessed are they who to observe
   His statutes are inclined;
And who do seek the living God
   With their whole heart and mind.

3 Such in his ways do walk, and they
   Do no iniquity.
4 Thou hast commanded us to keep
   Thy precepts carefully.
5 O that thy statutes to observe
   Thou wouldst my ways direct!
6 Then shall I not be shamed when I
   Thy precepts all respect.

7 Then with integrity of heart
   Thee will I praise and bless,
When I the judgments all have learned
   Of thy pure righteousness.

8 That I will keep thy statutes all
   Firmly resolved have I:
 O do not then, most gracious God,
   Forsake me utterly.

       BETH. The 2nd Part. Gräfenberg, 25.

9 By what means shall a young man learn
   His way to purify?
 If he according to thy word
   Thereto attentive be.
10 Unfeignedly thee have I sought
   With all my soul and heart:
 O let me not from the right path
   Of thy commands depart.
11 Thy word I in my heart have hid,
   That I offend not thee.
12 O Lord, thou ever blessed art,
   Thy statutes teach thou me.
13 The judgments of thy mouth each one
   My lips declared have:
14 More joy thy testimonies' way
   Than riches all me gave.
15 Thy holy precepts I will make
   My meditation still:
 And have respect unto thy ways
   Most carefully I will.
16 Upon thy statutes my delight
   Shall constantly be set:
 And, by thy grace, I never will
   Thy holy word forget.

       GIMEL. The 3rd Part. Evan, 20.

17 With me thy servant, in thy grace,
   Deal bountifully, Lord;

>   That by thy favour I may live,
>   And duly keep thy word.
> 18 Open mine eyes, that of thy law
>   The wonders I may see.
> 19 I am a stranger on the earth,
>   Hide not thy laws from me.
>
> 20 My soul within me breaks, and doth
>   Much fainting still endure,
>   Through longing that it hath all times
>   Unto thy judgments pure.
> 21 Thou hast rebuked the cursed proud,
>   Who from thy precepts swerve.
> 22 Reproach and shame remove from me,
>   For I thy laws observe.
>
> 23 Though princes in assembly sit,
>   And counsel 'gainst me take,
>   Thy statutes I, thy servant, still
>   My meditation make.
> 24 My comfort, and my heart's delight,
>   Thy testimonies be;
>   And they, in all my doubts and fears,
>   Are counsellors to me.

DALETH. The 4th Part. Newington, 34.

> 25 My soul to dust cleaves; quicken me,
>   According to thy word.
> 26 My ways I showed, and me thou heardst;
>   Teach me thy statutes, Lord.
> 27 The way of thy commandments teach,
>   And make me well to know;
>   So all thy works that wondrous are
>   I shall to others show.

28 My soul doth melt, and drop away,
   For heaviness and grief:
To me, according to thy word,
   Give strength and send relief.
29 O let the way of falsehood far
   From me removed be;
And graciously thy holy law
   Do thou grant unto me.

30 I chosen have the perfect way
   Of truth and verity:
Thy judgments that most righteous are
   Before me laid have I.
31 I to thy testimonies cleave;
   Shame do not on me cast.
32 I'll run thy precepts' way, for thou
   My heart enlarged hast.

HE. The 5th Part.   Durham, 16.

33 Teach me, O Lord, the perfect way
   Of thy precepts divine,
And to observe it to the end
   I shall my heart incline.
34 Give understanding unto me,
   So keep thy law shall I;
Yea, even with my whole heart I shall
   Observe it carefully.

35 In thy law's paths make me to go;
   For I delight therein.
36 My heart unto thy testimonies,
   And not to greed, incline.
37 Turn thou away my sight and eyes
   From viewing vanity;

    And in thy good and holy way
      Be pleased to quicken me.

38 Confirm to me thy gracious word,
      Which I did gladly hear;
    To me thy servant, Lord, who am
      Devoted to thy fear.
39 Turn thou away my feared reproach;
      For good thy judgments be.
40 Lo, for thy precepts I have longed;
      In thy truth quicken me.

VAU. The 6th Part.   Belmont, 11.

41 Let thy sweet mercies also come
      And visit me, O Lord:
    Let thy salvation come to me,
      According to thy word.
42 So shall I have wherewith I may
      Give him an answer just,
    Who spitefully reproacheth me;
      For in thy word I trust.

43 The word of truth out of my mouth
      Take thou not utterly;
    For on thy righteous judgments still
      Doth all my hope rely.
44 So shall I keep for evermore
      Thy law continually.
45 Because I have thy precepts sought,
      I'll walk at liberty.

46 I'll speak thy word to kings, and I
      Shall not be moved with shame;
47 And in thy laws I will delight,
      For I have loved the same.

48 To thy commandments, which I loved,
   My hands lift up I will;
And I will also meditate
   Upon thy statutes still.

ZAIN. The 7th Part. Gräfenberg, 25.

49 The promise keep in mind, which thou
   Didst to thy servant make,
The word, which as my ground of hope
   Thou causedst me to take.
50 By this, in time of my distress,
   Great comfort I have known;
For in my straits I am revived
   By this thy word alone.
51 The arrogant and proud in heart
   Did greatly me deride;
Yet from thy good and holy law
   I have not turned aside.
52 Thy righteous judgments, which of old
   Thou didst make known, O Lord,
I have remembered, and to me
   They comfort did afford.
53 Horror took hold on me, because
   Ill men thy law forsake.
54 I in my house of pilgrimage
   Thy laws my songs do make.
55 Thy name by night, Lord, I did mind,
   And I have kept thy law.
56 And this I had, because thy word
   I kept, and stood in awe.

CHETH. The 8th Part. Evan, 20.

57 Thou my sure portion art alone,
   Which I did choose, O Lord;

I have resolved, and said, that I
    Would keep thy holy word.
58 With my whole heart I did entreat
    Thy face and favour free:
According to thy gracious word
    Be merciful to me.

59 I thought upon my former ways,
    And did my life well try;
And to thy testimonies pure
    My feet then turned I.
60 I did not stay, nor linger long,
    As those that slothful are;
But hastily thy laws to keep
    Myself I did prepare.

61 Bands of the wicked me beset,
    Thy law I did not slight.
62 I'll rise at midnight thee to praise,
    Even for thy judgments right.
63 I am companion to all those
    Who fear, and thee obey.
64 O Lord, thy mercy fills the earth:
    Teach me thy laws, I pray.

TETH. The 9th Part.   Eden, 17.

65 Well hast thou with thy servant dealt,
    As thou didst promise give.
66 Good judgment me, and knowledge teach,
    For I thy word believe.
67 Ere I afflicted was I strayed;
    But now I keep thy word.
68 Good art thou, and thou doest good:
    Teach me thy statutes, Lord.

69 The men that are puffed up with pride
    Against me forged a lie;
But as for me, thy precepts keep
    With all my heart will I.
70 Their hearts, through worldly ease and
    As fat as grease they be;   [wealth,
But in thy holy law I take
    Delight continually.

71 It hath been very good for me
    That I afflicted was,
That I might well instructed be,
    And learn thy holy laws.
72 The word that cometh from thy mouth
    Is better unto me
Than many thousands and great sums
    Of gold and silver be.

JOD.   The 10th Part.   St. David, 45.

73 Thy hands have made and fashioned me;
    Teach me thy laws, O Lord.
74 They who thee fear see me with joy,
    For I trust in thy word.
75 That righteous are thy judgments, Lord,
    I know, and do confess;
And that thou hast afflicted me
    In truth and faithfulness.

76 O let thy kindness merciful,
    I pray thee, comfort me,
As to thy servant promised was
    In faithfulness by thee.
77 And let thy tender mercies come
    To me, that I may live;

Because thy holy laws to me
  Sweet delectation give.

78 O let the proud ashamed be;
  For they without a cause
With me have falsely dealt; but I
  Will muse upon thy laws.
79 Let such as fear thee, and have known
  Thy statutes, turn to me.
80 In thy laws let my heart be sound,
  That shamed I may not be.

CAPH. The 11th Part.   Dundee, 14.

81 My soul for thy salvation faints;
  Yet I thy word believe.
82 Mine eyes fail for thy word: I say,
  When wilt thou comfort give?
83 For like a bottle I'm become,
  That in the smoke is set:
But still thy righteous statutes, Lord,
  I never do forget.

84 How many are thy servant's days?
  When wilt thou execute
Just judgment on these wicked men
  That do me persecute?
85 The proud have digged pits for me,
  Which is against thy laws.
86 Thy words all faithful are: help me,
  Pursued without a cause.

87 They so consumed me, that on earth
  My life they scarce did leave:
Thy precepts yet forsook I not,
  But close to them did cleave.

88 After thy loving-kindness, Lord,
   Me quicken and preserve:
The testimony of thy mouth
   So shall I still observe.

LAMED. The 12th Part. *Leicester, 29.*

89 Thy word for ever is, O Lord,
   In heaven settled fast;
90 And unto generations all
   Thy faithfulness doth last:
The earth thou hast established,
   And it abides by thee.
91 This day they stand as thou ordain'dst;
   For all thy servants be.

92 Unless in thy most perfect law
   My soul delights had found,
I should have perished at the time
   My troubles did abound.
93 Thy precepts I will ne'er forget;
   They quickening to me brought.
94 Lord, I am thine; O save thou me:
   Thy precepts I have sought.

95 For me the wicked have laid **wait**,
   Me seeking to destroy:
But I thy testimonies true
   Consider will with joy.
96 An end of all perfection here
   Have I beheld, O God;
But thy command no limit **hath**,
   It is exceeding broad.

MEM. The 13th Part. *Farrant, 21*

97 O how I love thy law! it is
   My study all the day:

98 It makes me wiser than my foes;
    For it doth with me stay.
99 Than all my teachers now I have
    More understanding far;
    Because my meditation still
    Thy testimonies are.

100 In understanding I excel
    Even those that aged be;
    Because thy precepts to observe
    I have sought earnestly.
101 My feet from each ill way I stayed,
    That I may keep thy word.
102 I from thy judgments have not swerved;
    For thou hast taught me, Lord.

103 How sweet unto my taste, O Lord,
    Are all thy words of truth!
    Yea, I do find them sweeter far
    Than honey to my mouth.
104 I through thy precepts, that are pure,
    Do understanding get;
    I therefore every way that's false
    With all my heart do hate.

NUN. The 14th Part. *Martyrdom 30.*

105 Thy word is to my feet a lamp,
    And to my path a light.
106 Sworn have I, and I will perform,
    To keep thy judgments right.
107 I am afflicted very much
    And chastened sore, O Lord:
    In mercy raise and quicken me,
    According to thy word.

108 The free-will-offerings of my mouth
    Accept, I thee beseech:
And unto me thy servant, Lord,
    Thy judgments clearly teach.
109 Though still my soul be in my hand,
    Thy laws I'll not forget.
110 I erred not from them, though for me
    The wicked snares did set.

111 I of thy testimonies have
    Above all things made choice,
To be my heritage for aye;
    For they my heart rejoice.
112 I carefully inclined have
    My heart still to attend;
That I thy statutes may perform
    Alway unto the end.

SAMECH. The 15th Part. French, 22.

113 I hate the men of double mind,
    But love thy law do I.
114 My shield and hiding-place thou art:
    I on thy word rely.
115 All ye that evil-doers are
    From me depart away;
For the commandments of my God
    I purpose to obey.

116 According to thy faithful word
    Uphold and stablish me,
That I may live, and of my hope
    Ashamed never be.
117 Hold thou me up, so shall I be
    In peace and safety still;

And to thy statutes have respect
   Continually I will.

118 Thou tread'st down all that love to stray;
   False their deceit doth prove.
119 Vile men, like dross, thou putt'st away;
   Therefore thy law I love.
120 For fear of thee my very flesh
      Doth tremble, all dismayed;
   And of thy righteous judgments, Lord,
      My soul is much afraid.

AIN. The 16th Part.   St. James, 46.

121 To all men I have judgment done,
      Performing justice right;
   Then let me not be left unto
      My fierce oppressors' might.
122 For good unto thy servant, Lord,
      Thy servant's surety be:
   From the oppression of the proud
      Do thou deliver me.

123 Mine eyes do fail with looking long
      For thy salvation great,
   While for thy word of righteousness
      I earnestly do wait.
124 In mercy with thy servant deal,
      Thy statutes to me show.
125 I am thy servant, wisdom give,
      That I thy laws may know.

126 'Tis time to work, Lord; for they have
      Made void thy law divine.
127 Therefore thy precepts more I love
      Than gold, yea, gold most fine.

128 Concerning all things thy commands
    I therefore judge are right;
And every false and wicked way
    Is hateful in my sight.

PE. The 17th Part.   Belmont, 11.

129 Thy statutes, Lord, are wonderful,
    My soul them keeps with care.
130 The entrance of thy words gives light,
    Makes wise who simple are.
131 My mouth I also opened have,
    And panted earnestly;
For after thy commandments I
    Have longed exceedingly.

132 Look on me, Lord, and merciful
    Do thou unto me prove,
As thou art wont to do to those
    Thy name who truly love.
133 O let my footsteps in thy word
    Aright still ordered be:
Let no iniquity obtain
    Dominion over me.

134 From man's oppression save thou me;
    So keep thy laws I will.
135 Thy face make on thy servant shine:
    Teach me thy statutes still.
136 Rivers of water from mine eyes
    Ran down, because I saw
That wicked men go on in sin,
    And do not keep thy law.

TSADDI. The 18th Part.   Gauntlett, 23.

137 O Lord, thou ever righteous art;
    Thy judgments upright be.

138 Ordained thy testimonies are
   In faithfulness by thee.
139 My zeal hath even consumed me,
   Because mine enemies
   Thy holy words forgotten have,
   And do thy laws despise.

140 Thy word is very pure, on it
   Thy servant's love is set.
141 Small and despised I am, yet I
   Thy laws do not forget.
142 Thy righteousness is righteousness
   Which ever doth endure;
   Thy holy law, Lord, also is
   The very truth most pure.

143 Distress and anguish have me found,
   Fast hold on me they take:
   Yet in my trouble my delight
   I thy commandments make.
144 Eternal righteousness is in
   Thy testimonies all:
   Give understanding unto me,
   And ever live I shall.

KOPH. The 19th Part. Kilmarnock, 23.

145 With my whole heart I cried, Lord, hear;
   I will thy word obey.
146 I cried to thee; save me, and I
   Will keep thy laws alway.
147 I of the morning did prevent
   The dawning with my cry,
   For all my hope and confidence
   Did on thy word rely.

148 Mine eyes did wakefully prevent
      The watches of the night,
    That in thy word with careful mind
      Then meditate I might.
149 After thy loving-kindness hear
      My voice, that calls on thee:
    According to thy judgment, Lord,
      Revive and quicken me.

150 The men who mischief seek draw nigh,
      They from thy law are far:
151 But thou art near, O Lord; and truth
      All thy commandments are.
152 From thine own testimonies, long
      Hath this been known to me,
    That thou hast founded them to last
      Unto eternity.

RESH. The 20th Part.   Gloucester, 24.

153 On my affliction do thou look,
      And me in safety set:
    Deliver me, O Lord, for I
      Thy law do not forget.
154 After thy word revive thou me;
      Save me, and plead my cause.
155 Salvation is from sinners far;
      For they seek not thy laws.

156 O Lord, both great and manifold
      Thy tender mercies be:
    According to thy judgments just
      Revive and quicken me.
157 My persecutors many are,
      And foes that do combine;

    Yet from thy testimonies pure
      My heart doth not decline.

158 I saw transgressors, and was grieved;
      For they keep not thy word.
159 Behold, thy precepts I have loved,
      In love me quicken, Lord.
160 The sum of thy most holy word
      Is only truth most pure:
    Thy righteous judgments every one
      For evermore endure.

SCHIN. The 21st Part. *Jackson, 26.*

161 Princes have persecuted me,
      Although no cause they saw:
    But still of thy most holy word
      My hand doth stand in awe.
162 I at thy word rejoice, as one
      Of spoil that finds great store.
163 Thy law I love; but lying all
      I hate and do abhor.

164 Seven times a-day it is my care
      To give due praise to thee;
    Because of all thy judgments, Lord,
      Which righteous ever be.
165 Great peace have they who love thy law;
      Offence they shall have none.
166 I hoped for thy salvation, Lord,
      And thy commands have done.

167 My soul thy testimonies pure
      Observed carefully;
    On them my heart is set, and them
      I love exceedingly.

168 Thy testimonies and thy laws
    I kept with special care;
    For all my works and ways each one
    Before thee open are.

TAU. The 22nd Part.   Patton, 41.

169 O let my earnest prayer and cry
    Come near before thee, Lord:
    Give understanding unto me,
    According to thy word.
170 Let my request before thee come:
    After thy word me free.
171 My lips shall utter praise, when thou
    Hast taught thy laws to me.
172 My tongue of thy most blessed word
    Shall speak, and it confess;
    For truly thy commandments all
    Are perfect righteousness.
173 O let thy hand be help to me:
    Thy precepts are my choice.
174 I longed for thy salvation, Lord,
    And in thy law rejoice.
175 O let my soul live, and it shall
    Give praises unto thee;
    And let thy judgments righteous
    Be helpful unto me.
176 I, like a lost sheep, went astray;
    Thy servant seek, and find:
    For thy commands I suffered not
    To slip out of my mind.

PSALM CXX.   Martyrs, 31.

1 IN my strait cried to the Lord,
    And he gave ear to me.

2 From lying lips, and guileful tongue,
  O Lord, my soul set free.
3 What shall be given unto thee?
  What heaped on thee, false tongue?
4 The burning coals of juniper,
  Sharp arrows of the strong.

5 Woe's me that I in Mesech am
    A sojourner so long:
  That I beside the tents do dwell
    To Kedar that belong.
6 My soul with him that hateth peace
    Hath long a dweller been.
  I am for peace; but when I speak,
    For battle they are keen.

PSALM CXXI. French, 22.

1 I TO the hills will lift mine eyes,
    From whence doth come mine aid.
2 My safety cometh from the Lord,
    Who heaven and earth hath made.
3 Thy foot he'll not let slide, nor will
    He slumber that thee keeps.
4 Behold, he that keeps Israel,
    He slumbers not, nor sleeps.

5 The Lord thee keeps, the Lord thy shade
    On thy right hand doth stay:
6 The moon by night thee shall not smite,
    Nor yet the sun by day.
7 The Lord shall keep thy soul; he shall
    Preserve thee from all ill.
8 Henceforth thy going out and in
    God keep for ever will.

PSALM CXXII. St. Paul, 48.

1 I JOYED when to the house of God,
    Go up, they said to me.
2 Jerusalem, within thy gates
    Our feet shall standing be.
3 Jerusalem, as a city, is
    Compactly built together:
4 Unto that place the tribes go up,
    The tribes of God go thither,—

A statute this for Israel,—
    To God's name thanks to pay.
5 For thrones of judgment, even the thrones
    Of David's house there stay.
6 Pray that Jerusalem may have
    Peace and felicity:
Let them that love thee and thy peace
    Have still prosperity.

7 Therefore I wish that peace may still
    Within thy walls remain,
And ever may thy palaces
    Prosperity retain.
8 Now, for my friends' and brethren's sakes,
    Peace be in thee, I'll say.
9 And for the house of God the Lord,
    I'll seek thy good alway.

PSALM CXXIII. Evan, 20.

1 O THOU that dwellest in the heavens,
    I lift mine eyes to thee.
2 Behold, as servants' eyes are turned
    Their master's hand to see,

And as upon her mistress' hand
  A handmaid's eyes attend;
Our eyes are on the Lord our God,
  Till he us mercy send.

3 O Lord, be gracious unto us,
   Unto us gracious be;
  Because replenished with contempt
   Exceedingly are we.
4 Our soul is filled with scorn of those
   That at their ease abide,
  And with the insolent contempt
   Of those that swell in pride.

PSALM CXXIV.—1st Version. Gloucester, 24.

1 HAD not the Lord been on our side,
   May Israel now say;
2 Had not the Lord been on our side,
   When men rose us to slay;
3 Alive they had us swallowed then
   In rage beyond control;
4 The waters had us overwhelmed,
   The stream gone o'er our soul.

5 Then had the waters swelling high
   Over our soul made way.
6 Blessed be the Lord, who to their teeth
   Us gave not for a prey.
7 Our soul's escaped, as a bird
   Out of the fowler's snare;
  The snare asunder broken is,
   And we escaped are.

8 Our sure and all-sufficient help
   Is in Jehovah's name;

His name who did the heaven create,
   And who the earth did frame.

PSALM CXXIV.—2nd Version. Old 124th, 87.

1 NOW Israel
   May say, and that truly,
If that the Lord
   Had not our cause maintained,
2 If that the Lord
   Had not our right sustained,
When cruel men
   Who us desired to slay
Rose up in wrath,
   To make of us their prey;

3 Then certainly
   They had devoured us all,
And swallowed quick,
   For ought that we could deem;
Such was their rage,
   As we might well esteem.
4 And as fierce floods
   Before them all things drown,
So had they brought
   Our soul to death quite down.

5 The raging streams,
   With their proud swelling waves,
Had then our soul
   O'erwhelmed in the deep.
6 But blessed be God,
   Who doth us safely keep,
And gave us not
   A living prey to be

Unto their teeth
And bloody cruelty.

7 Even as a bird
Out of the fowler's snare
Escapes away,
So is our soul set free:
Rent is their net,
And thus escaped we.
8 Therefore our help
Is in the Lord's great name,
Who heaven and earth
By his great power did frame.

PSALM CXXV. Smart, 51.

1 THEY in the Lord that firmly trust
Shall be like Zion hill,
Which at no time can be removed,
But stand for ever will.
2 As round about Jerusalem
The mountains stand alway,
The Lord his folk doth compass so,
From henceforth and for aye.
3 For ill men's rod upon the lot
Of just men shall not lie;
Lest righteous men stretch forth their hands
Unto iniquity.
4 Do thou to all those that be good
Thy blessing, Lord, impart;
Thy blessing give thou unto all
Who upright are in heart.
5 But as for such as turn aside
After their crooked way,

With ill men God shall send them forth:
On Israel peace shall stay.

PSALM CXXVI. Durham, 16.

1 WHEN Zion's bondage God turned back,
  As men that dreamed were we.
2 Then filled with laughter was our mouth,
  Our tongue with melody.
  They 'mong the heathen said, The Lord
  Great things for them hath wrought.
3 The Lord hath done great things for us,
  Whence joy to us is brought.

4 As streams of water in the south,
  Our bondage, Lord, recall.
5 Who sow in tears, a reaping time
  Of joy enjoy they shall.
6 The man who, bearing precious seed,
  In going forth doth mourn,
  He doubtless, bringing back his sheaves,
  Rejoicing shall return.

PSALM CXXVII. Tallis, 53.

1 EXCEPT the Lord do build the house,
  The builders lose their pain:
  Except the Lord the city keep,
  The watchmen watch in vain.
2 'Tis vain for you to rise betimes,
  Or late from rest to keep,
  To feed on sorrows' bread; so gives
  He his beloved sleep.

3 Lo, children are God's heritage,
  The womb's fruit his reward.

4 The sons of youth as arrows are,
   For strong men's hands prepared.
5 O happy is the man that hath
   His quiver filled with those;
 They unashamed in the gate
   Shall speak unto their foes.

PSALM CXXVIII.   Dunfermline, 15.

1 BLEST is each one that fears the Lord,
   And walketh in his ways;
2 For of thy labour thou shalt eat,
   And prosper all thy days.
3 Thy wife shall as a fruitful vine
   By thy house' sides be found;
 Thy children like to olive-plants
   About thy table round.

4 Behold, the man that fears the Lord,
   Thus blessed shall he be.
5 The Lord shall out of Zion give
   His blessing unto thee:
 Thou shalt Jerusalem's good behold
   Whilst thou on earth dost dwell.
6 Thou shalt thy children's children see,
   And peace on Israel.

PSALM CXXIX.   Elgin, 18.

1 OFT did they vex me from my youth,
   May Israel now declare;
2 Oft did they vex me from my youth,
   Yet not victorious were.
3 The ploughers ploughed upon my back;
   They long their furrows made;

4 The righteous Lord hath cut the cords
   The wicked round me laid.

5 Let Zion's haters back be turned,
   Into confusion thrown;
6 As grass on housetops let them be,
   Which fades ere it be grown:
7 Whereof enough to fill his hand
   The mower cannot find;
   Nor can the man his bosom fill
   Whose work is sheaves to bind.

8 Nor is it said by passers by,
   God's blessing on you rest:
   We in the Lord's most holy name
   Pray that ye may be blest.

PSALM CXXX. Farrant, 21.

1 LORD, from the depths to thee I cried.
2 My voice, Lord, do thou hear:
   Unto my supplication's voice
   Give an attentive ear.
3 Lord, who shall stand, if thou, O Lord,
   Should'st mark iniquity?
4 But yet with thee forgiveness is,
   That feared thou mayest be.

5 I wait for God, my soul doth wait,
   My hope is in his word.
6 More than they that for morning watch,
   My soul waits for the Lord;
   Yea, even more than they that watch
   The morning light to see.
7 Let Israel in Jehovah hope,
   For with him mercies be;

Redemption also plenteous
   Is ever found with him.
8 And from all his iniquities
   He Israel shall redeem.

PSALM CXXXI. Stainer, 52.

1 MY heart not haughty is, O Lord,
      Mine eyes not lofty be;
   Nor do I deal in matters great,
      Or things too high for me.
2 I surely have myself behaved
      With spirit calm and mild,
   As child of mother weaned; my soul
      Is like a weaned child.

3 Upon the Lord let all the hope
      Of Israel placed be,
   Even from the time that present is
      Unto eternity.

PSALM CXXXII.—1st Version. St. David, 45.

1 DAVID, and his afflictions all,
      O Lord, remember thou;
2 How he unto the Lord did swear,
      To Jacob's Strong One vow.
3 I will not come into my house,
      Nor on my bed repose;
4 No slumber on mine eyes shall fall,
      Nor sleep mine eyelids close;

5 Till for the Lord a place I find,
      Where he may make abode,
   A place of habitation meet
      For Jacob's mighty God.

6 That in the land of Ephratah
  It lay we understood;
 We found it in the forest-fields,
  The city of the wood.

7 We'll to his tabernacles go,
  And at his footstool bow.
8 Arise, O Lord, into thy rest,
  The ark of thy strength, and thou.
9 O let thy priests be clothed, Lord,
  With truth and righteousness;
 And let all those that are thy saints
  Shout loud for joyfulness.

10 For thine own servant David's sake,
   Do not deny thy grace;
  Nor of thine own anointed one
   Turn thou away the face.
11 The Lord in truth to David sware,
   He will not turn from it,
  I of thy body's fruit will make
   Upon thy throne to sit.

12 My covenant if thy sons will keep,
   And laws to them made known,
  Their children then shall also sit
   For ever on thy throne.
13 For God of Zion hath made choice;
   There he desires to dwell.
14 This is my rest, here still I'll stay;
   For I do like it well.

15 Her food I'll greatly bless; her poor
   With bread will satisfy.
16 Her priests I'll with salvation clothe,
   Her saints shall shout for joy.

17 And there will I make David's horn
    To bud forth pleasantly:
For him that mine anointed is
    A lamp ordained have I.

18 As with a garment I will clothe
    With shame his enemies all:
But yet the crown that he doth wear
    Upon him flourish shall.

PSALM CXXXII.—2nd Version.   Breslau, 57.

1 DAVID, and all his anxious care,
    Do thou, O Lord, remember now;
How he unto the Lord did swear,
To Jacob's Mighty One did vow:
2 Into my house I will not go,
Nor will I on my bed repose;
Sleep to mine eyes I will not know,
Slumber shall not mine eyelids close;

3 Till I a place find for the Lord,
A house for Jacob's Strong One build.
Of it at Ephratah we heard,
We found it in the forest-field.
4 We'll go into his courts, and bow
Before the footstool of his grace.
Arise, thine ark of strength, and thou,
O Lord, into thy resting-place.

5 O clothe thy priests with righteousness,
And let thy saints glad shoutings make;
Avert not thine anointed's face,
For thine own servant David's sake.
6 The Lord hath unto David sworn
In truth, he will not turn from it,

  I of the sons unto thee born
  Will make upon thy throne to sit.

7 If they my covenant will obey,
  And testimonies I make known,
  Their children I will bless, and they
  Shall sit for ever on thy throne.
8 The Lord hath chosen Zion hill;
  For there he hath desired to dwell.
  This is my rest, and here I will
  Abide; for I do like it well.

9 I'll her provision richly bless;
  With bread her poor I'll satisfy:
  Her priests I'll clothe with righteousness;
  Her saints shall shout aloud for joy.
10 To bud I'll there make David's horn,
  And for my king a lamp I'll trim;
  His enemies I'll clothe with scorn,
  But flourish shall his crown on him.

PSALM CXXXIII. Evan, 20.

1 BEHOLD, how good a thing it is,
  And how becoming well,
  Together such as brethren are
  In unity to dwell!
2 Like precious ointment on the head,
  That down the beard did flow,
  Even Aaron's beard, and to the skirts
  Did of his garments go.

3 As Hermon's dew, the dew that doth
  On Zion hills descend:
  For there the blessing God commands,
  Life that shall never end.

PSALM CXXXIV. Paisley, 39.

1 BEHOLD, bless ye the Lord, all ye
    That his attendants are,
Who in Jehovah's temple be,
    And praise him nightly there.
2 Your hands within the holy place
    Lift up, and bless his name.
3 From Zion hill the Lord thee bless,
    Who heaven and earth did frame.

PSALM CXXXV. St. Stephen, 50.

1 PRAISE ye the Lord, the Lord's name
    His servants, praise ye God: [praise;
2 Who stand in God's house, in the courts
    Of our God make abode.
3 Praise ye the Lord, for he is good:
    Unto him praises sing:
Sing praises to his name, because
    It is a pleasant thing.

4 For Jacob to himself the Lord
    Did choose of his own will.
For his peculiar treasure he
    Hath chosen Israel.
5 Because I know assuredly
    The Lord is very great,
And that our Lord above all gods
    In glory hath his seat.

6 What things soever pleased the Lord,
    That in the heaven did he,
And in the earth, the seas, and all
    The places deep that be.

7 He from the ends of earth doth make
  The vapours to ascend;
 For rain he lightnings makes, and wind
  Doth from his treasures send.

8 Of Egypt's land the first-born all,
  Both man and beast, smote he;
9 Sent Pharaoh and his servant signs,
  Egypt, in midst of thee.
10 He smote great nations, great kings slew:
11   Sihon the Am'rite king,
 And Og of Bashan, and to nought
  Did Canaan's kingdoms bring:

12 And for a goodly heritage
  Their pleasant land he gave,
 An heritage which Israel,
  His chosen folk, should have.
13 Thy name, O Lord, shall still endure,
  And thy memorial
 With honour shall continued be
  To generations all.

14 Because the righteous God will judge
  His people righteously;
 Concerning those that do him serve
  Himself repent will he.
15 The idols of the nations are
  Of silver and of gold,
 And from the hands of men they take
  Their fashion and their mould.

16 Mouths have they, but they do not speak;
  Eyes, but they do not see;
17 Ears have they, but hear not; and in
  Their mouth no breathings be.

18 Their makers like them are; and all
   Their trust in them that place.
19 Bless ye the Lord, O Israel's house;
   O bless him, Aaron's race.

20 O bless the Lord, of Levi's house
   Ye who his servants be;
   And all ye that the Lord do fear,
   His holy name bless ye.
21 From Zion, his own holy hill,
   Blessed let Jehovah be,
   Who dwelleth at Jerusalem.
   Praise to the Lord give ye.

PSALM CXXXVI.—1st Version. Shepherd, 82

1 GIVE thanks to God, for good is he:
   For mercy hath he ever.
2 Thanks to the God of gods give ye:
   For his grace faileth never.
3 Thanks give the Lord of lords unto:
   For mercy hath he ever:
4 Who only wonders great can do:
   For his grace faileth never.

5 The heavens by wisdom fashioned he;
   For mercy hath he ever:
6 And stretched the earth above the sea;
   For his grace faileth never.
7 To him that made great lights to shine;
   For mercy hath he ever:
8 The sun to rule till day decline;
   For his grace faileth never:

9 The moon and stars to rule by night;
   For mercy hath he ever:

10 Who Egypt's first-born all did smite;
  For his grace faileth never:
11 And Israel brought out from their land;
  For mercy hath he ever:
12 With outstretched arm, and with strong
  For his grace faileth never: [hand;
13 By whom the Red Sea parted was;
  For mercy hath he ever:
14 Who through its midst made Israel pass;
  For his grace faileth never:
15 But Pharaoh and his hosts he drowned;
  For mercy hath he ever:
16 Paths for his own in desert found;
  For his grace faileth never.

17 To him great kings who overthrew;
  For he hath mercy ever:
18 Yea, famous kings in battle slew;
  For his grace faileth never:
19 Sihon, king of the Amorites;
  For he hath mercy ever:
20 And Og, king of the Bashanites;
  For his grace faileth never.

21 Their land as heritage to have,
  (For mercy hath he ever,)
22 His servant Israel right he gave;
  For his grace faileth never.
23 In our low state who on us thought;
  For he hath mercy ever:
24 And from our foes our freedom wrought;
  For his grace faileth never.
25 Who giveth food to all that live;
  For he hath mercy ever.

26 Thanks to the God of heaven give;
   For his grace faileth never.

PSALM CXXXVI.—2nd Version. Darwall, 70.

1 PRAISE God, for he is kind:
      His mercy lasts for aye.
2 Give thanks with heart and mind
   To God of gods alway:
      For certainly
         His mercies dure
         Most firm and sure
      Eternally.

3 The Lord of lords praise ye,
   Whose mercies ever stand.
4 Great wonders only he
   Doth work with mighty hand:
      For certainly, &c.

5 Give praise to his great name,
   Who, by his wisdom high,
   The heaven above did frame,
   And built the lofty sky:
      For certainly, &c.

6 To him who did outstretch
   The earth so great and wide;
   Above the waters' reach
   Who made it to abide:
      For certainly, &c.

7 Great lights who made of old;
   For his grace lasteth aye:
8 The sun, which we behold,
   To rule the lightsome day:
      For certainly, &c.

9 Also the moon so clear,
   Which shineth in our sight;
   The stars that do appear,
   To rule the darksome night:
      For certainly, &c.

10 Who smote Egyptian foes,
   That did his message scorn;
   And in his anger rose,
   And slew all their first-born:
      For certainly, &c.

11 Thence Israel out he brought;
   His mercies ever stand:
12 With outstretched arm he wrought,
   And with a mighty hand:
      For certainly, &c.

13 The sea he clave in twain;
   For his grace lasteth still:
14 And through the parted main
   Led his own Israel:
      For certainly, &c.

15 But cast down Pharaoh then
   Beneath the Red Sea's wave,
   And all his mighty men
   Unto destruction gave:
      For certainly, &c.

16 Who, in his faithfulness,
   His chosen people led
   Through the great wilderness,
   And in his love them fed:
      For certainly, &c.

17 To him great kings who smote;
   For his grace hath no bound:
18 Who slew, and spared not,
   Kings famous and renowned:
      For certainly, &c.

19 Sihon the Am'rites' prince;
   For his grace lasteth aye:
20 And mighty Og, who once
   In Bashan's land had sway:
      For certainly, &c.

21 By lot he gave their land,
   For his grace faileth never,
22 Into his Israel's hand,
   An heritage for ever:
      For certainly, &c.

23 Who also on us thought
   When in our low estate;
24 And from the hand us brought
   Of those who did us hate:
      For certainly, &c.

25 Who to all flesh gives food;
   For his grace faileth never.
26 Give thanks to God most good,
   The God of heaven, for ever:
      For certainly, &c.

PSALM CXXXVII. *Durham, 16.*

1 BY Babel's streams we sat and wept,
      When Zion we thought on.
2 In midst thereof we hung our harps
   The willow trees upon.

3 For there a song required they,
    Who did us captive bring:
  Our spoilers called for mirth, and said,
    A song of Zion sing.

4 O how the Lord's song shall we sing
    Within a foreign land?
5 If thee, Jerusalem, I forget,
    Skill part from my right hand.
6 My tongue to my mouth's roof let cleave,
    If I do thee forget,
  Jerusalem, and thee above
    My chief joy do not set.

7 Remember Edom's children, Lord,
    Who in Jerusalem's day,
  Even unto its foundation raze,
    Yea, raze it quite, did say.
8 O thou unto destruction doomed,
    Daughter of Babylon;
  Happy the man that doth to thee
    As thou to us hast done.

9 Yea, happy surely shall he be,
    Thy tender little ones
  Who shall lay hold upon, and them
    Shall dash against the stones.

PSALM CXXXVIII. Paisley, 39.

1 THEE will I praise with all my heart,
    I will sing praise to thee
2 Before the gods: And worship will
    Toward thy sanctuary.
  I'll praise thy name, even for thy truth,
    And kindness of thy love;

For thou thy word hast magnified
     All thy great name above.

3 Thou didst me answer in the day
     When I did cry to thee;
   And thou with strength my fainting soul
     Didst strengthen inwardly.
4 All kings upon the earth that are
     Shall give thee praise, O Lord:
   What time they from thy mouth shall hear
     Thy true and faithful word.
5 Yea, in the righteous ways of God
     With gladness they shall sing:
   For great's the glory of the Lord,
     Who is for ever king.
6 The Lord is high, yet he regards
     All those that lowly be;
   Whereas the proud and lofty ones
     Afar off knoweth he.

7 Though I in midst of trouble walk,
     I life from thee shall have:
   'Gainst my foes' wrath thou'lt stretch thine
     Thy right hand shall me save.   [hand;
8 All that which me concerns the Lord
     Will surely perfect make:
   Lord, still thy mercy lasts; do not
     Thine own hands' works forsake.

PSALM CXXXIX.—1st Version. _{Abbey, s.}

1 O LORD, thou hast me searched and known.
2 Thou knowest my sitting down,
   And rising up; yea, all my thoughts
     Afar to thee are known.

3 My footsteps, and my lying down,
    Thou compassest always;
  Thou also most entirely art
    Acquaint with all my ways.

4 For in my tongue, before I speak,
    Not any word can be,
  But altogether, lo, O Lord,
    It is well known to thee.
5 Behind, before, thou hast beset,
    And laid on me thine hand.
6 Such knowledge is too strange for me,
    Too high to understand.

7 Where from thy spirit shall I go?
    Or from thy presence fly?
8 Ascend I heaven, lo, thou art there;
    There, if in hell I lie.
9 Take I the wings of morn, and dwell
    In utmost parts of sea;
10 Even there, Lord, shall thy hand me lead,
    Thy right hand hold shall me.

11 If I do say that darkness shall
    Me cover from thy sight,
  Then surely shall the very night
    About me be as light.
12 Yea, darkness hideth not from thee,
    But night doth shine as day:
  To thee the darkness and the light
    Are both alike alway.

13 Because thou hast possessed my reins,
    And thou didst cover me,
  When I within my mother's womb
    Inclosed was by thee.

14 Thee will I praise, for fearfully
    And strangely made I am:
Thy works are wonderful, and well
    My soul doth know the same.
15 When I was made in secret place,
    My substance thou didst see;
When in the lowest parts of earth
    I was wrought curiously.
16 While yet unformed my substance was,
    Thine eyes on it did look;
My days, while yet not one had dawned,
    Were written in thy book.
17 How precious also are thy thoughts,
    O gracious God, to me!
And in their sum how passing great
    And numberless they be!
18 If I should count them, than the sand
    They more in number be:
What time soever I awake,
    I ever am with thee.
19 Thou, Lord, wilt sure the wicked slay:
    Hence from me bloody men.
20 Thy foes against thee loudly speak,
    And take thy name in vain.
21 Do not I hate all those, O Lord,
    That hatred bear to thee?
With those that up against thee rise
    Can I but grieved be?
22 With perfect hatred them I hate,
    My foes I them do hold.
23 Search me, O God, and know my heart,
    Try me, my thoughts unfold:

24 And see if any wicked way
    There be at all in me;
And in thine everlasting way
    To me a leader be.

PSALM CXXXIX.—2nd Version. Cannons, 59.

1 LORD, thou hast search'd me, and hast
    My rising up and lying down; [known
And from afar thy searching eye
    Beholds my thoughts that secret lie.
2 Thou know'st my path and lying down,
    And all my ways to thee are known;
For in my tongue no word can be,
    But lo! O Lord, 'tis known to thee.
3 Behind, before me, thou dost stand,
    And lay on me thy mighty hand.
Such knowledge is for me too strange,
    'Tis high beyond my utmost range.
4 O, whither shall my footsteps fly,
    Beyond thy Spirit's searching eye?
To what retreat shall I repair,
    And find not still thy presence there?
5 If I to heaven shall ascend,
    Thy presence there will me attend;
If in the grave I make my bed,
    Lo! there I find thy presence dread.
6 If on the morning wings I flee,
    And dwell in utmost parts of sea,
Ev'n there thy hand shall guide my way,
    And thy right hand shall be my stay.
7 Or if I say, to shun thine eye,
    In shades of darkness I will lie,

Around me then the very night
Will shine as shines the noonday light.
8 From thee the shades can nought disguise;
The night is day before thine eyes;
The darkness is to thee as bright
As are the beams of noonday light.

9 My very reins belong to thee;
Thou in the womb didst cover me;
And I to thee will praise proclaim,
For fearful, wondrous is my frame.
10 Thy works are wonderful, I know;
And when, in depths of earth below,
This complicated frame was made,
'Twas all before thine eyes displayed

11 My substance, yet unformed by thee,
Thy searching eye did clearly see:
My days were written, every one,
Within thy books, ere yet begun.
12 Thy thoughts, O God, to me are dear;
How vast their numbers do appear!
More than the sand my reckonings make.
I'm still with thee when I awake.

13 Thou wilt the wicked slay, O God;
Depart from me, ye men of blood,
Who speak of thee for ends profane,
Thy foes who take thy name in vain.
14 Do not I hate thy haters, Lord?
And thy assailants hold abhorred?
A perfect hatred them I show,
And count each one to me a foe.

15 Search me, O God, my heart discern.
Try me, my very thoughts to learn;

See if in evil paths I stray,
And guide me in the eternal way.

PSALM CXL. Moravia, 32.

1 LORD, from the ill and froward man
　　Give me deliverance,
　And do thou safe preserve me from
　　The man of violence:
2 Who in their heart things mischievous
　　Do meditate alway:
　And they for war together are
　　Assembled every day.

3 Even like unto a serpent's tongue
　　Their tongues they sharp do make;
　And underneath their lips there lies
　　The poison of a snake.
4 Lord, keep me from the wicked's hands,
　　From violent men me save;
　Who utterly to overthrow
　　My goings purposed have.

5 The proud have hid a snare and cords,
　　For me have spread a net;
　Close by the path they have it spread,
　　And gins for me have set.
6 Then to the Lord thus did I say,
　　My God art thou, O Lord;
　Then hear my supplication's voice,
　　And help to me afford.

7 Jehovah, Lord, thou who the strength
　　Of my salvation art,
　Thou to my head in day of war
　　Protection dost impart.

8 Unto the wicked man, O Lord,
   His wishes do not grant;
 Nor further thou his ill device,
   Lest they themselves should vaunt.

9 As for the head of those that do
   About encompass me,
 Even by the mischief of their lips
   Let thou them covered be.

10 Let burning coals upon them fall,
   Them cast into the flame,
 And pits so deep, that they no more
   May rise out of the same.

11 A man of evil tongue shall not
   On earth established be:
 Mischief shall hunt the violent
   And waste him utterly.

12 The Lord, I know, will judge the poor,
   Maintain the afflicted's right.

13 The righteous shall extol thy name:
   The just dwell in thy sight.

PSALM CXLI. Newington, 3'.

1 O LORD, I unto thee do cry,
     Do thou make haste to me,
 And give an ear unto my voice,
     When I cry unto thee.

2 As incense let my prayer be
     Directed in thine eyes;
 And the uplifting of my hands
     As the evening sacrifice.

3 Set, Lord, a watch before my mouth,
     Keep of my lips the door.

4 My heart incline thou not unto
   The ills I should abhor,
  To practise wicked works with men
   That work iniquity;
  And of their dainties let me not
   With them partaker be.
5 Let him that righteous is me smite,
   It shall a kindness be;
  Let him reprove, I shall it count
   A precious oil to me;
  Such oil my head shall not refuse;
   For yet shall come the day
  When I, in their calamities,
   To God for them shall pray.
6 When down the sides of rugged rocks
   Their judges shall be cast,
  Then shall they hear my words; for they
   Shall sweet be to their taste.
7 About the grave's devouring mouth
   Our bones are scattered round,
  As wood which men do cut and cleave
   Lies scattered on the ground.
8 But unto thee, O God the Lord,
   Mine eyes uplifted be:
  My soul do not leave destitute;
   My trust is set on thee.
9 Lord, keep me safely from the snares
   Which they for me prepare;
  And from the subtle gins of those
   That evil-doers are.
10 Let workers of iniquity
    Into their own nets fall,

Whilst I do, by thy help, escape
The danger of them all.

PSALM CXLII. Chester, 12.

1 I WITH my voice cried to the Lord,
    With it made my request:
2 Poured out to him my plaint, to him
    My trouble I expressed.
3 When overwhelmed my spirit is,
    Then knowest thou my way;
  Where I did walk a snare for me
    They privily did lay.

4 Look on the right hand, and behold,
    There's none to know me there;
  All refuge hath me failed, and none
    Doth for my soul take care.
5 I cried to thee; I said, Thou art
    A refuge, Lord, to me;
  Thou art my portion in the land
    Of those that living be.

6 Because I am brought very low,
    Attend unto my cry:
  Me from my persecutors save,
    Who stronger are than I.
7 From prison bring my soul, that I
    Thy name may glorify:
  The just shall compass me, when thou
    With me deal'st bounteously.

PSALM CXLIII.—1st Version. St. Mary, 47.

1 LORD, hear my prayer, regard my cries;
    And in thy faithfulness

Give thou an answer unto me,
    And in thy righteousness.
2 Thy servant also bring thou not
    In judgment to be tried:
  Because no living man can be
    In thy sight justified.

3 Because the foe pursues my soul,
    My life to earth doth tread;
  In darkness he hath made me dwell,
    As those that are long dead.
4 My spirit, then, is overwhelmed
    With sore perplexity;
  Within me is my very heart
    Amazed wondrously.

5 I call to mind the days of old,
    I think upon thy deeds;
  On all the work I meditate
    Which from thy hand proceeds.
6 My hands to thee I stretch; my soul
    Thirsts as dry land for thee.
7 Haste, Lord, to hear, my spirit fails:
    Hide not thy face from me;

  Lest like to them I do become
    That go down to the dust.
8 At morn let me thy kindness hear;
    For in thee do I trust.
  Teach me the way that I should walk:
    I lift my soul to thee.
9 Lord, free me from my foes; I flee
    To thee to cover me.
10 Because thou art my God, to do
    Thy will do me instruct;

> Good is thy Spirit, in a land
> That plain is me conduct.
11 Revive and quicken me, O Lord,
> Even for thine own name's sake;
> And do thou, in thy righteousness,
> My soul from trouble take.

12 And of thy mercy slay my foes;
> Let all destroyed be
> That do afflict my soul: for I
> A servant am to thee.

PSALM CXLIII.—2nd Version. Broadlands, 69.

1 O LORD, my prayer hear,
> And to my suppliant cry
> In faithfulness give ear,
> In righteousness reply.
2 In judgment call not me
> Thy servant to be tried,
> No living man can be
> In thy sight justified.

3 The foe my soul hath sought,
> My life to earth doth tread;
> To darkness me hath brought,
> As those that long are dead.
4 My spirit therefore vexed
> O'erwhelmed is me within;
> My heart in me perplexed,
> And desolate hath been.

5 Yet I to mind recall
> What ancient days record,
> Thy works I ponder all,
> I muse on them, O Lord.

6 To thee I stretch my hands,
   Do thou my helper be;
   Behold as thirsty lands
   My soul doth long for thee.

7 Lord, let my prayer prevail,
   To answer it make speed;
   My spirit quite doth fail:
   Hide not thy face in need;
   Lest I be like to those
   That do in darkness sit,
   Or him that downward goes
   Into the dreadful pit.

8 Because I trust in thee,
   O Lord, cause me to hear
   Thy loving-kindness free,
   When morning doth appear:
   Make me to know the way
   Wherein my path should be;
   Because my soul each day
   I do lift up to thee.

9 O Lord, deliver me
   From all who me oppose:
   To thee, my God, I flee,
   To hide me from my foes.

10 No God have I but thee,
    Teach me to do thy will:
    Thy Spirit's good, lead me
    In a plain pathway still.

11 Lord, for thine own name's sake,
    Be pleased to quicken me;
    In righteousness O take
    My soul from misery.

12 In mercy cut off those
   That enemies are to me;
   Slay of my soul the foes:
   I servant am to thee.

PSALM CXLIV. New London, 3s.

1 O BLESSED ever be the Lord,
   Who is my strength and might,
Who doth instruct my hands to war,
   My fingers teach to fight:
2 My goodness, fortress, my high tower,
   Deliverer, and shield,
In whom I trust: who under me
   My people makes to yield.

3 Lord, what is man, that thou of him
   Dost so much knowledge take?
Or son of man, that thou of him
   So great account dost make?
4 Man is like vanity; his days,
   As shadows, pass away.
5 Lord, bow thy heavens, come down, touch
   The hills, and smoke shall they.   [thou

6 Cast forth thy lightning, scatter them;
   Thine arrows shoot, them rout.
7 Thine hand send from above, me save;
   From great depths draw me out;
   And from the hand of children strange,
8   Whose mouth speaks vanity;
   And their right hand a right hand is
      That works deceitfully.

9 A new song I to thee will sing,
   Lord, on a psaltery;

I on a ten-stringed instrument
  Will praises sing to thee.
10 Even he it is that unto kings
  Doth his salvation send;
Who his own servant David doth
  From hurtful sword defend.

11 O free me from strange children's hand,
  Whose mouth speaks vanity:
And their right hand a right hand is
  That works deceitfully.
12 That like to well-grown plants our sons
  In time of youth may be;
Our daughters like to pillars carved
  In palace fair to see.
13 That all our garners may be full,
  Store of all kinds may yield;
And that our flocks may thousands bear,
  Ten thousands in the field.
14 That strong our oxen be for work,
  That no inbreaking be,
Nor going forth; and that our streets
  From outcry may be free.

15 Blest is the people that is found
  In such a case as this;
Yea, greatly is the people blest,
  Whose God Jehovah is.

PSALM CXLV.—1st Version. Nottingham, 37.

1 I'LL thee extol, my God, O King;
  I'll bless thy name always.
2 Thee will I bless each day, and will
  Thy name for ever praise.

3 Great is the Lord, much to be praised;
　　His greatness search exceeds.
4 Race unto race shall praise thy works,
　　And show thy mighty deeds.

5 I of thy glorious majesty
　　The honour will record;
　I'll speak of all thy mighty works,
　　Which wondrous are, O Lord.
6 Men of thine acts the might shall show,
　　Thine acts that dreadful are;
　And I, thy glory to advance,
　　Thy greatness will declare.

7 The memory of thy goodness great
　　They largely shall express;
　With songs of praise they shall extol
　　Thy perfect righteousness.
8 Jehovah very gracious is,
　　In him compassions flow;
　In mercy he is very great,
　　And is to anger slow.

9 The Lord most bountiful extends
　　His goodness unto all:
　And over all that he hath made
　　His tender mercies fall.
10 Thee all thy works shall praise, O Lord,
　　And thee thy saints shall bless;
11 They shall thy kingdom's glory show,
　　Thy power by speech express:

12 To make the sons of men to know
　　His acts done mightily,
　And of his kingdom excellent
　　The glorious majesty.

13 Thy kingdom shall endure for aye,
 Thy reign through ages all.
14 God raiseth all that are bowed down,
 Upholdeth all that fall.

15 The eyes of all things wait on thee,
 The giver of all good;
 And thou in time convenient dost
 Bestow on them their food.
16 Thy bounteous hand thou openest,
 And dost in kindness give
 Enough to satisfy the wants
 Of all on earth that live.

17 The Lord is just in all his ways,
 Holy in his works all.
18 He's near to all that call on him,
 In truth that on him call.
19 He will accomplish the desire
 Of those that do him fear:
 He also will deliver them,
 And he their cry will hear.

20 The Lord preserves all who him love,
 That nought can them annoy:
 But he all those that wicked are
 Will utterly destroy.
21 My mouth the praises of the Lord
 Shall constantly proclaim;
 And let all flesh for ever give
 Praise to his holy name.

PSALM CXLV.—2nd Version. New Winchester, 64.

1 O LORD, thou art my God and King;
 Thee will I magnify and praise:

 I will thee bless, and gladly sing
 Unto thy holy name always.
2 Each day I rise I will thee bless,
 And praise thy name time without end.
3 Much to be praised, and great God is;
 His greatness none can comprehend.

4 Race shall thy works praise unto race,
 The mighty acts show done by thee.
5 I will speak of the glorious grace,
 And honour of thy majesty;
 Thy wondrous works I will record.
6 By men the might shall be extolled
 Of all thy dreadful acts, O Lord;
 And I thy greatness will unfold.

7 They utter shall abundantly
 The memory of thy goodness great;
 And shall sing praises cheerfully,
 Whilst they thy righteousness relate.
8 The Lord is very gracious,
 And he doth great compassion show;
 In mercy he is plenteous,
 But unto wrath and anger slow.

9 Good unto all men is the Lord:
 O'er all his works his mercy is.
10 Thy works all praise to thee afford;
 Thy saints, O Lord, thy name shall bless.
11 The glory of thy kingdom show
 Shall they, and of thy power tell;
12 That so men's sons his deeds may know,
 His kingdom's glories that excel.

13 Thy kingdom hath none end at all,
 It doth through ages all remain.

14 The Lord upholdeth all that fall,
   The cast-down raiseth up again.
15 The eyes of all things, Lord, attend,
   And on thee wait that here do live,
   And thou, in season due, dost send
   Sufficient food them to relieve.

16 Yea, thou thine hand dost open wide,
   And everything dost satisfy
   That lives and doth on earth abide,
   Of thy great liberality.
17 The Lord is just in his ways all,
   And holy in his works each one.
18 He's near to all that on him call,
   Who call in truth on him alone.

19 The Lord will the desire fulfil
   Of such as truly do him fear:
   In time of need them save he will,
   For he their earnest cry will hear.
20 The Lord keeps all in faithfulness,
   That bear to him a loving heart:
   But workers all of wickedness
   Destroy will he, and quite subvert.

21 My mouth the praises of the Lord
   Shall therefore constantly proclaim:
   And let all flesh with one accord
   For ever bless his holy name.

PSALM CXLVI. St. Peter, 49.

1 PRAISE ye the Lord: him praise, my soul.
2 I'll praise God while I live;
   While I have being to my God
   In songs I'll praises give.

3 Trust not in princes, nor man's son,
　　In whom there is no stay:
4 His breath departs, to's earth he turns;
　　That day his thoughts decay.

5 O happy is that man and blest,
　　Whom Jacob's God doth aid;
　Whose hope upon the Lord doth rest,
　　And on his God is stayed:
6 Who made the earth and heavens high,
　　Who made the swelling deep,
　And all that is within the same;
　　Who truth doth ever keep:

7 Who righteous judgment executes
　　For those oppressed that be,
　Who to the hungry giveth food,
　　And sets the prisoners free.
8 The Lord doth give the blind their sight,
　　The bowed down doth raise:
　The Lord doth dearly love all those
　　Who walk in upright ways.

9 The stranger's shield, the widow's stay,
　　The orphan's help is he:
　But yet by him the wicked's way
　　Turned upside down shall be.
10 The Lord shall reign for evermore:
　　Thy God, O Zion, he
　To generations all shall reign.
　　Praise to the Lord give ye.

PSALM CXLVII.—1st Version. St. Stephen, 50.

1　PRAISE ye the Lord; for it is good
　　Praise to our God to sing:

For it is pleasant, and to praise
  Is a becoming thing.
2 The Lord builds up Jerusalem,
  And he it is alone
That the dispersed of Israel
  Doth gather into one.

3 Those that are broken in their heart
  And grieved in their minds
He healeth, and their painful wounds
  He tenderly up-binds.
4 He counts the number of the stars;
  He names them every one.
5 Great is our Lord, and of great power;
  His wisdom search can none.

6 The Lord lifts up the meek; and casts
  The wicked to the ground.
7 Sing to the Lord, and give him thanks;
  On harp his praises sound;
8 Who covereth the heaven with clouds,
  Who for the earth below
Prepareth rain, who maketh grass
  Upon the mountains grow.

9 He gives the beast his food, he feeds
  The ravens young that cry.
10 His pleasure not in horse's strength,
  Nor in man's legs doth lie.
11 But in all those that do him fear
  The Lord doth pleasure take;
In those that to his mercy do
  In hope themselves betake.

12 The Lord praise, O Jerusalem;
  Zion, thy God confess:

13 For thy gates' bars he maketh strong;
   Thy sons in thee doth bless.
14 He in thy borders maketh peace;
   With fine wheat filleth thee.
15 He sends forth his command on earth,
   His word runs speedily.

16 Hoar-frost, like ashes, scattereth he;
   Like wool he snow doth give:
17 Like morsels casteth forth his ice;
   Who in its cold can live?
18 He sendeth forth his mighty word,
   And melteth them again;
   His wind he makes to blow, and then
   The waters flow amain.

19 The doctrine of his holy word
   To Jacob he doth show;
   His statutes and his judgments he
   Gives Israel to know.
20 Of other nations unto none
   Such favour shown hath he:
   And they his judgments have not known.
   Praise to the Lord give ye.

PSALM CXLVII.—2nd Version.   Bremen, 74.

1 PRAISE God! 'tis good and pleasant,
     And comely to adore;
  Jehovah builds up Salem,
     Her outcasts doth restore.
2 He heals the broken-hearted,
     And makes the wounded live;
  The starry hosts he numbers,
     And names to all doth give.

3 Our Lord is great and mighty;
   His wisdom none can know;
The Lord doth raise the lowly,
   And sinners overthrow.
4 O thank and praise Jehovah!
   Praise him on harp with mirth,
The heaven with clouds who covers,
   And sends his rain on earth.

5 He clothes with grass the mountains,
   And gives the beasts their food;
He hears the crying ravens,
   And feeds their tender brood.
6 In horse's strength delights not,
   Nor speed of man loves he;
The Lord loves all who fear him,
   And to his mercy flee.

7 O Salem, praise Jehovah,
   Thy God, O Zion, praise;
For he thy gates has strengthened,
   And blessed thy sons with grace.
8 With peace he'll bless thy borders,
   The finest wheat afford;
He sends forth his commandment,
   And swiftly speeds his word.

9 Like wool the snow he giveth,
   Spreads hail o'er all the land,
Hoar frost like ashes scatters;
   Who can his cold withstand?
10 Then forth his word he sendeth,
   He makes his wind to blow;
The snow and ice are melted,
   Again the waters flow.

11 He shows his word to Jacob,
    To Israel's seed alone;
   His statutes and his judgments
    The heathen have not known.
     Praise ye the Lord!

PSALM CXLVIII.—1st Version. Zwingle, 55.

1 PRAISE ye the Lord. From heavens him
   In heights praise to him be. [praise;
2 All ye his angels, praise ye him;
   His hosts all, praise him ye.
3 O praise ye him, both sun and moon,
   Praise him, all stars of light.
4 Ye heavens of heavens him praise, and floods
   Above the heavens' height.

5 Let all the creatures praise the name
   Of the almighty Lord:
  For he commanded, and they were
   Created by his word.
6 He also, for all times to come,
   Hath them established sure;
  He hath appointed them a law,
   Which ever shall endure.

7 Praise ye Jehovah from the earth,
   Dragons, and every deep:
8 Fire, hail, snow, vapour, stormy wind,
   His word that fully keep:
9 All hills and mountains, fruitful trees,
   And all ye cedars high:
10 Beasts, and all cattle, creeping things,
   And all ye birds that fly:

11 Kings of the earth, all tribes of men,
    Princes, earth's judges all:
12 Young men, and youthful maidens too,
    Old men, and children small.
13 Let them the Lord's name praise, for it
    Alone is excellent:
His glory reacheth far above
    The earth and firmament.

14 A horn he raiseth for his folk,
    To all his saints a praise,
To Israel's seed so near to him.
    Jehovah's glory raise.

PSALM CXLVIII.—2nd Version. Dykes, 72.

1 FROM heaven the Lord confess,
    In heights his glory raise.
2 Him let all angels bless,
    Him all his armies praise.
3   Him glorify
      Sun, moon, and stars;
4   Ye higher spheres,
    And cloudy sky.

5 Jehovah gave you birth,
    Him therefore glorious make;
To being ye came forth,
    When he the word but spake.
6   And from that place,
      Where fixed you be
      By his decree,
You cannot pass.

7 Praise him from earth below,
    Ye dragons, and ye deeps:

8 Fire, hail, clouds, wind, and snow,
    Which in command he keeps.
9   Praise ye his name,
      Hills great and small,
      Trees low and tall,
10   Beasts wild and tame.

  All things that creep or fly,
11   Kings, tribes of every tongue,
  All princes mean or high,
12   Both men and virgins young;
    Even young and old,
13   Exalt his name;
      For much his fame
    Should be extolled.

  Jehovah's name be praised
    Above both earth and sky;
14 For he his saints hath raised,
    And set their horn on high:
     Even those that be
      Of Israel's race,
      Near to his grace.
     The Lord praise ye.

PSALM CXLIX.—1st Version.   Leicester, 29.

1 PRAISE ye the Lord: unto him sing
    A new song, and his praise
  In the assembly of his saints
    In sweet psalms do ye raise.
2 Let Israel in his Maker joy,
    And to him praises sing:
  Let all that Zion's children are
    Be joyful in their King.

3 O let them unto his great name
    Give praises in the dance;
Let them with timbrel and with harp
    In songs his praise advance.
4 For God doth pleasure take in those
    That his own people be;
And he with his salvation sure
    The meek will beautify.

5 And in his glory excellent
    Let all his saints rejoice:
Let them to him upon their beds
    Aloud lift up their voice.
6 Let in their mouth aloft be raised
    The high praise of the Lord,
And let them have in their right hand
    A sharp two-edged sword;

7 To execute the vengeance due
    Upon the heathen all,
And make deserved punishment
    Upon the people fall;
8 With chains as prisoners to bind
    Their kings that them command;
Yea, and with iron fetters strong,
    The nobles of their land.

9 On them the judgment to perform
    Found written in his word:
An honour this to all his saints.
    O do ye praise the Lord.

PSALM CXLIX.—2nd Version. *Houghton, 6s.*

1 O PRAISE ye the Lord!
    Prepare your glad voice,

New songs with his saints
  Assembled to sing;
Before his Creator
  Let Israel rejoice,
And children of Zion
  Be glad in their King.

2 And let them his name
    Extol in the dance;
  With timbrel and harp
    His praises express;
  Who always takes pleasure
    His saints to advance,
  And with his salvation
    The humble to bless.

3 His saints shall sing loud
    With glory and joy,
  And rest undismayed;
    With songs in the night
  The praise of Jehovah
    Their lips shall employ;
  A sword in their right hand
    Two-edged for the fight;

4 The heathen to judge,
    Their pride to consume,
  To fetter their kings,
    Their princes to bind;
  To execute on them
    The long-decreed doom;
  Such honour for ever
    The holy shall find.   Hallelujah.

PSALM CL.

Nativity, 33.

1 PRAISE ye the Lord. God's praise within
   His sanctuary raise;
And to him in the firmament
   Of his power give ye praise.
2 Because of all his mighty acts,
   With praise him magnify:
O praise him, as he doth excel
   In glorious majesty.

3 Praise him with trumpet's sound; his praise
   With psaltery advance:
4 With timbrel, harp, stringed instruments,
   And organs in the dance.
5 Praise him on cymbals loud; him praise
   On cymbals sounding high.
6 Let each thing breathing praise the Lord.
   Praise to the Lord give ye.

A TABLE OF FIRST LINES OF THE PSALMS.

	Psalm
As pants the hart for water-brooks,	42
Against a wicked race, O God,	43
All people, clap your hands; to God,	47
After thy loving-kindness, Lord,	51
All lands to God, in joyful sounds,	66
Attend, my people, to my law,	78
All people that on earth do dwell,	100
Blessed is he that carefully,	41
Be merciful to me, O God,	57
Bless God, my soul. O Lord my God,	104
Blessed are they that undefiled,	119
Blest is each one that fears the Lord,	128
Behold, how good a thing it is,	133
Behold, bless ye the Lord, all ye,	134
By Babel's streams we sat and wept,	137
Do ye, O congregation, then,	58
David, and his afflictions all,	132
David, and all his anxious care,	132
Except the Lord do build the house,	127
For evil-doers fret thou not,	37
From all that dwell below the skies,	117
From heaven the Lord confess,	148
Give ear unto me when I call,	4
Give ear unto my words, O Lord,	5
Give ye unto the Lord, ye sons,	29
Give ye to Jehovah, O sons of the mighty,	29
God will I bless all times; his praise,	34
God is our refuge and our strength,	46

	Psalm
God is our sure defence, our aid,	46
Great is the Lord, and greatly he,	48
God's mercies I will ever sing,	89
God reigneth, let the earth be glad,	97
Give thanks to God, call on his name,	105
Give praise and thanks unto the Lord,	106
Give thanks to God, for good is he,	136
How excellent in all the earth,	8
Help, Lord, because the godly man,	12
How long wilt thou forget me, Lord?	13
How long wilt thou forget me?	13
Hear this, all people, and give ear,	49
Hear thou my prayer, O God, hide not,	55
Hear, Israel's Shepherd! like a flock,	80
How lovely is thy dwelling-place,	84
He that doth in the secret place,	91
Had not the Lord been on our side,	124
In thy great indignation, Lord,	6
I in the Lord do put my trust,	11
In thee, O Lord, I put my trust,	31
In thy great indignation, Lord,	38
I said, I will look to my ways,	39
I will of my ways be heedful,	39
I waited for the Lord my God,	40
In Judah God is known, his name,	76
In gods' assembly God doth judge,	82
I mercy will and judgment sing,	101
I love the Lord, because my voice,	116
I in my strait cried to the Lord,	120
I to the hills will lift mine eyes,	121
I joyed when to the house of God,	122
I with my voice cried to the Lord,	142
I'll thee extol, my God, O King,	145
Jehovah hear thee in the day,	20
Jehovah, in thy strength the king,	21
Judge me, O Lord, for I have walked,	26
Jehovah is my light,	27
Jehovah is enthroned as king,	99

FIRST LINES OF THE PSALMS.

	Psalm
Jehovah said unto my Lord,	110
Keep not, O God, we thee entreat,	83
Lord, in thy wrath rebuke me not,	6
Lord, thee I'll praise with all my heart,	9
Lord, keep me, for I trust in thee,	16
Lord, hear the right, regard my cry,	17
Lord, I will thee extol, for thou,	30
Lord, I will thee extol,	30
Lord, hear my voice, my prayer attend,	61
Lord, thee my God, I'll early seek,	63
Lord, bless and pity us,	67
Let God arise, and scattered,	68
Lord, thine heart in love hath yearned,	85
Lord God, my Saviour, day and night,	88
Lord, thou hast been our dwelling-place,	90
Lord, thou hast been a dwelling-place,	90
Lord, hear my prayer, and let my cry,	102
Lord, from the depths to thee I cried,	130
Lord, thou hast search'd me, and hast known,	139
Lord, from the ill and froward man,	140
Lord, hear my prayer, regard my cries,	143
My God, my God, wherefore is it,	22
My heart brings forth a goodly thing,	45
My heart inditing is,	45
My God, deliver me from those,	59
My soul with expectation doth,	62
Make haste, O God, me to preserve,	70
My voice I will lift up to God,	77
My soul, praise the Lord,	104
My heart is fixed, O God; I'll sing,	108
My heart not haughty is, O Lord,	131
Not unto us, Lord, not to us,	115
Not ours the glory make,	115
Now Israel may say,	124
O Lord, how are my foes increas'd!	3
O Lord my God, in thee do I,	7

	Psalm
O Lord, our Lord, how excellent,	8
O blessed is the man to whom,	32
O God, we with our ears have heard,	44
O God, thou hast rejected us,	60
O God, give ear unto my cry,	61
O God, be merciful to us,	67
O God, to save me haste,	70
O Lord, my hope and confidence,	71
O Lord, thy judgments give the king,	72
O God, why hast thou cast us off?	74
O God, why hast thou cast us off?	74
O God, into thy heritage,	79
O Lord, do thou bow down thine ear,	86
O Lord, the God to whom alone,	94
O come, and let us to the Lord,	95
O come, let us sing to the Lord,	95
O sing a new song to the Lord,	96
O sing a new song to the Lord,	98
O all ye lands, unto the Lord,	100
O Lord, unto my prayer give ear,	102
O thou my soul, bless God the Lord,	103
O thou the God of all my praise,	109
O all ye nations of the earth,	117
O praise the Lord, for he is good,	118
O thou that dwellest in the heavens,	123
Oft did they vex me from my youth,	129
O Lord, thou hast me searched and known,	139
O Lord, I unto thee do cry,	141
O Lord, my prayer hear,	143
O blessed ever be the Lord,	144
O Lord, thou art my God and King,	145
O praise ye the Lord!	149
Plead, Lord, with those that plead; and fight,	35
Praise waits for thee in Zion, Lord,	65
Praise ye the Lord, for he is good,	107
Praise ye the Lord: with my whole heart,	111
Praise ye the Lord. The man is blessed,	112
Praise ye the Lord: who serve the Lord,	113
Praise ye the Lord, the Lord's name praise,	135
Praise God, for he is kind,	136

FIRST LINES OF THE PSALMS.

	Psalm
Praise ye the Lord: him praise, my soul,	146
Praise ye the Lord; for it is good,	147
Praise God! 'tis good and pleasant,	147
Praise ye the Lord. From heavens him praise,	148
Praise ye the Lord: unto him sing,	149
Praise ye the Lord. God's praise within,	150
Save me, O God, by thy great name,	54
Show mercy, Lord, to me, for man,	56
Save me, O God, because the floods,	69
Sing loud to God our strength; with joy,	81
Sing a new song to Jehovah,	98
That man hath perfect blessedness,	1
That there is not a God, the fool,	14
Thee will I love, O Lord, my strength,	18
The heavens God's glory do declare,	19
The lofty heavens proclaim,	19
The Lord's my shepherd, I'll not want,	23
The earth belongs unto the Lord,	24
To thee I lift my soul,	25
To thee I lift my soul, O Lord,	25
The Lord's my light and saving health,	27
To thee I'll cry, O Lord, my rock,	28
To thee, Jehovah, will I cry,	28
The wicked man's transgression speaks,	36
The mighty God, the Lord,	50
The mighty God, the Lord, doth speak,	50
That there is not a God, the fool,	53
Thy mercy, Lord, to me extend.	57
To thee, O God, do we give thanks,	75
Thou hast been favourable, Lord,	85
To render thanks unto the Lord,	92
The Lord doth reign, and clothed is he,	93
The Lord is king and weareth,	93
They in the Lord that firmly trust,	125
Thee will I praise with all my heart,	138
Unto the voice of my complaint,	64
Upon the hills of holiness,	87
Unto my Lord Jehovah said,	110

	Psalm
Why rage the heathen? and vain things,	2
Wherefore is it that thou, O Lord,	10
Within thy tabernacle, Lord,	15
Why boast thyself, O mighty man,	52
When Israel out of Egypt went,	114
When Israel had from Egypt gone,	114
When Zion's bondage God turned back,	126
Ye righteous, in the Lord rejoice,	33
Ye dwellers all on earth, give ear,	49
Yea, God is good to Israel,	73

TRANSLATIONS AND PARAPHRASES

IN VERSE

OF SEVERAL PASSAGES OF

SACRED SCRIPTURE.

NOTE.

In appending the Paraphrases and Hymns, the Committee are instructed to state, that the Book of Psalms forms the only Psalmody authorized by the General Assembly.

BLACKIE & SON:
89 TALBOT STREET, DUBLIN, AND
97 DONEGAL STREET, BELFAST.
1880.

TRANSLATIONS AND PARAPHRASES,

IN VERSE,

OF SEVERAL PASSAGES OF SACRED SCRIPTURE.

I. Gen. i.

1 LET heav'n arise, let earth appear,
    Said the Almighty Lord:
The heav'n arose, the earth appear'd,
    At his creating word.
2 Thick darkness brooded o'er the deep:
    God said, "Let there be light:"
The light shone forth with smiling ray,
    And scatter'd ancient night.

3 He bade the clouds ascend on high;
    The clouds ascend, and bear
A wat'ry treasure to the sky,
    And float upon the air.
4 The liquid element below
    Was gather'd by his hand;
The rolling seas together flow,
    And leave the solid land.

5 With herbs, and plants, and fruitful trees,
    The new-form'd globe he crown'd,
Ere there was rain to bless the soil,
    Or sun to warm the ground.
6 Then high in heav'n's resplendent arch
    He plac'd two orbs of light,

  He set the sun to rule the day,
   The moon to rule the night.

7 Next, from the deep, th' Almighty King
   Did vital beings frame;
  Fowls of the air of ev'ry wing,
   And fish of ev'ry name.
8 To all the various brutal tribes
   He gave their wondrous birth;
  At once the lion and the worm
   Sprung from the teeming earth.

9 Then, chief o'er all his works below,
   At last was Adam made;
  His Maker's image bless'd his soul,
   And glory crown'd his head.
10 Fair in the Almighty Maker's eye
   The whole creation stood.
  He view'd the fabric he had rais'd;
   His word pronounc'd it good.

II. Gen. xxviii. 20–22.

1 O GOD of Bethel! by whose hand
   Thy people still are fed;
  Who through this weary pilgrimage
   Hast all our fathers led:
2 Our vows, our pray'rs, we now present
   Before thy throne of grace:
  God of our fathers! be the God
   Of their succeeding race.

3 Through each perplexing path of life
   Our wand'ring footsteps guide;
  Give us each day our daily bread,
   And raiment fit provide.

4 O spread thy cov'ring wings around,
   Till all our wand'rings cease,
And at our Father's lov'd abode
   Our souls arrive in peace.

5 Such blessings from thy gracious hand
   Our humble pray'rs implore;
And thou shalt be our chosen God,
   And portion evermore.

III. Job i. 21.

1 NAKED as from the earth we came,
      And enter'd life at first;
   Naked we to the earth return,
      And mix with kindred dust.
2 Whate'er we fondly call our own
      Belongs to heav'n's great Lord;
   The blessings lent us for a day
      Are soon to be restor'd.
3 'Tis God that lifts our comforts high,
      Or sinks them in the grave:
   He gives; and, when he takes away,
      He takes but what he gave.
4 Then, ever blessed be his name!
      His goodness swell'd our store;
   His justice but resumes its own;
      'Tis ours still to adore.

IV. Job iii. 17–20.

1 HOW still and peaceful is the grave!
      Where, life's vain tumults past,
   Th' appointed house, by Heav'n's decree,
      Receives us all at last.

2 The wicked there from troubling cease,
   Their passions rage no more;
 And there the weary pilgrim rests
   From all the toils he bore.

3 There rest the pris'ners, now releas'd
   From slav'ry's sad abode;
 No more they hear th' oppressor's voice,
   Or dread the tyrant's rod.

4 There servants, masters, small and great,
   Partake the same repose;
 And there, in peace, the ashes mix
   Of those who once were foes.

5 All, levell'd by the hand of Death,
   Lie sleeping in the tomb;
 Till God in judgment calls them forth,
   To meet their final doom.

V. Job v. 6–12.

1 THOUGH trouble springs not from the
     Nor sorrow from the ground; [dust,
 Yet ills on ills, by Heav'n's decree,
   In man's estate are found.

2 As sparks in close succession rise,
   So man, the child of woe,
 Is doom'd to endless cares and toils
   Through all his life below.

3 But with my God I leave my cause;
   From him I seek relief;
 To him, in confidence of pray'r,
   Unbosom all my grief.

4 Unnumber'd are his wondrous works,
   Unsearchable his ways;

'Tis his the mourning soul to cheer,
   The bowed down to raise.

VI. Job viii. 11–22.

1 THE rush may rise where waters flow,
   And flags beside the stream;
But soon their verdure fades and dies
   Before the scorching beam:
2 So is the sinner's hope cut off;
   Or, if it transient rise,
'Tis like the spider's airy web,
   From ev'ry breath that flies.

3 Fix'd on his house he leans; his house
   And all its props decay:
He holds it fast; but, while he holds,
   The tott'ring frame gives way.
4 Fair, in his garden, to the sun,
   His boughs with verdure smile;
And, deeply fix'd, his spreading roots
   Unshaken stand a while.

5 But forth the sentence flies from Heav'n,
   That sweeps him from his place;
Which then denies him for its lord,
   Nor owns it knew his face.
6 Lo! this the joy of wicked men,
   Who Heav'n's high laws despise:
They quickly fall; and in their room
   As quickly others rise.

7 But, for the just, with gracious care,
   God will his pow'r employ;
He'll teach their lips to sing his praise,
   And fill their hearts with joy.

VII. Job ix. 2-10.

1 HOW should the sons of Adam's race
    Be pure before their God?
If he contends in righteousness,
    We sink beneath his rod.
2 If he should mark my words and thoughts
    With strict inquiring eyes,
Could I for one of thousand faults
    The least excuse devise?

3 Strong is his arm, his heart is wise;
    Who dares with him contend?
Or who, that tries th' unequal strife,
    Shall prosper in the end?
4 He makes the mountains feel his wrath,
    And their old seats forsake;
The trembling earth deserts her place,
    And all her pillars shake.

5 He bids the sun forbear to rise;
    Th' obedient sun forbears:
His hand with sackcloth spreads the skies,
    And seals up all the stars.
6 He walks upon the raging sea;
    Flies on the stormy wind:
None can explore his wondrous way,
    Or his dark footsteps find.

VIII. Job xiv. 1-15.

1 FEW are thy days, and full of woe,
    O man, of woman born!
Thy doom is written, "Dust thou art,
    And shalt to dust return."

2 Behold the emblem of thy state
    In flow'rs that bloom and die,
  Or in the shadow's fleeting form,
    That mocks the gazer's eye.

3 Guilty and frail, how shalt thou stand
    Before thy sov'reign Lord?
  Can troubled and polluted springs
    A hallow'd stream afford?

4 Determin'd are the days that fly
    Successive o'er thy head;
  The number'd hour is on the wing
    That lays thee with the dead.

5 Great God! afflict not in thy wrath
    The short allotted span,
  That bounds the few and weary days
    Of pilgrimage to man.

6 All nature dies, and lives again:
    The flow'r that paints the field,
  The trees that crown the mountain's brow,
    And boughs and blossoms yield,

7 Resign the honours of their form
    At Winter's stormy blast,
  And leave the naked leafless plain
    A desolated waste.

8 Yet soon reviving plants and flow'rs
    Anew shall deck the plain;
  The woods shall hear the voice of Spring,
    And flourish green again.

9 But man forsakes this earthly scene,
    Ah! never to return:
  Shall any foll'wing spring revive
    The ashes of the urn?

10 The mighty flood that rolls along
    Its torrents to the main,
Can ne'er recall its waters lost
    From that abyss again.

11 So days, and years, and ages past,
    Descending down to night,
Can henceforth never more return
    Back to the gates of light;
12 And man, when laid in lonesome grave,
    Shall sleep in Death's dark gloom,
Until th' eternal morning wake
    The slumbers of the tomb.

13 O may the grave become to me
    The bed of peaceful rest,
Whence I shall gladly rise at length,
    And mingle with the blest!
14 Cheer'd by this hope, with patient mind,
    I'll wait Heav'n's high decree,
Till the appointed period come,
    When death shall set me free.

IX. JOB xxvi. 6, to the end.

1 WHO can resist th' Almighty arm
        That made the starry sky?
Or who elude the certain glance
    Of God's all-seeing eye?
2 From him no cov'ring vails our crimes;
    Hell opens to his sight;
And all Destruction's secret snares
    Lie full disclos'd in light.

3 Firm on the boundless void of space
    He pois'd the steady pole,

  And in the circle of his clouds
   Bade secret waters roll.
4 While nature's universal frame
   Its Maker's pow'r reveals,
  His throne, remote from mortal eyes,
   An awful cloud conceals.

5 From where the rising day ascends,
   To where it sets in night,
  He compasses the floods with bounds,
   And checks their threat'ning might.
6 The pillars that support the sky
   Tremble at his rebuke;
  Through all its caverns quakes the earth,
   As though its centre shook.

7 He brings the waters from their beds,
   Although no tempest blows,
  And smites the kingdom of the proud
   Without the hand of foes.
8 With bright inhabitants above
   He fills the heav'nly land,
  And all the crooked serpent's breed
   Dismay'd before him stand.

9 Few of his works can we survey;
   These few our skill transcend:
  But the full thunder of his pow'r
   What heart can comprehend?

X. Prov. i. 20–31.

1 IN streets, and op'nings of the gates,
   Where pours the busy crowd,
  Thus heav'nly Wisdom lifts her voice,
   And cries to men aloud:

2 How long, ye scorners of the truth,
  Scornful will ye remain?
How long shall fools their folly love,
  And hear my words in vain?

3 O turn, at last, at my reproof!
  And, in that happy hour,
His bless'd effusions on your heart
  My Spirit down shall pour.

4 But since so long, with earnest voice,
  To you in vain I call,
Since all my counsels and reproofs
  Thus ineffectual fall;

5 The time will come, when humbled low,
  In Sorrow's evil day,
Your voice by anguish shall be taught,
  But taught too late, to pray.

6 When, like the whirlwind, o'er the deep
  Comes Desolation's blast:
Pray'rs then extorted shall be vain,
  The hour of mercy past.

7 The choice you made has fix'd your doom;
  For this is Heav'n's decree,
That with the fruits of what he sow'd
  The sinner fill'd shall be.

XI. Prov. iii. 13–17.

1 O HAPPY is the man who hears
    Instruction's warning voice;
And who celestial Wisdom makes
  His early, only choice.

2 For she has treasures greater far
  Than east or west unfold;

And her rewards more precious are
   Than all their stores of gold.

3 In her right hand she holds to view
   A length of happy days;
Riches, with splendid honours join'd,
   Are what her left displays.
4 She guides the young with innocence,
   In pleasure's paths to tread,
A crown of glory she bestows
   Upon the hoary head.

5 According as her labours rise,
   So her rewards increase;
Her ways are ways of pleasantness,
   And all her paths are peace.

XII. Prov. vi. 6–12.

1 YE indolent and slothful! rise,
   View the ant's labours, and be wise;
She has no guide to point her way,
No ruler chiding her delay:
2 Yet see with what incessant cares
She for the winter's storm prepares;
In summer she provides her meat,
And harvest finds her store complete.

3 But when will slothful man arise?
How long shall sleep seal up his eyes?
Sloth more indulgence still demands;
Sloth shuts the eyes, and folds the hands.
4 But mark the end; want shall assail,
When all your strength and vigour fail;
Want, like an armed man, shall rush
The hoary head of age to crush.

XIII. Prov. viii. 22, to the end.

1 KEEP silence, all ye sons of men,
    And hear with rev'rence due;
Eternal Wisdom from above
    Thus lifts her voice to you:
2 I was th' Almighty's chief delight
    From everlasting days,
Ere yet his arm was stretched forth
    The heav'ns and earth to raise.

3 Before the sea began to flow,
    And leave the solid land,
Before the hills and mountains rose,
    I dwelt at his right hand.
4 When first he rear'd the arch of heav'n,
    And spread the clouds on air,
When first the fountains of the deep
    He open'd, I was there.

5 There I was with him, when he stretch'd
    His compass o'er the deep,
And charg'd the ocean's swelling waves
    Within their bounds to keep.
6 With joy I saw th' abode prepar'd
    Which men were soon to fill:
Them from the first of days I lov'd,
    Unchang'd, I love them still.

7 Now therefore hearken to my words,
    Ye children, and be wise:
Happy the man that keeps my ways;
    The man that shuns them dies.
8 Where dubious paths perplex the mind,
    Direction I afford;

Life shall be his that follows me,
      And favour from the Lord.

9 But he who scorns my sacred laws
      Shall deeply wound his heart,
   He courts destruction who contemns
      The counsel I impart.

XIV. Eccles. vii. 2–6.

1 WHILE others crowd the house of mirth,
      And haunt the gaudy show,
   Let such as would with Wisdom dwell,
      Frequent the house of woe.
2 Better to weep with those who weep,
      And share th' afflicted's smart,
   Than mix with fools in giddy joys
      That cheat and wound the heart.
3 When virtuous sorrow clouds the face,
      And tears bedim the eye,
   The soul is led to solemn thought,
      And wafted to the sky.
4 The wise in heart revisit oft
      Grief's dark sequester'd cell:
   The thoughtless still with levity
      And mirth delight to dwell.
5 The noisy laughter of the fool
      Is like the crackling sound
   Of blazing thorns, which quickly fall
      In ashes to the ground.

XV. Eccles. ix. 4–6, 10.

1 AS long as life its term extends,
      Hope's blest dominion never ends;

    For while the lamp holds on to burn,
    The greatest sinner may return.
2 Life is the season God hath giv'n
    To fly from hell, and rise to heav'n;
    That day of grace fleets fast away,
    And none its rapid course can stay.

3 The living know that they must die;
    But all the dead forgotten lie:
    Their mem'ry and their name is gone,
    Alike unknowing and unknown.
4 Their hatred and their love is lost,
    Their envy bury'd in the dust;
    They have no share in all that's done
    Beneath the circuit of the sun.

5 Then what thy thoughts design to do,
    Still let thy hands with might pursue;
    Since no device nor work is found,
    Nor wisdom underneath the ground.
6 In the cold grave, to which we haste,
    There are no acts of pardon past:
    But fix'd the doom of all remains,
    And everlasting silence reigns.

XVI. Eccles. xii. 1.

1 IN life's gay morn, when sprightly youth
    With vital ardour glows,
  And shines in all the fairest charms
    Which beauty can disclose;
2 Deep on thy soul, before its pow'rs
    Are yet by vice enslav'd,
  Be thy Creator's glorious name
    And character engrav'd.

3 For soon the shades of grief shall cloud
    The sunshine of thy days;
  And cares, and toils, in endless round,
    Encompass all thy ways.
4 Soon shall thy heart the woes of age
    In mournful groans deplore,
  And sadly muse on former joys,
    That now return no more.

XVII. Isaiah i. 10–19.

1 RULERS of Sodom! hear the voice
    Of heav'n's eternal Lord;
  Men of Gomorrah! bend your ear
    Submissive to his word.
2 'Tis thus he speaks: To what intent
    Are your oblations vain?
  Why load my altars with your gifts,
    Polluted and profane?

3 Burnt-off'rings long may blaze to heav'n,
    And incense cloud the skies;
  The worship and the worshipper
    Are hateful in my eyes.
4 Your rites, your fasts, your pray'rs, I scorn,
    And pomp of solemn days:
  I know your hearts are full of guile,
    And crooked are your ways.

5 But cleanse your hands, ye guilty race,
    And cease from deeds of sin;
  Learn in your actions to be just,
    And pure in heart within.
6 Mock not my name with honours vain,
    But keep my holy laws;

Do justice to the friendless poor,
    And plead the widow's cause.

7 Then though your guilty souls are stain'd
    With sins of crimson dye,
Yet, through my grace, with snow itself
    In whiteness they shall vie.

XVIII. Isaiah ii. 2–6.

1 BEHOLD! the mountain of the Lord
    In latter days shall rise
On mountain tops above the hills,
    And draw the wond'ring eyes.
2 To this the joyful nations round,
    All tribes and tongues shall flow;
Up to the hill of God, they'll say,
    And to his house we'll go.

3 The beam that shines from Sion hill
    Shall lighten ev'ry land;
The King who reigns in Salem's tow'rs
    Shall all the world command.
4 Among the nations he shall judge;
    His judgments truth shall guide;
His sceptre shall protect the just,
    And quell the sinner's pride.

5 No strife shall rage, nor hostile feuds
    Disturb those peaceful years; [swords,
To ploughshares men shall beat their
    To pruning-hooks their spears.
6 No longer hosts encount'ring hosts
    Shall crowds of slain deplore:
They hang the trumpet in the hall,
    And study war no more.

7 Come then, O house of Jacob! come
    To worship at his shrine;
And, walking in the light of God,
    With holy beauties shine.

XIX. Isaiah ix. 2–8.

1 THE race that long in darkness pin'd
    Have seen a glorious light;
The people dwell in day, who dwelt
    In death's surrounding night.
2 To hail thy rise, thou better Sun!
    The gath'ring nations come,
Joyous, as when the reapers bear
    The harvest treasures home.

3 For thou our burden hast remov'd,
    And quell'd th' oppressor's sway,
Quick as the slaughter'd squadrons fell
    In Midian's evil day.
4 To us a Child of hope is born;
    To us a Son is giv'n;
Him shall the tribes of earth obey,
    Him all the hosts of heav'n.

5 His name shall be the Prince of Peace,
    For evermore ador'd,
The Wonderful, the Counsellor,
    The great and mighty Lord.
6 His pow'r increasing still shall spread,
    His reign no end shall know;
Justice shall guard his throne above,
    And peace abound below.

XX. Isaiah xxvi. 1–7.

1 HOW glorious Sion's courts appear,
　　The city of our God!
　His throne he hath establish'd here,
　　Here fix'd his lov'd abode.
2 Its walls, defended by his grace,
　　No pow'r shall e'er o'erthrow,
　Salvation is its bulwark sure
　　Against th' assailing foe.

3 Lift up the everlasting gates,
　　The doors wide open fling;
　Enter, ye nations, who obey
　　The statutes of our King.
4 Here shall ye taste unmingled joys,
　　And dwell in perfect peace,
　Ye, who have known Jehovah's name,
　　And trusted in his grace.

5 Trust in the Lord, for ever trust,
　　And banish all your fears;
　Strength in the Lord Jehovah dwells
　　Eternal as his years.
6 What though the wicked dwell on high,
　　His arm shall bring them low;
　Low as the caverns of the grave
　　Their lofty heads shall bow.

7 Along the dust shall then be spread
　　Their tow'rs, that brave the skies:
　On them the needy's feet shall tread,
　　And on their ruins rise.

XXI. Isaiah xxxiii. 13-18.

1 ATTEND, ye tribes that dwell remote,
  Ye tribes at hand, give ear;
Th' upright in heart alone have hope,
  The false in heart have fear.
2 The man who walks with God in truth,
  And ev'ry guile disdains;
Who hates to lift oppression's rod,
  And scorns its shameful gains;

3 Whose soul abhors the impious bribe
  That tempts from truth to stray,
And from th' enticing snares of vice
  Who turns his eyes away:
4 His dwelling, 'midst the strength of rocks,
  Shall ever stand secure;
His Father will provide his bread,
  His water shall be sure.

5 For him the kingdom of the just
  Afar doth glorious shine;
And he the King of kings shall see
  In majesty divine.

XXII. Isaiah xl. 27, to the end.

1 WHY pour'st thou forth thine anxious
    Despairing of relief,   [plaint,
As if the Lord o'erlook'd thy cause,
  And did not heed thy grief?
2 Hast thou not known, hast thou not heard,
  That firm remains on high
The everlasting throne of Him
  Who form'd the earth and sky?

3 Art thou afraid his power shall fail
  When comes thy evil day?
 And can an all-creating arm
  Grow weary or decay?
4 Supreme in wisdom as in pow'r
  The Rock of ages stands;
 Though him thou canst not see, nor trace
  The working of his hands.

5 He gives the conquest to the weak,
  Supports the fainting heart;
 And courage in the evil hour
  His heav'nly aids impart.
6 Mere human pow'r shall fast decay,
  And youthful vigour cease;
 But they who wait upon the Lord,
  In strength shall still increase.

7 They with unweary'd feet shall tread
  The path of life divine;
 With growing ardour onward move,
  With growing brightness shine.
8 On eagles' wings they mount, they soar,
  Their wings are faith and love,
 Till, past the cloudy regions here,
  They rise to heav'n above.

XXIII. Isaiah xlii. 1–13.

1 BEHOLD my Servant! see him rise
   Exalted in my might!
 Him have I chosen, and in him
  I place supreme delight.
2 On him, in rich effusion pour'd,
  My Spirit shall descend;

My truths and judgments he shall show
    To earth's remotest end.

3 Gentle and still shall be his voice,
    No threats from him proceed;
  The smoking flax he shall not quench,
    Nor break the bruised reed.
4 The feeble spark to flames he'll raise;
    The weak will not despise;
  Judgment he shall bring forth to truth,
    And make the fallen rise.

5 The progress of his zeal and pow'r
    Shall never know decline,
  Till foreign lands and distant isles
    Receive the law divine.
6 He who erected heav'n's bright arch,
    And bade the planets roll,
  Who peopled all the climes of earth,
    And form'd the human soul,

7 Thus saith the Lord, Thee have I rais'd,
    My Prophet thee install;
  In right I've rais'd thee, and in strength
    I'll succour whom I call.
8 I will establish with the lands
    A covenant in thee,
  To give the Gentile nations light;
    And set the pris'ners free:

9 Asunder burst the gates of brass;
    The iron fetters fall;
  And gladsome light and liberty
    Are straight restor'd to all.
10 I am the Lord, and by the name
    Of great Jehovah known;

No idol shall usurp my praise,
   Nor mount into my throne.

11 Lo! former scenes, predicted once,
      Conspicuous rise to view;
   And future scenes, predicted now,
      Shall be accomplish'd too.
12 Sing to the Lord in joyful strains!
      Let earth his praise resound,
   Ye who upon the ocean dwell,
      And fill the isles around!

13 O city of the Lord! begin
      The universal song;
   And let the scatter'd villages
      The cheerful notes prolong.
14 Let Kedar's wilderness afar
      Lift up its lonely voice;
   And let the tenants of the rock
      With accents rude rejoice;

15 Till 'midst the streams of distant lands
      The islands sound his praise;
   And all combin'd, with one accord,
      Jehovah's glories raise.

XXIV. Isaiah xlix. 13–17.

1 YE heav'ns, send forth your song of praise!
      Earth, raise your voice below!
   Let hills and mountains join the hymn,
      And joy through nature flow.
2 Behold how gracious is our God!
      Hear the consoling strains,
   In which he cheers our drooping hearts,
      And mitigates our pains.

3 Cease ye, when days of darkness come,
   In sad dismay to mourn,
  As if the Lord could leave his saints
   Forsaken or forlorn.
4 Can the fond mother e'er forget
   The infant whom she bore?
  And can its plaintive cries be heard,
   Nor move compassion more?

5 She may forget: nature may fail
   A parent's heart to move;
  But Sion on my heart shall dwell
   In everlasting love.
6 Full in my sight, upon my hands
   I have engrav'd her name:
  My hands shall build her ruin'd walls,
   And raise her broken frame.

XXV. Isaiah liii.

1 HOW few receive with cordial faith
   The tidings which we bring?
  How few have seen the arm reveal'd
   Of heav'n's eternal King?
2 The Saviour comes! no outward pomp
   Bespeaks his presence nigh;
  No earthly beauty shines in him
   To draw the carnal eye.

3 Fair as a beauteous tender flow'r
   Amidst the desert grows,
  So slighted by a rebel race
   The heav'nly Saviour rose.
4 Rejected and despis'd of men,
   Behold a man of woe!

  Grief was his close companion still
   Through all his life below.

5 Yet all the griefs he felt were ours,
   Ours were the woes he bore:
  Pangs, not his own, his spotless soul
   With bitter anguish tore.
6 We held him as condemn'd by Heav'n,
   An outcast from his God,
  While for our sins he groan'd, he bled,
   Beneath his Father's rod.
7 His sacred blood hath wash'd our souls
   From sin's polluted stain;
  His stripes have heal'd us, and his death
   Reviv'd our souls again.
8 We all, like sheep, have gone astray
   In ruin's fatal road:
  On him were our transgressions laid;
   He bore the mighty load.
9 Wrong'd and oppress'd, how meekly he
   In patient silence stood!
  Mute, as the peaceful, harmless lamb,
   When brought to shed its blood.
10 Who can his generation tell?
   From prison see him led!
  With impious show of law condemn'd,
   And number'd with the dead.
11 'Midst sinners low in dust he lay;
   The rich a grave supply'd:
  Unspotted was his blameless life;
   Unstain'd by sin he dy'd.
12 Yet God shall raise his head on high,
   Though thus he brought him low;

His sacred off'ring, when complete,
  Shall terminate his woe.

13 For, saith the Lord, my pleasure then
  Shall prosper in his hand;
  His shall a num'rous offspring be,
  And still his honours stand.
14 His soul, rejoicing, shall behold
  The purchase of his pain;
  And all the guilty whom he sav'd
  Shall bless Messiah's reign.
15 He with the great shall share the spoil,
  And baffle all his foes;
  Though rank'd with sinners, here he fell,
  A conqueror he rose.
16 He dy'd to bear the guilt of men,
  That sin might be forgiv'n:
  He lives to bless them and defend,
  And plead their cause in heav'n.

XXVI. Isaiah lv.

1 HO! ye that thirst, approach the spring
    Where living waters flow:
  Free to that sacred fountain all
    Without a price may go.
2 How long to streams of false delight
    Will ye in crowds repair?
  How long your strength and substance waste
    On trifles, light as air?

3 My stores afford those rich supplies
    That health and pleasure give:
  Incline your ear, and come to me;
    The soul that hears shall live.

4 With you a cov'nant I will make,
   That ever shall endure;
The hope which gladden'd David's heart
   My mercy hath made sure.

5 Behold he comes! your leader comes,
   With might and honour crown'd;
A witness who shall spread my name
   To earth's remotest bound.

6 See! nations hasten to his call
   From ev'ry distant shore;
Isles, yet unknown, shall bow to him,
   And Israel's God adore.

7 Seek ye the Lord while yet his ear
   Is open to your call;
While offer'd mercy still is near,
   Before his footstool fall.

8 Let sinners quit their evil ways,
   Their evil thoughts forego,
And God, when they to him return,
   Returning grace will show.

9 He pardons with o'erflowing love:
   For, hear the voice divine!
My nature is not like to yours,
   Nor like your ways are mine:

10 But far as heav'n's resplendent orbs
    Beyond earth's spot extend,
As far my thoughts, as far my ways,
    Your ways and thoughts transcend.

11 And as the rains from heav'n distil,
    Nor thither mount again,
But swell the earth with fruitful juice,
    And all its tribes sustain:

12 So not a word that flows from me
    Shall ineffectual fall;
But universal nature prove
    Obedient to my call.

13 With joy and peace shall then be led
    The glad converted lands;
The lofty mountains then shall sing,
    The forests clap their hands.

14 Where briers grew 'midst barren wilds,
    Shall firs and myrtles spring;
And nature, through its utmost bounds,
    Eternal praises sing.

XXVII. Isaiah lvii. 15, 16.

1 THUS speaks the high and lofty One;
    Ye tribes of earth, give ear;
The words of your Almighty King
    With sacred rev'rence hear:

2 Amidst the majesty of heav'n
    My throne is fix'd on high;
And through eternity I hear
    The praises of the sky:

3 Yet, looking down, I visit oft
    The humble hallow'd cell;
And with the penitent who mourn
    'Tis my delight to dwell;

4 The downcast spirit to revive,
    The sad in soul to cheer;
And from the bed of dust the man
    Of heart contrite to rear.

5 With me dwells no relentless wrath
    Against the human race;

The souls which I have form'd shall find
A refuge in my grace.

XXVIII. Isaiah lviii. 5–9.

1 ATTEND, and mark the solemn fast
    Which to the Lord is dear;
Disdain the false unhallow'd mask
    Which vain dissemblers wear.

2 Do I delight in sorrow's dress?
    Saith he who reigns above;
The hanging head and rueful look,
    Will they attract my love?

3 Let such as feel oppression's load
    Thy tender pity share:
And let the helpless, homeless poor,
    Be thy peculiar care.

4 Go, bid the hungry orphan be
    With thy abundance blest;
Invite the wand'rer to thy gate,
    And spread the couch of rest.

5 Let him who pines with piercing cold
    By thee be warm'd and clad;
Be thine the blissful task to make
    The downcast mourner glad.

6 Then, bright as morning, shall come forth,
    In peace and joy, thy days;
And glory from the Lord above
    Shall shine on all thy ways.

XXIX. Lam. iii. 37–40.

1 AMIDST the mighty, where is he
    Who saith, and it is done?

Each varying scene of changeful life
    Is from the Lord alone.
2 He gives in gladsome bow'rs to dwell,
    Or clothes in sorrow's shroud;
His hand hath form'd the light, his hand
    Hath form'd the dark'ning cloud.

3 Why should a living man complain
    Beneath the chast'ning rod?
Our sins afflict us; and the cross
    Must bring us back to God.
4 O sons of men! with anxious care
    Your hearts and ways explore;
Return from paths of vice to God:
    Return, and sin no more!

XXX. Hosea vi. 1–4.

1 COME, let us to the Lord our God
    With contrite hearts return;
Our God is gracious, nor will leave
    The desolate to mourn.
2 His voice commands the tempest forth,
    And stills the stormy wave;
And though his arm be strong to smite,
    'Tis also strong to save.

3 Long hath the night of sorrow reign'd;
    The dawn shall bring us light:
God shall appear, and we shall rise
    With gladness in his sight.
4 Our hearts, if God we seek to know,
    Shall know him, and rejoice;
His coming like the morn shall be,
    Like morning songs his voice.

5 As dew upon the tender herb,
    Diffusing fragrance round;
As show'rs that usher in the spring,
    And cheer the thirsty ground:
6 So shall his presence bless our souls,
    And shed a joyful light;
That hallow'd morn shall chase away
    The sorrows of the night.

XXXI. MICAH vi. 6–9.

1 THUS speaks the heathen: How shall man
    The Pow'r Supreme adore?
With what accepted off'rings come
    His mercy to implore?
2 Shall clouds of incense to the skies
    With grateful odour speed?
Or victims from a thousand hills
    Upon the altar bleed?

3 Does justice nobler blood demand
    To save the sinner's life?
Shall, trembling, in his offspring's side
    The father plunge the knife?
4 No: God rejects the bloody rites
    Which blindfold zeal began;
His oracles of truth proclaim
    The message brought to man.

5 He what is good hath clearly shown,
    O favour'd race! to thee;
And what doth God require of those
    Who bend to him the knee?
6 Thy deeds, let sacred justice rule;
    Thy heart, let mercy fill;

And, walking humbly with thy God,
  To him resign thy will.

XXXII. Hab. iii. 17, 18.

1 WHAT though no flow'rs the fig-tree clothe,
  Though vines their fruit deny,
The labour of the olive fail,
  And fields no meat supply?
2 Though from the fold, with sad surprise,
  My flock cut off I see;
Though famine pine in empty stalls,
  Where herds were wont to be?

3 Yet in the Lord will I be glad,
  And glory in his love:
In him I'll joy, who will the God
  Of my salvation prove.
4 He to my tardy feet shall lend
  The swiftness of the roe;
Till, rais'd on high, I safely dwell
  Beyond the reach of woe.

5 God is the treasure of my soul,
  The source of lasting joy;
A joy which want shall not impair,
  Nor death itself destroy.

XXXIII. Mat. vi. 9-14.

1 FATHER of all! we bow to thee,
  Who dwell'st in heav'n ador'd;
But present still through all thy works,
  The universal Lord.
2 For ever hallow'd be thy name
  By all beneath the skies;

      And may thy kingdom still advance,
        Till grace to glory rise.

3 A grateful homage may we yield
    With hearts resign'd to thee;
And as in heav'n thy will is done,
    On earth so let it be.
4 From day to day we humbly own
    The hand that feeds us still:
Give us our bread, and teach to rest
    Contented in thy will.

5 Our sins before thee we confess;
    O may they be forgiven!
As we to others mercy show,
    We mercy beg from Heav'n.
6 Still let thy grace our life direct;
    From evil guard our way;
And in temptation's fatal path
    Permit us not to stray.

7 For thine the pow'r, the kingdom thine;
    All glory's due to thee:
Thine from eternity they were,
    And thine shall ever be.

    XXXIV.   Mat. xi. 25, to the end.

1 THUS spoke the Saviour of the world,
    And rais'd his eyes to heav'n:
To thee, O Father! Lord of all,
    Eternal praise be given.
2 Thou to the pure and lowly heart
    Hast heav'nly truth reveal'd;
Which from the self-conceited mind
    Thy wisdom hath conceal'd.

3 Ev'n so! thou, Father, hast ordain'd
   Thy high decree to stand;
 Nor men nor angels may presume
   The reason to demand.
4 Thou only know'st the Son: from thee
   My kingdom I receive;
 And none the Father know but they
   Who in the Son believe.

5 Come then to me, all ye who groan,
   With guilt and fears opprest;
 Resign to me the willing heart,
   And I will give you rest.
6 Take up my yoke, and learn of me
   The meek and lowly mind;
 And thus your weary troubled souls
   Repose and peace shall find.

7 For light and gentle is my yoke;
   The burden I impose
 Shall ease the heart, which groan'd before
   Beneath a load of woes.

XXXV. Mat. xxvi. 26–29.

1 'TWAS on that night, when doom'd to know
   The eager rage of ev'ry foe,
 That night in which he was betray'd,
 The Saviour of the world took bread:
2 And, after thanks and glory giv'n
 To him that rules in earth and heav'n,
 That symbol of his flesh he broke,
 And thus to all his foll'wers spoke:

3 My broken body thus I give
 For you, for all; take, eat, and live;

  And oft the sacred rite renew,
  That brings my wondrous love to view.
4 Then in his hands the cup he rais'd,
  And God anew he thank'd and prais'd;
  While kindness in his bosom glow'd,
  And from his lips salvation flow'd.

5 My blood I thus pour forth, he cries,
  To cleanse the soul in sin that lies;
  In this the covenant is seal'd,
  And Heav'n's eternal grace reveal'd.
6 With love to man this cup is fraught,
  Let all partake the sacred draught;
  Through latest ages let it pour,
  In mem'ry of my dying hour.

XXXVI. Luke i. 46–56.

1 MY soul and spirit, fill'd with joy,
  My God and Saviour praise,
 Whose goodness did from poor estate
  His humble handmaid raise.
2 Me bless'd of God, the God of might,
  All ages shall proclaim;
 From age to age his mercy lasts,
  And holy is his name.

3 Strength with his arm th' Almighty show'd:
  The proud his looks abas'd;
 He cast the mighty to the ground,
  The meek to honour rais'd.
4 The hungry with good things were fill'd,
  The rich with hunger pin'd:
 He sent his servant Isr'el help,
  And call'd his love to mind;

5 Which to our fathers' ancient race
    His promise did ensure,
To Abrah'm and his chosen seed,
    For ever to endure.

XXXVII.   Luke ii. 8–15.

1 WHILE humble shepherds watch'd their
    In Bethleh'm's plains by night, [flocks
An angel sent from heav'n appear'd,
    And fill'd the plains with light.
2 Fear not, he said, (for sudden dread
    Had seiz'd their troubled mind;)
Glad tidings of great joy I bring
    To you, and all mankind.

3 To you, in David's town, this day
    Is born, of David's line,
The Saviour, who is Christ the Lord;
    And this shall be the sign:
4 The heav'nly Babe you there shall find
    To human view display'd,
All meanly wrapt in swaddling-bands,
    And in a manger laid.

5 Thus spake the seraph; and forthwith
    Appear'd a shining throng
Of angels, praising God; and thus
    Address'd their joyful song:
6 All glory be to God on high,
    And to the earth be peace;
Good-will is shown by Heav'n to men,
    And never more shall cease.

XXXVIII. Luke ii. 25–33.

1 JUST and devout old Simeon liv'd;
  To him it was reveal'd,
That Christ, the Lord, his eyes should see
  Ere death his eyelids seal'd.
2 For this consoling gift of Heav'n
  To Isr'el's fallen state,
From year to year with patient hope
  The aged saint did wait.

3 Nor did he wait in vain; for, lo!
  Revolving years brought round,
In season due, the happy day,
  Which all his wishes crown'd.
4 When Jesus, to the temple brought
  By Mary's pious care,
As Heav'n's appointed rites requir'd,
  To God was offer'd there,

5 Simeon into those sacred courts
  A heav'nly impulse drew;
He saw the Virgin hold her Son,
  And straight his Lord he knew.
6 With holy joy upon his face
  The good old father smil'd;
Then fondly in his wither'd arms
  He clasp'd the promis'd child:

7 And while he held the heav'n-born Babe,
  Ordain'd to bless mankind,
Thus spoke, with earnest look, and heart
  Exulting, yet resign'd:
8 Now, Lord! according to thy word,
  Let me in peace depart;

Mine eyes have thy salvation seen,
  And gladness fills my heart.

9 At length my arms embrace my Lord,
  Now let their vigour cease:
 At last my eyes my Saviour see,
  Now let them close in peace.
10 This great salvation, long prepar'd,
  And now disclos'd to view,
 Hath prov'd thy love was constant still,
  And promises were true.

11 That Sun I now behold, whose light
  Shall heathen darkness chase;
 And rays of brightest glory pour
  Around thy chosen race.

XXXIX. Luke iv. 18, 19.

1 HARK, the glad sound, the Saviour comes!
  The Saviour promised long;
 Let ev'ry heart exult with joy,
  And ev'ry voice be song!
2 On him the Spirit, largely shed,
  Exerts its sacred fire;
 Wisdom and might, and zeal and love,
  His holy breast inspire.

3 He comes! the pris'ners to relieve,
  In Satan's bondage held;
 The gates of brass before him burst,
  The iron fetters yield.
4 He comes! from dark'ning scales of vice
  To clear the inward sight;
 And on the eye-balls of the blind
  To pour celestial light.

5 He comes! the broken hearts to bind,
   The bleeding souls to cure;
  And with the treasures of his grace
   T' enrich the humble poor.
6 The sacred year has now revolv'd,
   Accepted of the Lord,
  When Heav'n's high promise is fulfill'd,
   And Isr'el is restor'd.

7 Our glad hosannahs, Prince of Peace!
   Thy welcome shall proclaim;
  And heav'n's exalted arches ring
   With thy most honour'd name.

XL. Luke xv. 13–25.

1 THE wretched prodigal behold
   In mis'ry lying low,
  Whom vice had sunk from high estate,
   And plung'd in want and woe.
2 While I, despis'd and scorn'd, he cries,
   Starve in a foreign land,
  The meanest in my father's house
   Is fed with bounteous hand:

3 I'll go, and with a mourning voice,
   Fall down before his face:
  Father! I've sinn'd 'gainst Heav'n and thee,
   Nor can deserve thy grace.
4 He said, and hasten'd to his home,
   To seek his father's love:
  The father sees him from afar,
   And all his bowels move.

5 He ran, and fell upon his neck,
   Embrac'd and kiss'd his son:

    The grieving prodigal bewail'd
      The follies he had done.
6 No more, my father, can I hope
      To find paternal grace;
    My utmost wish is to obtain
      A servant's humble place.

7 Bring forth the fairest robe for him,
      The joyful father said;
    To him each mark of grace be shown,
      And ev'ry honour paid.
8 A day of feasting I ordain;
      Let mirth and song abound:
    My son was dead, and lives again!
      Was lost, and now is found!

9 Thus joy abounds in paradise
      Among the hosts of heav'n,
    Soon as the sinner quits his sins,
      Repents, and is forgiv'n.

XLI. JOHN iii. 14–19.

1 AS when the Hebrew prophet rais'd
      The brazen serpent high,
    The wounded look'd, and straight were cur'd,
      The people ceas'd to die:
2 So from the Saviour on the cross
      A healing virtue flows;
    Who looks to him with lively faith
      Is sav'd from endless woes.

3 For God gave up his Son to death,
      So gen'rous was his love,
    That all the faithful might enjoy
      Eternal life above.

4 Not to condemn the sons of men
    The Son of God appear'd;
No weapons in his hand are seen,
    Nor voice of terror heard:

5 He came to raise our fallen state,
    And our lost hopes restore:
Faith leads us to the mercy-seat,
    And bids us fear no more.

6 But vengeance just for ever lies
    On all the rebel race,
Who God's eternal Son despise,
    And scorn his offer'd grace.

XLII. John xiv. 1–7.

1 LET not your hearts with anxious thoughts
    Be troubled or dismay'd;
But trust in Providence divine,
    And trust my gracious aid.

2 I to my Father's house return;
    There num'rous mansions stand,
And glory manifold abounds
    Through all the happy land.

3 I go your entrance to secure,
    And your abode prepare;
Regions unknown are safe to you,
    When I, your friend, am there.

4 Thence shall I come, when ages close,
    To take you home with me;
There we shall meet to part no more,
    And still together be.

5 I am the way, the truth, the life:
    No son of human race,

But such as I conduct and guide,
　　Shall see my Father's face.

XLIII. John xiv. 25–28.

1 YOU now must hear my voice no more;
　　My Father calls me home;
But soon from heav'n the Holy Ghost,
　　Your Comforter, shall come.
2 That heav'nly Teacher, sent from God,
　　Shall your whole soul inspire;
Your minds shall fill with sacred truth,
　　Your hearts with sacred fire.

3 Peace is the gift I leave with you;
　　My peace to you bequeath;
Peace that shall comfort you through life,
　　And cheer your souls in death.
4 I give not as the world bestows,
　　With promise false and vain;
Nor cares, nor fears, shall wound the heart
　　In which my words remain.

XLIV. John xix. 30.

1 BEHOLD the Saviour on the cross,
　　A spectacle of woe!
See from his agonizing wounds
　　The blood incessant flow;
2 Till death's pale ensigns o'er his cheek
　　And trembling lips were spread;
Till light forsook his closing eyes,
　　And life his drooping head!

3 'Tis finish'd—was his latest voice;
　　These sacred accents o'er,

He bow'd his head, gave up the ghost,
  And suffer'd pain no more.
4 'Tis finish'd—The Messiah dies
  For sins, but not his own;
The great redemption is complete,
  And Satan's pow'r o'erthrown.

5 'Tis finish'd—All his groans are past;
  His blood, his pain, and toils,
Have fully vanquished our foes,
  And crown'd him with their spoils.
6 'Tis finish'd—Legal worship ends,
  And gospel ages run;
All old things now are past away,
  And a new world begun.

XLV. Romans ii. 4–8.

1 UNGRATEFUL sinners! whence this
    Of God's long-suff'ring grace? [scorn
  And whence this madness that insults
    Th' Almighty to his face?
2 Is it because his patience waits,
    And pitying bowels move,
  You multiply transgressions more,
    And scorn his offer'd love?

3 Dost thou not know, self-blinded man!
    His goodness is design'd
  To wake repentance in thy soul,
    And melt thy harden'd mind?
4 And wilt thou rather chuse to meet
    Th' Almighty as thy foe,
  And treasure up his wrath in store
    Against the day of woe?

5 Soon shall that fatal day approach
    That must thy sentence seal,
And righteous judgments, now unknown,
    In awful pomp reveal;
6 While they, who full of holy deeds
    To glory seek to rise,
Continuing patient to the end,
    Shall gain th' immortal prize.

XLVI. Romans iii. 19–22.

1 VAIN are the hopes the sons of men
    Upon their works have built;
Their hearts by nature are unclean,
    Their actions full of guilt.
2 Silent let Jew and Gentile stand,
    Without one vaunting word;
And, humbled low, confess their guilt
    Before heav'n's righteous Lord.

3 No hope can on the law be built
    Of justifying grace;
The law, that shows the sinner's guilt,
    Condemns him to his face.
4 Jesus! how glorious is thy grace!
    When in thy name we trust,
Our faith receives a righteousness
    That makes the sinner just.

XLVII. Romans vi. 1–7.

1 AND shall we then go on to sin,
    That grace may more abound?
Great God, forbid that such a thought
    Should in our breast be found!

2 When to the sacred font we came,
   Did not the rite proclaim,
That, wash'd from sin, and all its stains,
   New creatures we became?

3 With Christ the Lord we dy'd to sin;
   With him to life we rise,
To life, which now begun on earth,
   Is perfect in the skies.

4 Too long enthrall'd to Satan's sway,
   We now are slaves no more;
For Christ hath vanquish'd death and sin,
   Our freedom to restore.

XLVIII. Romans viii. 31, to the end.

1 LET Christian faith and hope dispel
   The fears of guilt and woe;
The Lord Almighty is our friend,
   And who can prove a foe?

2 He who his Son, most dear and lov'd,
   Gave up for us to die,
Shall he not all things freely give
   That goodness can supply?

3 Behold the best, the greatest gift,
   Of everlasting love!
Behold the pledge of peace below,
   And perfect bliss above!

4 Where is the judge who can condemn,
   Since God hath justify'd?
Who shall charge those with guilt or crime
   For whom the Saviour dy'd?

5 The Saviour dy'd, but rose again
   Triumphant from the grave;

And pleads our cause at God's right hand,
   Omnipotent to save.
6 Who then can e'er divide us more
   From Jesus and his love,
Or break the sacred chain that binds
   The earth to heav'n above?

7 Let troubles rise, and terrors frown,
   And days of darkness fall;
Through him all dangers we'll defy,
   And more than conquer all.
8 Nor death nor life, nor earth nor hell,
   Nor time's destroying sway,
Can e'er efface us from his heart,
   Or make his love decay.

9 Each future period that will bless
   As it has bless'd the past;
He lov'd us from the first of time,
   He loves us to the last.

XLIX. 1 Cor. xiii.

1 THOUGH perfect eloquence adorn'd
   My sweet persuading tongue,
Though I could speak in higher strains
   Than ever angel sung;
2 Though prophecy my soul inspir'd,
   And made all myst'ries plain:
Yet, were I void of Christian love,
   These gifts were all in vain.

3 Nay, though my faith with boundless pow'r
   Ev'n mountains could remove,
I still am nothing, if I'm void
   Of charity and love.

4 Although with lib'ral hand I gave
   My goods the poor to feed,
Nay, gave my body to the flames,
   Still fruitless were the deed.

5 Love suffers long: love envies not;
   But love is ever kind;
She never boasteth of herself,
   Nor proudly lifts the mind.

6 Love harbours no suspicious thought,
   Is patient to the bad;
Griev'd when she hears of sins and crimes,
   And in the truth is glad.

7 Love no unseemly carriage shows,
   Nor selfishly confin'd;
She glows with social tenderness,
   And feels for all mankind.

8 Love beareth much, much she believes,
   And still she hopes the best;
Lovely meekly suffers many a wrong,
   Though sore with hardship press'd.

9 Love still shall hold an endless reign
   In earth and heav'n above,
When tongues shall cease, and prophets fail,
   And ev'ry gift but love.

10 Here all our gifts imperfect are;
   But better days draw nigh,
When perfect light shall pour its rays,
   And all those shadows fly.

11 Like children here we speak and think,
   Amus'd with childish toys;
But when our pow'rs their manhood reach,
   We'll scorn our present joys.

12 Now dark and dim, as through a glass,
   Are God and truth beheld;
   Then shall we see as face to face,
   And God shall be unveil'd.

13 Faith, Hope, and Love, now dwell on earth,
   And earth by them is blest;
   But Faith and Hope must yield to Love,
   Of all the graces best.

14 Hope shall to full fruition rise,
   And Faith be sight above:
   These are the means, but this the end;
   For saints for ever love.

L. 1 Cor. xv. 52, to the end.

1 WHEN the last trumpet's awful voice
   This rending earth shall shake,
  When op'ning graves shall yield their charge,
   And dust to life awake;

2 Those bodies that corrupted fell
   Shall incorrupted rise,
  And mortal forms shall spring to life
   Immortal in the skies.

3 Behold what heav'nly prophets sung
   Is now at last fulfill'd,
  That Death should yield his ancient reign,
   And, vanquish'd, quit the field.

4 Let Faith exalt her joyful voice,
   And thus begin to sing;
  O Grave! where is thy triumph now?
   And where, O Death! thy sting?

5 Thy sting was sin, and conscious guilt,
   'Twas this that arm'd thy dart;

  The law gave sin its strength and force
   To pierce the sinner's heart:
6 But God, whose name be ever bless'd!
   Disarms that foe we dread,
  And makes us conqu'rors when we die,
   Through Christ our living head.

7 Then stedfast let us still remain,
   Though dangers rise around,
  And in the work prescrib'd by God
   Yet more and more abound;
8 Assur'd that though we labour now,
   We labour not in vain,
  But, through the grace of heaven's great
   Th' eternal crown shall gain.   [Lord,

LI. 2 Cor. v. 1–11.

1 SOON shall this earthly frame, dissolv'd,
   In death and ruins lie;
  But better mansions wait the just,
   Prepar'd above the sky.
2 An house eternal, built by God,
   Shall lodge the holy mind;
  When once those prison-walls have fall'n
   By which 'tis now confin'd.

3 Hence, burden'd with a weight of clay,
   We groan beneath the load,
  Waiting the hour which sets us free,
   And brings us home to God.
4 We know, that when the soul, uncloth'd,
   Shall from this body fly,
  'Twill animate a purer frame
   With life that cannot die.

5 Such are the hopes that cheer the just:
   These hopes their God hath giv'n;
   His Spirit is the earnest now,
   And seals their souls for heav'n.
6 We walk by faith of joys to come,
   Faith grounded on his word;
   But while this body is our home,
   We mourn an absent Lord.

7 What faith rejoices to believe,
   We long and pant to see;
   We would be absent from the flesh,
   And present, Lord! with thee.
8 But still, or here, or going hence,
   To this our labours tend,
   That, in his service spent, our life
   May in his favour end.

9 For, lo! before the Son, as judge,
   Th' assembled world shall stand,
   To take the punishment or prize
   From his unerring hand.
10 Impartial retributions then
   Our different lives await;
   Our present actions, good or bad,
   Shall fix our future fate.

LII. PHIL. ii. 6–12.

1 YE who the name of Jesus bear,
   His sacred steps pursue;
   And let that mind which was in him
   Be also found in you.
2 Though in the form of God he was,
   His only Son declar'd,

  Nor to be equally ador'd
   As robb'ry did regard;

3 His greatness he for us abas'd,
  For us his glory vail'd;
 In human likeness dwelt on earth,
  His majesty conceal'd:
4 Nor only as a man appears,
  But stoops a servant low,
 Submits to death, nay, bears the cross,
  In all its shame and woe.

5 Hence God this gen'rous love to men
  With honours just hath crown'd,
 And rais'd the name of Jesus far
  Above all names renown'd:
6 That at this name, with sacred awe,
  Each humble knee should bow,
 Of hosts immortal in the skies,
  And nations spread below:

7 That all the prostrate pow'rs of hell
  Might tremble at his word,
 And ev'ry tribe, and ev'ry tongue
  Confess that he is Lord.

  LIII. 1 Thes. iv 13, to the end.

1 TAKE comfort, Christians, when your
  In Jesus fall asleep;   [friends
 Their better being never ends;
  Why then dejected weep?
2 Why inconsolable, as those
  To whom no hope is giv'n?
 Death is the messenger of peace,
  And calls the soul to heav'n.

3 As Jesus dy'd, and rose again
   Victorious from the dead;
So his disciples rise, and reign
   With their triumphant Head.
4 The time draws nigh, when from the clouds
   Christ shall with shouts descend,
And the last trumpet's awful voice
   The heavens and earth shall rend.

5 Then they who live shall changed be,
   And they who sleep shall wake;
The graves shall yield their ancient charge,
   And earth's foundations shake.
6 The saints of God, from death set free,
   With joy shall mount on high;
The heav'nly hosts with praises loud
   Shall meet them in the sky.

7 Together to their Father's house
   With joyful hearts they go;
And dwell for ever with the Lord,
   Beyond the reach of woe.
8 A few short years of evil past,
   We reach the happy shore,
Where death-divided friends at last
   Shall meet, to part no more.

LIV. 2 Tim. i. 12.

1 I'M not asham'd to own my Lord,
   Or to defend his cause,
Maintain the glory of his cross,
   And honour all his laws.
2 Jesus, my Lord! I know his name,
   His name is all my boast;

>   Nor will he put my soul to shame,
>   Nor let my hope be lost.
>
> 3 I know that safe with him remains,
>   Protected by his pow'r,
>   What I've committed to his trust,
>   Till the decisive hour.
> 4 Then will he own his servant's name
>   Before his Father's face,
>   And in the New Jerusalem
>   Appoint my soul a place.

LV. 2 Tim. iv. 6–8, 18.

> 1 MY race is run; my warfare's o'er;
>   The solemn hour is nigh,
>   When, offer'd up to God, my soul,
>   Shall wing its flight on high.
> 2 With heav'nly weapons I have fought
>   The battles of the Lord;
>   Finish'd my course, and kept the faith,
>   Depending on his word.
>
> 3 Henceforth there is laid up for me
>   A crown which cannot fade;
>   The righteous Judge at that great day
>   Shall place it on my head.
> 4 Nor hath the Sov'reign Lord decreed
>   This prize for me alone;
>   But for all such as love like me
>   Th' appearance of his Son.
>
> 5 From ev'ry snare and evil work
>   His grace shall me defend,
>   And to his heav'nly kingdom safe
>   Shall bring me in the end.

LVI. Titus iii. 3 9.

1 How wretched was our former state,
    When, slaves to Satan's sway,
  With hearts disorder'd and impure,
    O'erwhelm'd in sin we lay!
2 But, O my soul! for ever praise,
    For ever love his name,
  Who turn'd thee from the fatal paths
    Of folly, sin, and shame.

3 Vain and presumptuous is the trust
    Which in our works we place,
  Salvation from a higher source
    Flows to the human race.
4 'Tis from the mercy of our God
    That all our hopes begin;
  His mercy sav'd our souls from death,
    And wash'd our souls from sin.

5 His Spirit, through the Saviour shed,
    Its sacred fire imparts,
  Refines our dross, and love divine
    Rekindles in our hearts.
6 Thence rais'd from death, we live anew;
    And, justify'd by grace,
  We hope in glory to appear,
    And see our Father's face.

7 Let all who hold this faith and hope
    In holy deeds abound;
  Thus faith approves itself sincere,
    By active virtue crown'd.

LVII. Heb. iv. 14, to the end.

1 JESUS, the Son of God, who once
    For us his life resign'd,
Now lives in heav'n, our great High Priest,
    And never-dying friend.
2 Through life, through death, let us to him
    With constancy adhere;
Faith shall supply new strength, and hope
    Shall banish ev'ry fear.

3 To human weakness not severe
    Is our High Priest above;
His heart o'erflows with tenderness,
    His bowels melt with love.
4 With sympathetic feelings touch'd,
    He knows our feeble frame;
He knows what sore temptations are,
    For he has felt the same.

5 But though he felt temptation's pow'r
    Unconquer'd he remain'd;
Nor, 'midst the frailty of our frame,
    By sin was ever stain'd.
6 As, in the days of feeble flesh,
    He pour'd forth cries and tears;
So, though exalted, still he feels
    What ev'ry Christian bears.

7 Then let us, with a filial heart,
    Come boldly to the throne
Of grace supreme, to tell our griefs,
    And all our wants make known:
8 That mercy we may there obtain
    For sins and errors past,

And grace to help in time of need,
  While days of trial last.

LVIII. *Another version of the same passage.*

1 WHERE high the heav'nly temple stands,
  The house of God not made with hands,
  A great High Priest our nature wears,
  The guardian of mankind appears.
2 He who for men their surety stood,
  And pour'd on earth his precious blood,
  Pursues in heav'n his mighty plan,
  The Saviour and the friend of man.
3 Though now ascended up on high,
  He bends on earth a brother's eye;
  Partaker of the human name,
  He knows the frailty of our frame.
4 Our fellow-suff'rer yet retains
  A fellow-feeling of our pains;
  And still remembers in the skies
  His tears, his agonies, and cries.
5 In ev'ry pang that rends the heart,
  The Man of sorrows had a part;
  He sympathizes with our grief,
  And to the suff'rer sends relief.
6 With boldness, therefore, at the throne,
  Let us make all our sorrows known;
  And ask the aids of heav'nly pow'r
  To help us in the evil hour.

LIX. Heb. xii. 1–13.

1 BEHOLD what witnesses unseen
  Encompass us around;

Men, once like us, with suff'ring try'd,
  But now with glory crown'd.
2 Let us, with zeal like theirs inspir'd,
  Begin the Christian race,
And, freed from each encumb'ring weight,
  Their holy footsteps trace.

3 Behold a witness nobler still,
  Who trod affliction's path,
Jesus, at once the finisher
  And author of our faith.
4 He for the joy before him set,
  So gen'rous was his love,
Endur'd the cross, despis'd the shame,
  And now he reigns above.

5 If he the scorn of wicked men
  With patience did sustain,
Becomes it those for whom he dy'd
  To murmur or complain?
6 Have ye like him to blood, to death,
  The cause of truth maintain'd?
And is your heav'nly Father's voice
  Forgotten or disdain'd?

7 My son, saith he, with patient mind
  Endure the chast'ning rod;
Believe, when by afflictions try'd,
  That thou art lov'd by God.
8 His children thus most dear to him,
  Their heav'nly Father trains,
Through all the hard experience led
  Of sorrows and of pains.

9 We know he owns us for his sons,
  When we correction share;

Nor wander as a bastard race,
    Without our Father's care.
10 A father's voice with rev'rence we
    On earth have often heard;
  The Father of our spirits now
    Demands the same regard.

11 Parents may err; but he is wise,
    Nor lifts the rod in vain;
  His chast'nings serve to cure the soul
    By salutary pain.
12 Affliction, when it spreads around,
    May seem a field of woe;
  Yet there, at last, the happy fruits
    Of righteousness shall grow.

13 Then let our hearts no more despond,
    Our hands be weak no more;
  Still let us trust our Father's love,
    His wisdom still adore.

LX. Heb. xiii. 20, 21.

1 FATHER of peace, and God of love!
    We own thy pow'r to save,
  That pow'r by which our Shepherd rose
    Victorious o'er the grave.
2 Him from the dead thou brought'st again,
    When, by his sacred blood,
  Confirm'd and seal'd for evermore,
    Th' eternal cov'nant stood.
3 O may thy Spirit seal our souls,
    And mould them to thy will,
  That our weak hearts no more may stray,
    But keep thy precepts still;

4 That to perfection's sacred height
  We nearer still may rise,
And all we think, and all we do,
  Be pleasing in thine eyes.

LXI. 1 Peter i. 3–5.

1 BLESS'D be the everlasting God,
    The Father of our Lord;
  Be his abounding mercy prais'd,
    His majesty ador'd.
2 When from the dead he rais'd his Son,
    And call'd him to the sky,
  He gave our souls a lively hope
    That they should never die.

3 To an inheritance divine
    He taught our hearts to rise;
  'Tis uncorrupted, undefil'd,
    Unfading in the skies.
4 Saints by the pow'r of God are kept
    Till the salvation come:
  We walk by faith as strangers here;
    But Christ shall call us home.

LXII. 2 Peter iii. 3–14.

1 LO! in the last of days behold
    A faithless race arise;
  Their lawless lust their only rule;
    And thus the scoffer cries;
2 Where is the promise, deem'd so true,
    That spoke the Saviour near?
  E'er since our fathers slept in dust,
    No change has reach'd our ear.

3 Years roll'd on years successive glide,
   Since first the world began,
  And on the tide of time still floats,
   Secure, the bark of man.
4 Thus speaks the scoffer; but his words
   Conceal the truth he knows,
  That from the waters' dark abyss
   The earth at first arose.

5 But when the sons of men began
   With one consent to stray,
  At Heav'n's command a deluge swept
   The godless race away.
6 A diff'rent fate is now prepar'd
   For Nature's trembling frame;
  Soon shall her orbs be all enwrapt
   In one devouring flame.

7 Reserv'd are sinners for the hour
   When to the gulf below,
  Arm'd with the hand of sov'reign pow'r,
   The Judge consigns his foe.
8 Though now, ye just! the time appears
   Protracted, dark, unknown,
  An hour, a day, a thousand years,
   To heav'n's great Lord are one.

9 Still all may share his sov'reign grace,
   In ev'ry change secure;
  The meek, the suppliant contrite race,
   Shall find his mercy sure.
10 The contrite race he counts his friends,
   Forbids the suppliant's fall;
  Condemns reluctant, but extends
   The hope of grace to all.

11 Yet as the night-wrapt thief who lurks
    To seize th' expected prize,
  Thus steals the hour when Christ shall come,
    And thunder rend the skies.
12 Then at the loud, the solemn peal,
    The heav'ns shall burst away;
  The elements shall melt in flame
    At Nature's final day.

13 Since all this frame of things must end,
    As Heav'n has so decreed,
  How wise our inmost thoughts to guard,
    And watch o'er ev'ry deed;
14 Expecting calm th' appointed hour,
    When, Nature's conflict o'er,
  A new and better world shall rise,
    Where sin is known no more.

LXIII.   1 John iii. 1–4.

1 BEHOLD th' amazing gift of love
    The Father hath bestow'd
  On us, the sinful sons of men,
    To call us sons of God!
2 Conceal'd as yet this honour lies,
    By this dark world unknown,
  A world that knew not when he came,
    Ev'n God's eternal Son.

3 High is the rank we now possess;
    But higher we shall rise;
  Though what we shall hereafter be
    Is hid from mortal eyes:
4 Our souls, we know, when he appears,
    Shall bear his image bright;

For all his glory, full disclos'd,
  Shall open to our sight.

5 A hope so great, and so divine,
  May trials well endure;
And purge the soul from sense and sin,
  As Christ himself is pure.

LXIV. Rev. i. 5–9.

1 TO him that lov'd the souls of men,
    And wash'd us in his blood,
  To royal honours rais'd our head,
    And made us priests to God;
2 To him let ev'ry tongue be praise,
    And ev'ry heart be love!
  All grateful honours paid on earth,
    And nobler songs above!
3 Behold, on flying clouds he comes!
    His saints shall bless the day;
  While they that pierc'd him sadly mourn
    In anguish and dismay.
4 I am the First, and I the Last;
    Time centres all in me;
  Th' Almighty God, who was, and is,
    And evermore shall be.

LXV. Rev. v. 6, to the end.

1 BEHOLD the glories of the Lamb
    Amidst his Father's throne;
  Prepare new honours for his name,
    And songs before unknown.
2 Lo! elders worship at his feet;
    The church adores around,

With vials full of odours rich,
    And harps of sweetest sound.

3 These odours are the pray'rs of saints,
    These sounds the hymns they raise;
God bends his ear to their requests,
    He loves to hear their praise.

4 Who shall the Father's record search,
    And hidden things reveal?
Behold the Son that record takes,
    And opens ev'ry seal!

5 Hark how th' adoring hosts above
    With songs surround the throne!
Ten thousand thousand are their tongues;
    But all their hearts are one.

6 Worthy the Lamb that dy'd, they cry,
    To be exalted thus;
Worthy the Lamb, let us reply,
    For he was slain for us.

7 To him be pow'r divine ascrib'd,
    And endless blessings paid;
Salvation, glory, joy, remain
    For ever on his head!

8 Thou hast redeem'd us with thy blood,
    And set the pris'ners free;
Thou mad'st us kings and priests to God,
    And we shall reign with thee.

9 From ev'ry kindred, ev'ry tongue,
    Thou brought'st thy chosen race;
And distant lands and isles have shar'd
    The riches of thy grace.

10 Let all that dwell above the sky,
    Or on the earth below,

With fields, and floods, and ocean's shores,
   To thee their homage show.

11 To Him who sits upon the throne,
   The God whom we adore,
 And to the Lamb that once was slain,
   Be glory evermore.

LXVI. REV. vii. 13, to the end.

1 HOW bright these glorious spirits shine!
   Whence all their white array?
 How came they to the blissful seats
   Of everlasting day?

2 Lo! these are they from suff'rings great,
   Who came to realms of light,
 And in the blood of Christ have wash'd
   Those robes which shine so bright.

3 Now, with triumphal palms, they stand
   Before the throne on high,
 And serve the God they love, amidst
   The glories of the sky.

4 His presence fills each heart with joy,
   Tunes ev'ry mouth to sing:
 By day, by night, the sacred courts
   With glad hosannahs ring.

5 Hunger and thirst are felt no more,
   Nor suns with scorching ray;
 God is their sun, whose cheering beams
   Diffuse eternal day.

6 The Lamb which dwells amidst the throne
   Shall o'er them still preside;
 Feed them with nourishment divine,
   And all their footsteps guide.

7 'Mong pastures green he'll lead his flock,
  Where living streams appear;
And God the Lord from every eye
  Shall wipe off ev'ry tear.

LXVII. Rev. xxi. 1-9.

1 LO! what a glorious sight appears
    To our admiring eyes!
  The former seas have pass'd away,
    The former earth and skies.
2 From heav'n the New Jerus'lem comes,
    All worthy of its Lord;
  See all things now at last renew'd,
    And paradise restor'd!
3 Attending angels shout for joy,
    And the bright armies sing;
  Mortals! behold the sacred seat
    Of your descending King!
4 The God of glory down to men
    Removes his bless'd abode;
  He dwells with men; his people they,
    And he his people's God.
5 His gracious hand shall wipe the tears
    From ev'ry weeping eye;
  And pains and groans, and griefs and fears,
    And death itself, shall die.
6 Behold, I change all human things!
    Saith he, whose words are true;
  Lo! what was old is pass'd away,
    And all things are made new!
7 I am the First, and I the Last,
    Through endless years the same;

I AM, is my memorial still,
  And my eternal name.
8 Ho, ye that thirst! to you my grace
  Shall hidden streams disclose,
And open full the sacred spring,
  Whence life for ever flows.

9 Bless'd is the man that overcomes;
  I'll own him for a son;
A rich inheritance rewards
  The conquests he hath won.
10 But bloody hands and hearts unclean,
  And all the lying race,
The faithless, and the scoffing crew,
  Who spurn at offer'd grace;

11 They, seiz'd by justice, shall be doom'd
  In dark abyss to lie,
And in the fiery burning lake
  The second death shall die.
12 O may we stand before the Lamb,
  When earth and seas are fled,
And hear the Judge pronounce our name,
  With blessings on our head!

HYMNS.

HYMN I.

1 WHEN all thy mercies, O my God!
    My rising soul surveys,
Transported with the view, I'm lost
    In wonder, love, and praise.

2 O how shall words, with equal warmth,
    The gratitude declare
That glows within my ravish'd heart!
    But Thou canst read it there.

3 Thy Providence my life sustain'd,
    And all my wants redrest,
When in the silent womb I lay,
    And hung upon the breast.

4 To all my weak complaints and cries
    Thy mercy lent an ear,
Ere yet my feeble thoughts had learn'd
    To form themselves in pray'r.

5 Unnumber'd comforts to my soul
    Thy tender care bestow'd,
Before my infant heart conceiv'd
    From whom these comforts flow'd.

6 When in the slipp'ry paths of youth
    With heedless steps I ran;
Thine arm, unseen, convey'd me safe,
    And led me up to man:

7 Through hidden dangers, toils, and deaths,
    It gently clear'd my way;
And through the pleasing snares of vice,
    More to be fear'd than they.

8 When worn with sickness, oft hast thou
   With health renew'd my face;
And, when in sins and sorrows sunk,
   Reviv'd my soul with grace.

9 Thy bounteous hand with worldly bliss
   Hath made my cup run o'er;
And, in a kind and faithful friend,
   Hath doubled all my store.

10 Ten thousand thousand precious gifts
   My daily thanks employ;
Nor is the least a cheerful heart,
   That tastes these gifts with joy.

11 Through ev'ry period of my life
   Thy goodness I'll proclaim;
And after death, in distant worlds,
   Resume the glorious theme.

12 When nature fails, and day and night
   Divide thy works no more,
My ever grateful heart, O Lord,
   Thy mercy shall adore.

13 Through all eternity to thee
   A joyful song I'll raise;
For, oh! eternity's too short
   To utter all thy praise.

HYMN II.

1 THE spacious firmament on high,
   With all the blue ethereal sky,
And spangled heav'ns, a shining frame,
Their great Original proclaim.

2 The unweary'd sun, from day to day,
Does his Creator's pow'r display;

And publishes to ev'ry land
The work of an Almighty hand.

3 Soon as the ev'ning shades prevail,
The moon takes up the wondrous tale,
And, nightly to the list'ning earth,
Repeats the story of her birth;

4 While all the stars that round her burn,
And all the planets in their turn,
Confirm the tidings as they roll,
And spread the truth from pole to pole.

5 What though in solemn silence all
Move round the dark terrestrial ball?
What though no real voice, nor sound,
Amidst their radiant orbs be found?

6 In Reason's ear they all rejoice,
And utter forth a glorious voice;
For ever singing, as they shine,
"The hand that made us is divine."

HYMN III.

1 WHEN rising from the bed of death,
O'erwhelm'd with guilt and fear,
I see my Maker face to face,
O how shall I appear!

2 If yet while pardon may be found,
And mercy may be sought,
My heart with inward horror shrinks,
And trembles at the thought;

3 When thou, O Lord! shalt stand disclos'd
In majesty severe,
And sit in judgment on my soul,
O how shall I appear!

4 But thou hast told the troubled mind,
    Who doth her sins lament,
That timely grief for errors past
    Shall future woe prevent.

5 Then see the sorrows of my heart,
    Ere yet it be too late;
And hear my Saviour's dying groans,
    To give those sorrows weight.
6 For never shall my soul despair
    Of mercy at thy throne,
Who knows thine only Son has dy'd
    Thy justice to atone.

HYMN IV.

1 BLEST morning! whose first dawning rays
    Beheld the Son of God
Arise triumphant from the grave,
    And leave his dark abode.
2 Wrapt in the silence of the tomb
    The great Redeemer lay,
Till the revolving skies had brought
    The third, th' appointed day.
3 Hell and the grave combin'd their force
    To hold our Lord in vain;
Sudden the Conqueror arose,
    And burst their feeble chain.
4 To thy great name, Almighty Lord!
    We sacred honours pay,
And loud hosannahs shall proclaim
    The triumphs of the day.

5 Salvation and immortal praise
    To our victorious King!

Let heav'n and earth, and rocks and seas,
  With glad hosannahs ring.
6 To Father, Son, and Holy Ghost,
  The God whom we adore,
Be glory, as it was, and is,
  And shall be evermore.

HYMN V.

1 THE hour of my departure's come;
  I hear the voice that calls me home;
At last, O Lord! let trouble cease,
And let thy servant die in peace.

2 The race appointed I have run;
The combat's o'er, the prize is won;
And now my witness is on high,
And now my record's in the sky.

3 Not in mine innocence I trust;
I bow before thee in the dust;
And through my Saviour's blood alone
I look for mercy at thy throne.

4 I leave the world without a tear,
Save for the friends I held so dear;
To heal their sorrows, Lord, descend,
And to the friendless prove a friend.

5 I come, I come, at thy command,
I give my spirit to thy hand;
Stretch forth thine everlasting arms,
And shield me in the last alarms.

6 The hour of my departure's come:
I hear the voice that calls me home:
Now, O my God! let trouble cease;
Now let thy servant die in peace.

PASSAGES OF SCRIPTURE PARAPHRASED.

No.		Page
1.	Gen. i.,	337
2.	Gen. xxviii. 20-22,	338
3.	Job i. 21,	339
4.	Job iii. 17-20,	339
5.	Job v. 6-12,	340
6.	Job viii. 11-22,	341
7.	Job ix. 2-10,	342
8.	Job xiv. 1-15	342
9.	Job xxvi. 6, to the end,	344
10.	Prov. i. 20-31,	345
11.	Prov. iii. 13-17,	346
12.	Prov. vi. 6-12,	347
13.	Prov. viii. 22, to the end,	348
14.	Eccles. vii. 2-6,	349
15.	Eccles. ix. 4-6, 10,	349
16.	Eccles. xii. 1,	350
17.	Isaiah i. 10-19,	351
18.	Isaiah ii. 2-6,	352
19.	Isaiah ix. 2-8,	353
20.	Isaiah xxvi. 1-7,	354
21.	Isaiah xxxiii. 13-18,	355
22.	Isaiah xl. 27, to the end,	355
23.	Isaiah xlii. 1-13,	356
24.	Isaiah xlix. 13-17,	358
25.	Isaiah liii.	359
26.	Isaiah lv.	361
27.	Isaiah lvii. 15, 16,	363
28.	Isaiah lviii. 5-9,	364
29.	Lam. iii. 37-40,	364
30.	Hosea vi. 1-4,	365
31.	Micah vi. 6-9,	366
32.	Hab. iii. 17, 18,	367
33.	Mat. vi. 9-14,	367
34.	Mat. xi. 25, to the end,	368
35.	Mat. xxvi. 26-29,	369
36.	Luke i. 46-56,	370
37.	Luke ii. 8-15,	371
38.	Luke ii. 25-33,	372

No.		Page
39.	Luke iv. 18, 19,	373
40.	Luke xv. 13-25,	374
41.	John iii. 14-19,	375
42.	John xiv. 1-7,	376
43.	John xiv. 25-28,	377
44.	John xix. 30, ...	377
45.	Romans ii. 4-8,	378
46.	Romans iii. 19-22,	379
47.	Romans vi. 1-7,	379
48.	Romans viii. 31, to the end,	380
49.	1 Cor. xiii.,	381
50.	1 Cor. xv. 52, to the end,	383
51.	2 Cor. v. 1-11,	384
52.	Phil. ii. 6-12,	385
53.	1 Thes. iv. 13, to the end,	386
54.	2 Tim. i. 12, ...	387
55.	2 Tim. iv. 6-8, 18,	388
56.	Titus iii. 3-9,	389
57.	Heb. iv. 14, to the end,	390
58.	Another version of the same passage,	391
59.	Heb. xii. 1-13,	391
60.	Heb. xiii. 20, 21,	393
61.	1 Peter i. 3-5,	394
62.	2 Peter iii. 3-14,	394
63.	1 John iii. 1-4,	396
64.	Rev. i. 5-9, ...	397
65.	Rev. v. 6, to the end,	397
66.	Rev. vii. 13, to the end,	399
67.	Rev. xxi. 1-9,	400

www.ingramcontent.com/pod-product-compliance
Lightning Source LLC
Chambersburg PA
CBHW022119290426
44112CB00008B/730